Blender

for Animation
and Film-Based
Production

Blender
for Animation and Film-Based Production

Michelangelo Manrique

CRC Press
Taylor & Francis Group
Boca Raton London New York

CRC Press is an imprint of the
Taylor & Francis Group, an **informa** business

AN A K PETERS BOOK

CRC Press
Taylor & Francis Group
6000 Broken Sound Parkway NW, Suite 300
Boca Raton, FL 33487-2742

© 2015 by Taylor & Francis Group, LLC
CRC Press is an imprint of Taylor & Francis Group, an Informa business

No claim to original U.S. Government works

Printed on acid-free paper
Version Date: 20140624

International Standard Book Number-13: 978-1-4822-0474-2 (Paperback)

Library of Congress Cataloging-in-Publication Data

Manrique, Michelangelo.
   Blender for animation and film-based production / Michelangelo Manrique.
      pages cm
   Includes bibliographical references and index.
   ISBN 978-1-4822-0474-2
   1. Blender (Computer file) 2. Computer Animation. 3. Three-dimensional display systems. I. Title.

TR897.72.B55M36 2015
777'.7--dc23   2014022786

Visit the Taylor & Francis Web site at
http://www.taylorandfrancis.com

and the CRC Press Web site at
http://www.crcpress.com

To my lovely wife and children.

Contents

Preface

THE IDEA FOR THIS book started quite some time ago—when I was working on the project that became my Blender Foundation Certified Trainer certificate. At that time, 2010, I wanted to write about how I created that animation project from scratch. I thought that sharing this experience may be useful to others with similar interests.

That project ended in my homemade studio, where I developed my personal projects. It was also the place where I carried out my professional and educational activities.

This book remained in a corner in that small studio waiting to be completed some day. In the meantime, Blender was upgraded several times, with new code and completely new features. For this reason, this book has been reviewed and updated several times to keep up with Blender's latest releases.

My intention is not to write a detailed manual about Blender's features, or where to find specific buttons. Nor is this a book laid out in the form of a structured tutorial. I would like to think of this book as a mixed bag, where I share my experiences with Blender, and discuss its usefulness in most of today's studios.

The purpose of this book is to show why Blender is perfect for animation films, demonstrating Blender's capability to do the job in each production department.

Some parts of this book may be oriented toward beginners, some to advanced learners, and some to professional users. I will not explain what every button does but what options are available. I like to let people explore, discover, and learn on their own. A positive approach toward Blender is always a good starting point in learning how it could be used for film production.

The reasons I chose to work with Blender will be detailed in Chapter 1, Why Blender, but how this application became my favorite is something you will discover in the rest of the pages. I will be very glad if you can understand and benefit from the possibilities of this wonderful suite.

My goal is to familiarize you with the animation industry, and to achieve this goal, demonstrating that Blender is as good as any other suite is my objective. The risks involved in choosing applications like Blender as a primary tool in animation studios is something we will see along the course of this book. Knowing this is important in understanding the way the film industry works.

Let us go ahead and see how film production works and why Blender should be taken into consideration.

Author

Born on May 20, 1980, Michelangelo Manrique has always been interested in the fine arts, which not only encouraged him to pursue university education in history of art, but also to work as a painter and an art curator. Michelangelo is also technologically adept, which led him to Blender in 2004. Blender caught his attention right away and he was fascinated by this 3D suite's workflow and many possibilities.

Currently, Michelangelo is a programmer and 3D artist. He is working toward developing animation productions and rigging. He is also involved in publishing tutorials and writing books, while he also conducts different courses on Blender. He is available for freelance or collaborative work with other studios. Michelangelo offers different Blender courses designed to suit individual student needs. For teaching, he uses video-conferencing software to interact with students and share each other's desktops. The topics covered in his courses are: Blender interface and basics, modeling, shading and textures, rigging, animation, lighting, rendering, compositing and nodes, dynamics, and Blender production pipeline.

## CHAPTER 1

Why Blender?

I CONSIDER BLENDER TO be the best 3D content creation suite I have ever used due to several reasons. It's not at the top of my list for sentimental reasons or because it's the only one I have used; it's at the top of my list simply because I feel really comfortable working with it.

You have probably come across a lot of *open source* and *free software*. Blender is one of the most popular applications not only in the open source community but also in the 3D content environment, and it has been climbing the list of 3D creation suites in recent years.

If you are interested in open source or free software, check the websites of the *Free Software Foundation* at http://fsf.org and the *Open Source Initiative* at http://opensource.org.

Blender has seen a lot of success throughout its history—not just in developing open-source movies but also in building a growing community around it.

But Blender has also had some hardships: refactoring stress, license issues, or the fear of studios introducing Blender in their pipeline.

It is worth comparing Blender supported by a small group of developers, mostly volunteers, with other 3D creation suites supported by a large number of official developers, a big infrastructure, and a lot of money invested in research and development. I want to emphasize that this doesn't mean a better product, but sufficient resources if organized well might end in a better product.

This is also comparable to the perspective on big and small studios. Big studios' films are not necessarily always the better ones or worthy of awards just because they have the infrastructure and funds for research and development (Figures 1.1 and 1.2). Small studios also have a lot of great ideas, but lack infrastructure or funds to put their ideas to work.

Blender's workflow and the strong community supporting Blender are probably the two best reasons to use Blender as your main 3D creation suite for small productions or homemade studios.

Is it only suitable for small projects and homemade studios? No, Blender is also suitable for enterprises, big studios, and universities and colleges because it is not only used for 3D films or by artists but also by professionals in varied disciplines like mathematics and science. A search on the Internet would reveal the various kinds of professional institutions that are successfully using Blender on a day-to-day basis, as shown in Figure 1.3.

FIGURE 1.1 **(See color insert.)** The Wind is Changing by Andy Goralczyk, 2006. Awesome rendering demonstrating how powerful Blender can be in the right hands. This still is an awesome render from 6 years ago. I can assure you that Blender has improved even more in its latest releases, so can you reach the limits?

A good example is the University of Castilla-La Mancha, which has been using Blender in many of its projects thanks to Dr. Carlos González Morcillo, Blender Foundation–certified trainer and associate professor of the Department of Technology and Information System at the University of Castilla-La Mancha.

One of the scientific projects developed in Blender is Ganas, a nonlinear animation of characters for sign language representation.

Blender conferences have showcased many projects in the field of science, education, and the like. A lot of interesting, non–3D film related projects are being developed by professionals or amateur artists in a very wide range of activities. Projects like BioBlender, and others developed by the TOSMI (Training in Open-Source Multimedia Instruments) group and for archaeological research do not use the 3D feature of Blender but have turned out to be of quite good quality.

"Blender is for artists" might have been the software's initial goal, but, in fact, Blender has been used in so many different areas that they are the ones that contribute much toward its improvement. A lot of new features are suggested and bugs are reported and fixed.

FIGURE 1.2 **(See color insert.)** Gorilla by Everett Gunther. Interesting use of Blender's particle system.

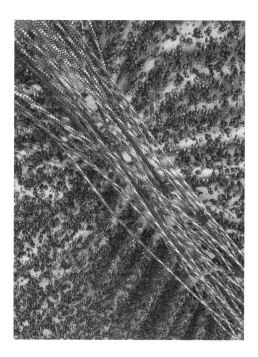

FIGURE 1.3 **(See color insert.)** Contractile Ring simulation by BioBlender. Here, we see how Blender is used in scientific projects.

The results you get with Blender are obviously based on your skills, like in any other application you use or activity you perform. The best thing about Blender is that an amateur can create projects with ease without prior knowledge of the software.

I know that it is hard to believe given Blender's complicated interface and I totally agree that it will look a bit scary for amateurs at the beginning but I'll tell you why this perception is wrong.

Sometime back I read something really interesting in Iker J. de los Mozos' blog, http://somosposmodernos.com. Iker is a great artist and rigger and has worked in very interesting projects, including movies like *Planet 51*, *The Missing Lynx*, *The Lady and the Reaper*, *Justin and the Knights of Valour*, and *Frozen*.

I came across some words in his blog that set me thinking about the way we have to approach new software. He basically said that we cannot learn to handle new software correctly if we approach it with preconceived notions.

In other words, we cannot learn and grasp everything that Blender can offer us if we approach Blender software with our knowledge of the Maya software. It's very interesting to start from scratch like a newbie, letting the software surprise us. This will result in a better learning curve than trying to do in Blender what you can do in Maya or any other 3D creation suite.

The Blender interface has been a highly debated topic in computer-generated imagery forums and communities. A whole range of new proposals, changes, and implements are available on the internet but we will be quite mistaken if we approach Blender with any other 3D suite in mind.

We must discard our conventional ideas and approach Blender as total newbies. Ultimately, Blender is not harder to learn than any other application is for people starting from scratch. The problem lies in the fact that people try to find the same things in the same place even when the applications are very different.

As mentioned earlier, the Blender interface has been a very hot topic in various communities and forums. Recently, a study by Andrew Price, http://blenderguru.com, revealed in the Blender Conference 2013 and titled *The Big Issues* demonstrated popular interest in the Blender user interface.

That study showed that although many people are comfortable with the new interface, a significant number of people totally disagree with it, and are the reason for Blender not being popular.

A couple of clicks, surfing between windows, areas and panels are all you need to navigate through Blender. You can argue that it is this aspect of Blender's user interface that makes you avoid it. I cannot blame you for thinking so because it can be confusing when you use it for the first time, but, believe me, it is not really so hard to understand.

When you get used to Blender's user interface—and you do not need much time for that—the workflow is one of the best as it allows you to develop your project in a comfortable way.

Once you learn to use the basic operators and their keyboard shortcuts, you will enjoy developing new objects, characters, and scenes; applying materials and textures to your models or providing an armature, and animating your characters.

FIGURE 1.4 **(See color insert.)** *Big Buck Bunny* project developed by the Blender Institute. The open movies developed by the BI represent a great example of Blender used for film production.

Over the years, I found people giving very different reasons for not using Blender, like *it's frustrating using Blender if you don't know the keyboard shortcuts*. I will concede that the earlier versions of Blender were difficult but in the recent versions of Blender, the user interface has been simplified to such an extent that this statement is baseless.

It is true that some conventions like the use of left and right mouse buttons can be improved but those shortcomings are like small drops in the ocean.

Blender is powerful and can be effective in animation studios as the main studio creation suite or, in the worst case, as a shared application helping in some specific areas. I will be honest and agree that adopting Blender in a big studio's pipeline could be taking too much of a risk for several reasons but I am confident it will work as well as any other private software as a shared tool (Figures 1.4 and 1.5).

Using Blender as the main tool in very big studios is not only an utopian because, we should be honest, there are a lot of economical interests in adopting one or another creation suite. Ultimately, everything is determined by the market and some applications, as mentioned earlier, expend a lot of human and economical resources to improve their position in the market (Figure 1.6).

The number and reliability of Blender's features and the variety available makes Blender the perfect application to use. Modular implementations and new features that people propose every day are introduced into Blender's trunk code a feature that others cannot claim they have.

Blender is an open-source software and has one of the biggest and most enthusiastic communities helping in source code development and sharing years of knowledge and experience. A growing number of educational institutions are also supporting it as partners.

FIGURE 1.5 **(See color insert.)** *Tears of Steel* is another great example not only for Blender used in animation films but also for vfx projects.

FIGURE 1.6 **(See color insert.)** *Sintel* became a very ambitious project for the Blender Foundation and served as an important test for new awesome features added to Blender's code.

Like other applications, Blender is always evolving, and improving its interface even while it is trying to become a really interesting and strong creation suite for artists. In the final analysis, as mentioned earlier, Blender is not only for artists but also for other disciplines such as education, architecture, and science.

The fine quality of the work produced by several artists using Blender is in itself proof that Blender suits artists' needs. Although we cannot claim that Blender is the best ever 3D application in the world, which no other software can also claim to be, we can argue that Blender is one of the most interesting 3D applications in the world with the additional point advantage of being completely free and open to you.

This book focuses on new Blender users but, from my point of view, it could also be interesting for those who are more knowledgeable in the subject, because they could use this book to recollect old stuff learned in the past or to update their current knowledge of recently added features.

I still use Blender's wiki documentation for information on something I am working on, which is not a bad practice at all. It will be futile to try to understand all the features in Blender at one go—in fact nobody should attempt to do so—for manuals and information sources like books are the only way to get all answers to our questions even when we are not connected to the Internet.

This book introduces you to many of these questions. I am sure there are different ways to solve any issue or to complete any Blender exercise successfully, however the solutions I propose in this book are those I have actually used in my homemade studio.

They are not necessarily the best solutions, but they will help you to get reasonably good results in your project. Remember that the purpose of this book is to create a Blender reference to help people manage projects from start to finish, to understand the different stages in any animation production, and to throw some light on how studios work and develop a complete animation project (Figures 1.7 and 1.8).

It will be difficult to provide all these in a single book—there could be something that I might miss—but I will make an honest effort to put down everything that is needed.

FIGURE 1.7 **(See color insert.)** *Tube,* an open movie developed by Bassam Kurdali and urchn.org.

FIGURE 1.8 **(See color insert.)** *Ara's Tale*, a movie developed by Martin Lubich.

In my opinion, this book will help you in the hard task of finding solutions for determined issues avoiding the loss of productive hours searching the net for any specific trouble with your production files or pipeline. We will see some different areas in-depth and others as simple introduction, depending on the purpose of the chapter but I will try to compile as much useful information as you might need.

I assume you are a committed artist and you are probably nervous looking to develop your project as soon as possible. If I have not mentioned it earlier, I will do so right now, *be patient because good results require hard work and this takes time.*

Read this book to learn how to set up your small home studio and produce a successful project, using Blender and any other open-source application.

Because Blender and other open-source applications are supported and developed mainly by volunteers, they are continuously evolving with new features being added and performance bugs being fixed constantly. At the moment of authoring this book, I am using the Blender 2.6 series, but you will find references to older versions, and sometimes comparison between both, old and modern versions.

Everything you learn in this book will be useful for other 3D applications. In other words, once you learn some basic principles about digital animation you can put them into practice in any other software. Remember, adapting your knowledge to different applications or different versions of the same software makes you valuable in the animation studios' market.

Everything you need is on http://www.blender.org.

## CHAPTER 2

History of Blender

BLENDER'S HISTORY IS CLOSELY connected to Ton Roosendaal, currently chairman of the Blender Foundation, where some open-content projects have been developed using Blender as the main tool.

The Blender Institute was founded in the summer of 2007 by Ton where he coordinates with Blender development and organizes some training DVDs on animation projects.

Ton founded the animation studio *NeoGeo* between 1988 and 1989, which quickly became one of the most important animation studios in the Netherlands. There, he was responsible for software development and in charge of the art department, when he noticed the NeoGeo's in-house 3D tool was too old to maintain and upgrade. A new rewrite of this tool was proposed by Ton, becoming one of the most important decisions for the current Blender state, because this new tool was later named *Blender*.

Ten years later, in 1998, Ton Roosendaal and Frank van Beek together founded a company called *Not a Number* (NaN) to support the Blender market and development. In January of that year, a free version of Blender was released.

The main objective of NaN was to offer professional 3D modeling and animation tools but because of low sales and the difficult economic climate in the Netherlands in those days, NaN investors decided to shut down all operations early in 2002, signifying the end of Blender's development. Two months later, in March 2002 Ton founded the nonprofit organization *Blender Foundation* that is the main organization supporting Blender in both development and artistic projects.

The Blender Foundation was created with the intention of continuing Blender's development and promotion based on the community and following an open-source model.

In July 2002, NaN investors agreed to the Blender Foundation's organization goals and released an open-source Blender version. The *Free Blender Campaign* raised 100,000 EUR for the Blender source and intellectual property rights from NaN investors signifying that Blender as an open-source tool under the *GNU General Public License* (GPL).

The blender development continues thanks to dedicated volunteer developers from around the world with some hired help and a great and committed community of Blender's fans and enthusiasts.

2.1 BLENDER'S ROAD MAP

The beginnings of Blender at NeoGeo and NaN

- 1.00—January 1995
- 1.23—January 1998
- 1.30—April 1998
- 1.3x—June 1998
- 1.40—September 1998
- 1.50—November 1998
- 1.60—April 1999
- 1.6x—June 1998
- 1.80—June 2000
- 2.00—August 2000
- 2.10—December 2000
- 2.20—August 2001
- 2.21—October 2001
- 2.2x—December 2001

Blender becomes open source on October 13, 2002, at the first Blender Conference scheduled.

- 2.25—October 2002.
- 2.26—February 2003.
- 2.27—May 2003.
- 2.28x—July 2003.
- 2.30—October 2003. Blender UI redesign, Knife tool, Mesh undo, Mesh drawmodes, new Transform functionality, Face Loop selection and subdivision, Python API, Radiosity render, Audio window as *frame slider*, and smaller fixes.
- 2.31—December 2003. New default startup file built in, Mesh subdivision surfaces, Python updates and fixes, and more bug fixes.
- 2.32—January 2004. Rendering improvements, Displacement mapping, YafRay support, and bug fixes.

- 2.33—April 2004. Game Engine is back, Ambient occlusion, Musgrave, Voronoi and Noise procedural textures, UV and Image editor, Python API, Render engine, YafRay export, and Localization.

- 2.34—August 2004. Particle forces and deflection, UV unwrapping with LSCM, YafRay improvements and further integration, Weighted creases for subdivision surface, Python API, Game Engine, Oversampling for render, Ramp Shading, Color picker, Interface upgrades, and bug fixes.

- 2.35—November 2004. Undo, Outliner, Mesh editing, Object hooks, Python API, Curve Deform, Taper Curves, Particle duplicators, Rendering updates, Stretch to constraint, UI drawing, Game Engine, and bug fixes.

- 2.36—December 2004. Normals and Textures, Normal Map support, and bug fixes.

- 2.37—June 2005. Transformation tools, Transformation widgets, Soft body, Force Fields and deflection, Incremental Subdivision Surfaces, Transparent filtering, Timeline, Python scripting, Game Engine, and bug fixes.

- 2.40—December 2005.

- 2.41—January 2006.
  The development and release of the *Elephants Dream* animation project by the Blender Institute *Project Orange* resulted in the release of Blender 2.42 as shown in Figure 2.1.

- 2.42—July 2006.

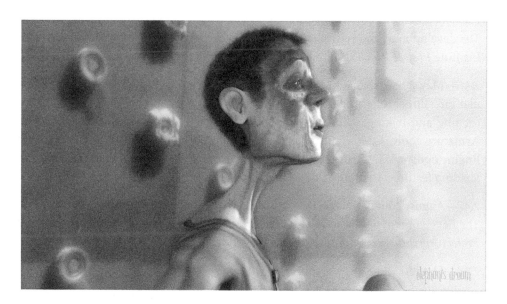

FIGURE 2.1 **(See color insert.)** *Project Orange* resulted in *Elephants Dream*, the first open movie developed by the Blender Foundation.

FIGURE 2.2 **(See color insert.)** Project Peach resulted in the *Big Buck Bunny* movie developed by the Blender Foundation as a result of which Blender was improved to end up with the 2.46 version.

- 2.43—February 2007.

- 2.44—May 2007. Sculpt and multires, Subsurface scattering, Python scripts and API, New Composite nodes, New modifiers, Character animation, Physics engine, Mesh primitives update, and bug fixes.

- 2.45—September 2007. Bug fixes.
  The development and release of the *Big Buck Bunny* animation project by the Blender Institute *Project Peach* resulted in the release of Blender 2.46 as shown in Figure 2.2.

- 2.46—May 2008. Hair and Fur, Particle system rewrite, Image browsing, Cloth simulation, Glossy reflections, Approximate AO, Render Baking, Mesh Deform, Physics caching and baking, Action editor updates, Armature drawing, Constraint system, Armature tools, QMC and adaptive sampling, Skinning update, Sequencer, Game Engine update, UV texture editing, Soft shadows, Compositing nodes, Render pipeline, Shading features, Python API.

- 2.47—August 2008. Bug fixes.
  The development and release of the *Yo Frankie!* game project by the Blender Institute *Project Apricot* resulted in the release of Blender 2.48 as shown in Figure 2.3.

- 2.48—October 2008.

- 2.49—June 2009.

Blender's refactor and new paradigms implemented. A whole review and redesign is programmed.

FIGURE 2.3 **(See color insert.)** Project Apricot was the first game developed by the Blender Foundation to be run within Blender Game Engine and resulted in the development of Blender 2.48.

- 2.5x—From 2009 to August 2011.
  The development and release of the *Sintel* animation project by the Blender Institute *Project Durian* resulted in the release of Blender 2.5 whose main purpose was to stabilize code and make sculpting tools improved at the same time that rendering quality was improved with Global Illumination rendering as shown in Figure 2.4.

- 2.60—October 2011.

- 2.61—December 2011.

FIGURE 2.4 **(See color insert.)** Project Durian represented a step forward in Blender development. With the new 2.5 redesign proposal, the *Sintel* movie ended up with the Blender appearance as we see it now.

FIGURE 2.5 **(See color insert.)** Project Mango, titled *Tears of Steel*, was a vfx and realistic rendering project using both real and cgi developments. The Blender Foundation developed this vfx movie involving real human actors together with visual effects developed entirely with Blender and resulting in the development and improvement of the most recent Blender versions.

- 2.62—February 2012.
- 2.63—April 2012.
  The development and release of the *Tears of Steel* movie project by the Blender Institute *Project Mango* resulted in the release of Blender 2.64 as shown in Figure 2.5.
- 2.64—October 2012.
- 2.65—December 2012.
- 2.66—February 2013.
- 2.67—May 2013.
- 2.67a—May 2013.
- 2.67b—May 2013.
- 2.68—July 2013.
- 2.68a—July 2013.
- 2.69 RC1—October 2013.
- 2.69 RC2—October 2013.

## CHAPTER 3

Blender User Interface

THERE ARE SEVERAL DOCUMENTS and videos on the Blender user interface available over the net and in many diverse formats like books, DVDs, and magazines. Most of the documentation meant for new users provides information on what a specific button does or in which panel we could find a specific feature; in general, they cover, in a very trivial manner, a lot of useless stuff in very large fonts that, in fact, are not really useful for new Blender users or students making the learning path hard, complex, stressful, and completely useless. This was the reason several people who wanted to use Blender gave up their attempt to use it.

In this book, we talk about those aspects we need to know to develop our project successfully. We will learn how animation studios develop their animation projects and the ways in which we can involve Blender in such a process. We will also provide in-depth technical lists about different types of editors, buttons, or properties and they will be provided as merely added information complementing the main idea.

We attempt to create here a comprehensible and solid learning path and focus on the important stuff, so once we know where to find things in the interface and how to use the different features, the rest will come with time and practice.

There is no magic rule that tells new users what they need to do at every moment, because as Blender evolves the position of some of the buttons are moved and some buttons that should not have been there in the first place are removed. Every project requires specific solutions as it evolves and grows on its own, and those solutions might vary depending on the version of Blender that is used.

In fact, has much of the 3D paradigms used in other applications such as Maya or 3ds Max are also found in Blender, but Blender also has its own principles. We need to understand those principles to build the foundation of our knowledge of Blender.

This chapter does not aim to give an in-depth explanation of each Blender button, panel, or feature, but aims to provide an overview of the most common editors, contexts, and workspaces within Blender to understand how this software could be introduced into the animation studios' workflow.

The current Blender user interface is modular and customizable, thanks to Open GL, allowing artists and other blender users to set it up and customize it to their needs or simply adapt it to their taste. That means we can join and split editors, open and collapse panels, drag and drop panels, or change all we need to accommodate our workspace layout to look exactly like we want. We talk more about the workspace layout later in Section 3.3.3.

This and the fact that Blender is also a cross-platform application officially supported by the most common desktop operating systems in the market, for example, Linux, Windows, or Mac OS X, makes Blender the perfect 3D application to get introduced to and to learn about because its user interface looks exactly the same on different machines with different hardware specifications.

This is also an advantage for colleges, universities, or freelances trying to teach Blender because this consistency opens relationships between teachers and students getting rid of useless old barriers and requirements like using the same operating system in order to use the same user interface. However, this doesn't get rid of other unknowns of the equation like keyboard shortcuts because, unlike the user interface, they are not the same over different operating systems and platforms.

We can say that the most recent Blender releases are the result of an in-depth refactor made from version 2.5 where the whole application was reviewed to improve code, appearance, and performance. That *2.5 refactor revolution* followed what is referred to *the three rules* criteria, that consists of

1. *Nonoverlapping*: This is based on the principle of having everything we need visible or easily accessible, for example, no boxes overlapping background context, control, or buttons.

2. *Nonblocking*: This is based on the principle of avoiding pop ups of useless windows or messages disrupting the user's work with useless questions regarding actions or operators to execute, for example, *Are you sure you want to add a Cube?*

3. *Nonmodal*: This is based on the principle of not changing commonly used methods. In other words, imagine we need to modify our object; those changes will not be visible until we click a confirmation button in a pop-up window. The aim is to avoid that and make the user focus on the work instead of the eventual tool itself.

3.1 START-UP BLENDER

As mentioned earlier, the first look at Blender is probably intimidating. For those who are familiar with any other 3D software, the Blender user interface could have some similarities with those applications, especially the latest Blender versions. But that does not mean that other applications are fine and Blender is adapting its user interface to them.

Blender has been faithful to its principles ever since the first releases. If we compare the different Blender versions down the years, we will find that visuals have remained pretty much the same and work in the same way, as shown in Figure 3.1.

Of course, the *2.5 refactor revolution* has meant an incredible step forward in user interface organization and user experience, but those who have had experience in using Blender will confirm that much of the current features were there even in the chaotic user interface of older Blender versions.

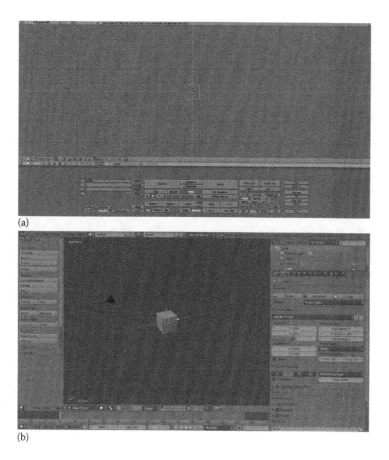

(a)

(b)

FIGURE 3.1   Blender user interface evolution along the years. Many of the paradigms of very old versions remain in the most recent versions. This picture represents the default layout for Blender 1.80 released in 2003 (a) and Blender 2.66.6 r56257 built in 2013 (b).

The first contact we have with the Blender user interface is called *splash screen*, that is, a small pop-up *square* that contains information on the Blender version and revision, a column with some useful links on the left and the latest or recently opened files on the right. We also can select the keymap preset in this screen like *Blender* or *Maya*. This option will change our relationship with Blender and the basic actions such *Scale*, *Translate*, or *Rotate*.

By default, the *Blender* keymap is selected, as shown in Figure 3.2. But didn't we say something about the paradigm of nonoverlapping and nonblocking pop up? Well, in fact, we're starting Blender and the splash screen is there to help in this initial state to speed up your work sessions with useful links to the most recently opened files.

One thing that people don't know is that it has been common practice for Blender to use the artwork of Blender community artists on their splash screens. The featured artworks were those from contests organized by the Blender Foundation and served as a great opportunity to promote both artists' works and open-source projects.

Coming back to the Blender user interface, it is important that we understand some user interface concepts because we will refer to them later in the book. The Blender user interface

FIGURE 3.2 The Blender user interface by default. Customizable and easily adaptable to our needs thanks to Open GL. In this example, we see a basic workspace layout distribution: Splash screen (a), 3D View Editor (b) with Object/Mesh operators (c) internal panel. Outliner (d) with a tree of all objects and data inside the scene. Property Editor (e) panel with buttons and Timeline (f).

is closely linked to elements like Editors, Headers, Context buttons, Regions, Panels, and Controls.

- *Editors* in Blender refer to those areas of work in the determined production pipeline, what some animation studios call departments. For example, we have to open 3D View Editor for object/mesh editing or extrapolation to those animation studios, modeling department, NLA Editor for animation and strips managing, Node Editor to work with nodes and compositing, and UV/Image Editor for renders and UV Unwrap actions, and so on.

    Sometimes there are divergences in the naming conventions regarding Editors, like in the Blender Wiki Documentation at *wiki.blender.org*, where we sometimes see two names for the same concept: Editor and Window. I honestly prefer to call them Blender Editors, because I don't see each of these areas like a window if we define it as we know in the IT world.

    The Blender editors are 3D View, Timeline, Graphic Editor, DopeSheet, NLA Editor, UV/Image Editor, Video Sequence Editor, Movie Clip Editor, Text Editor, Node Editor, Logic Editor, Properties Editor, Outliner, User Preferences, Info Window, File Browser, and Console. We can switch between editors with the *Editor Type Menu*, as shown in Figure 3.3.

- *Context buttons* are those giving access to other options, and they are usually placed on the editor header. An example is the Properties panel that allows us to switch to different options for Scene, Materials, Modifiers, and more.

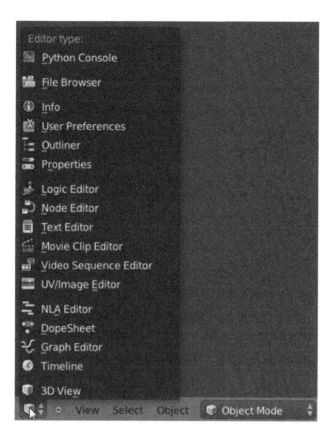

FIGURE 3.3 Editor Type Menu. By selecting the editor type we need at the determined moment from the Editor Type Menu, Blender will offer us different properties, features, and operators panels.

- *Panels* are those collapsible sections where control options are grouped.
- *Regions* are the spaces included in some editors where more panels and controls are placed. Sometimes the Blender user interface saves space by collapsing regions that are easily accessible by keys T and N also called the *Tool Shelf* and *Properties Region*.
- *Controls* are really the options allowing you to modify parameters and values or executing operators.

3.2 CONTROLS AND BUTTONS

In Blender, we call the elements that allow us to modify any value or setting controls. They display additional content or execute any specific function to confirm or refuse any operation. As mentioned earlier, Blender has been cleaning the face of the controls with respect to older versions since the *2.5 refactor revolution*, making them comprehensible and sensitive to the user. There are a few control types:

1. *Buttons*: They execute operators and provide access to tools like *Rotate* or *Scale*, for example. We don't need to remember where the buttons are located because many of these buttons have a keyboard shortcut.

This shortcut speeds up your work session in Blender because you don't need to localize the right button and click on it every time you want to execute any specific function.

However, sometimes it is useful to remember where the button is placed in case of keyboard shortcut issues. We must remember now that keyboard shortcuts for these buttons may differ in the different Blender distros, depending on whether the release is for Linux, Windows, Mac OS, or any other operating system.

Buttons organization is the main headache for new Blender users. My teaching experience has shown that they are overwhelmed, even frightened, on their first approach to Blender, by the keyboard shortcuts. They usually wonder why the Blender user interface gives such importance to keyboard shortcuts, and they worry that they may not be able to remember the shortcuts or to locate the corresponding button in the user interface.

a. *Operation Buttons*: As mentioned earlier, they apply the operator or function we want to execute, like *Duplicate Objects*. There is an interesting feature in the latest Blender releases that allows us to copy the Python command the operator executes by pressing Ctrl+C and then pasting it wherever we want to use it, say Python Console or any of our Python scripts or add-ons. For example: if we put our mouse over the button *Translate*, placed in the Tool Shelf panel, and we press Ctrl+C, we've now the Python command in the clipboard buffer. Then we can switch to *Text Editor* and paste using Ctrl+V, resulting in *bpy.ops.transform.translate()* being pasted within the text editor buffer.

b. *Toggle Buttons*: By enabling these buttons, we make available other kind of buttons, normally a number button, which lets us control value of influence.

c. *Radio Buttons*: This allows us to choose from different value selections.

d. *Number Buttons*: They allow us to switch values of the properties, say *Start Frame: 1*. We can modify those values by clicking on the little arrows at the side of the button, for increasing or decreasing the value and also by dragging the ranged value for percentages, like *50%*. We can also enter values manually by clicking on the button itself; if the button is labeled, this label disappears so we can enter our value, but will appear again after confirmation by pressing Enter or after cancellation of the edit by pressing Esc. As we noticed earlier, we can copy the value of any of these inputs by pressing Ctrl+C and paste it wherever we need, say on another number button, by pressing Ctrl+V.

2. *Checkboxes*: As we can expect, they allow us to enable/disable options. Some are simple checkboxes that instruct Blender to activate any function and some display hidden content related to the context, making visible more controls and buttons.

3. *Sliders*: These are used to enter a float value. The values can be limited by the source code, allowing us to enter from 0.0 to 100.0 but can also be unlimited so we can enter values from $-\infty$ to $+\infty$.

4. *Menus*: These are the lists of elements that allow us to select one of them, like *Render Presets*.

3.3 EDITOR SYSTEM

As we have discussed earlier, the Blender user interface may be strange the very first time we deal with it. When we start Blender, we see different windows, or again *editors* as I prefer to call them and they constitute the Blender environment. To understand this, we should get rid of the common concept of *window* as we know it. In Blender, we are not talking about window in this strict meaning, and we don't refer to the Blender window like these with the minimize, maximize, and close buttons we all know in the IT world.

When we start Blender, we have some editors within the main window and each one contains specific functions according to its purpose. For example, the default scene contains five basic editors: Info Window, 3D View, Timeline, Outliner, and Properties together with the splash screen we already know.

Each editor has its own functions and options, but they also have a couple of things in common. First, all editors have a header containing relevant information about the editor. Second, editors can be systematized, split, and joined, making the workspace layout customizable to our needs.

It's important to know that when we make a call to any operator using keyboard shortcuts, that will affect current selected editor. In other words, editors are automatically selected depending on where our mouse is. For example, if our mouse is over 3D View and we press key A, we are selecting or deselecting everything in our scene, but if our mouse is over Properties Editor and we press key A we open or close panels.

3.3.1 Editor's Header

Editor's headers contain important information about the editor purpose like icon buttons or menu lists, as shown in Figure 3.4. They do not have a fixed position over the editor because they could be at the top, like in the Outliner, or at the bottom like in the Timeline.

We can switch the header position by clicking RMB, right mouse button, over it and selecting the right option. The header itself can be made visible or hidden. To hide it, just drag the border and automatically a small + (plus) button will be visible. The opposite, that is to make the header visible, can be achieved by a click and drag on this small button.

We should not confuse those small + (plus) buttons in the header with the ones we have in the 3D View for *Tool Shelf* and *Transformation* panels visible on the left and right sides when those panels are collapsed.

3.3.2 Systematize Editors

The main purpose in using the nonoverlapping paradigm is to have a clean workspace layout to work with; that is, we can split or join editors and subdivide our main window into several editors and frames to customize the Blender's workspace to our needs. But, the paradigm of

FIGURE 3.4   3D View Header. Showing or hiding headers of editors is really easy; it can be done by dragging and dropping the border on the small + (plus) button.

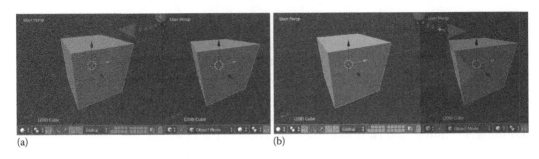

(a)   (b)

FIGURE 3.5 Editors' split and join. With the editors' split widgets, it is easy to customize the workspace layout to our needs. Click and drag to split editors (a) or to join and combine (b).

nonoverlapping is also broken by just a single case. In the latest Blender's releases, we have the option of splitting an editor and making it fit another window, intentionally made for multiple monitors support as we will see later in this section.

1. *Maximize editor*: We have ways to maximize any editor and make it full screen. The maximized editor will obviously contain its internal panels and header. We can maximize editors then by using the *View → Toggle Full Screen*, or using one of the following keyboard shortcuts: Shift+Spacebar or Ctrl+↓ or Ctrl+↑ keys.

2. *Split editors*: There are a couple of split editor widgets, on the left-bottom and top-right corners of each editor. If we want to split an editor into two, we can drag from any of those widgets; notice our cursor is a cross icon once we let the mouse hover over the widget, as shown in Figure 3.5.

3. *Join editors*: To join and combine two editors, we can drag the same split editor widget and drag it over the editors we want to combine. The editors that combine become darker and a big lighter arrow indicates that the previous editor has filled in, as shown in Figure 3.5.

4. *Editors size*: It's really easy to change our editor's size by dragging the editor's border with LMB, left mouse button.

5. *Switch editors' content*: In Blender, we can switch editor's content using the editors split widgets again. In this case, to switch content between editors, we need to use Ctrl+LMB.

6. *Open editor in a new window*: Blender, allows us to open editors in a new window supporting multimonitors. This is what I meant earlier when I spoke of the broken nonoverlapping paradigm.

   The paradigm is not broken if we move the recently opened window outside the Blender's main window, which is another monitor. We can open the selected editor in a new window by using Shift+LMB on the editor's split widgets and dragging.

   The new window follows the same principles this section talks about; for example, maximize, split, join, resize, and open in a new window. The content of the editor in the new window is automatically updated if we manipulate the main Blender window, that is, if we open 3D View editor in a new window and move it to our right monitor using a Camera view, then we have in the left monitor our main Blender window and another 3D View editor using Side view for modeling, and all changes we make in the latest one are automatically reflected in our recently opened right-side window.

3.3.3 Workspace Layout

Animation studios have very different areas to cover when working on any project. Each of these areas requires a specific layout to work efficiently, and 3D applications are working hard to allow maximum customization. But, sometimes, it's hard to customize everything we need by ourselves. Blender offers several different layouts by default, so we can switch from one to another depending on the stage of our project.

Everyone of those default screens is what we call *Workspace Layout*. To switch our workspace layout, we have a dropdown located in the *Info Window* header together, the Scene dropdown, as shown in Figure 3.6.

The integrated workspace layouts Blender currently has are as follows:

1. *3D View Full*: By selecting this workspace layout, we have the 3D View Editor full sized in the window using the option *Only Render*. The *Tool Shelf* panel, accessible with key T or by dragging the small + (plus) icon on the left, and the *Transformation Panel*, accessible with key N, or by dragging the small + (plus) icon on the right, are still working in this workspace.

2. *Animation*: This workspace is designed for a fluid animation stage. When working with animations, we need certain kinds of editors helping in the process as configuring everything from scratch could be tedious for many people. Blender supports, by default, a very useful Animation workspace layout containing the following editors: DopeSheet, Graphic Editor, 3D View, Timeline, 3D View with hidden header and Camera View selected, Outliner, and Properties Editor.

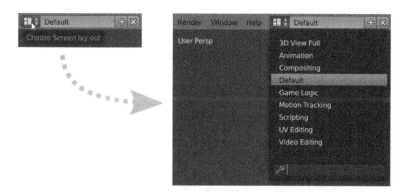

FIGURE 3.6 Workspace Layout options list. List of current available workspace layouts built-in within Blender.

3. *Compositing*: This workspace is designed to offer more control over the final appearance of the scene, specially for color correction, lights, effects, and more. This workspace contains the following editors: Node Editor, UV/Image Editor, 3D View with Camera View selected, Properties Editor, and Timeline.

4. *Default*: The default workspace layout is the one where we launch Blender. It contains the famous initial Blender's Cube. The default workspace is usually used for modeling stage. This workspace contains the following editors: 3D View with Tool Shelf open, Timeline, Outliner, and Properties Editor.

5. *Game Logic*: This workspace is designed to work with Blender's Game Engine in games development. This workspace contains the following editors: Outliner, 3D View, Text Editor, Logic Editor, and Properties Editor.

6. *Motion Track*: The Motion Track Editor has been added recently thanks to the Mango Project, and it's purposed to work with camera tracking. This workspace contains the following editors: Three Movie Clip Editors (for graph view, dopesheet view, and editing clip preview) and Timeline.

7. *Scripting*: The main purpose of this workspace is to offer a comfortable layout for documenting or script writing. This is useful to write new Blender scripts and to test whether they work as expected, for example, Blender add-ons or fixing Blender's bugs. This workspace contains the following editors: Text editor, 3D View, Outliner, Properties Editor, and Python Console.

8. *UV Editing*: This is designed to control how textures map the objects and customize projections. This workspace contains the following editors: UV/Image Editor and 3D View with Tool Shelf open.

9. *Video Editing*: The Video Editing workspace is targeted for postproduction tasks like cutting or joining animation pieces. This workspace contains the following editors: Graphic Editor, two Video Sequence Editors (preview and strip manager), and Timeline.

3.3.3.1 Configuring our Workspace Layout

Sometimes default workspace layouts built in Blender are not enough for our purpose. As we have already explained, we can configure our workspace layout to suit our needs by adding or deleting layouts.

1. *Add a new layout*: In the workspace layout widget, we can add, based on our current layout, a new one to the list by clicking on the *Add* button plus-like icon. Then we can rename our recently created workspace layout as we desire.

2. *Delete layout*: Close to the *Add* new workspace layout button there is another one, a cross-like icon, that we can use to delete the selected workspace layout. Blender will automatically switch its interface to the next workspace layout in the list. Take care to see that no confirmation pop-up message appears.

3.3.4 Scenes

It is very important we understand how scenes work in Blender. We will always be working on scenes, and if we can control their behavior, we can be more productive in our work. Scenes and workspace layouts are both very important bits to understand because they can change the entire Blender user interface and, hence, our approach to Blender. Scenes are independent and can store everything you can imagine, and can be totally different from one another; that is, we may have *Scene.001* for modeling the main character in our project and *Scene.002* for modeling props and environment objects. It's important to know that scenes don't remember the workspace layout; so, in our example, we will be in the same workspace layout even when we switch between scenes.

3.3.4.1 Configuring Our Scene

Like workspace layouts, our scenes can be configured as we need, not only by addition or deletion of scenes but also in their relationship with objects and data. We can configure our scene with the scene widget close to the workspace layout widget, as shown in Figure 3.7. Actually, both look the same.

1. *Add New Scene*: We are able to add a new scene to our current project by clicking on the *Add* button plus-like icon. When we add a new scene, Blender offers us a small list with options to select the way we want to create our new scene. This is important because what we select here will determine how we must work with the future scene:

   a. *New*: This makes a new empty default scene and sets the render settings to its default state.

   b. *Copy Settings*: This makes the same as previous one but, in this case, copies the render settings from the base scene.

   c. *Link Objects*: The link objects generate a new scene linking objects in the old scene to those in the new one. That means that changes in those objects affect both scenes because objects are actually shared between both scenes.

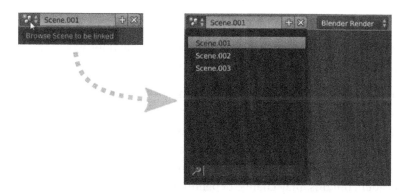

FIGURE 3.7 Select Scene dropdown. This widget allow us to switch between scenes, but at the same time, we might create new or delete current existing scenes.

d. *Link Object Data*: The new scene makes a copy of the old scene Objects but links to the Object Data; for example, materials, mesh. That means, that changes in those objects are independent in each scene but changes in any of the object data are shared. To avoid that we need to make *single-user* from the Properties Editor, the Object Data.

e. *Full Copy*: This makes a new a copy of the old scene, but nothing is shared. Objects are completely independent between scenes, and changes in the objects don't affect the other scene.

2. *Delete Scene*: We can delete scenes by clicking the cross-like icon close to the *Add* scene button.

3.4 EDITOR TYPES

We already know that studios' productions are usually divided into several areas and stages, and for big studios into actual departments. Each of these areas requires specific solutions and features, but accommodating them in the user interface for any of the 3D applications in the market is not easy. Blender uses different editor types for different purposes according to the requirement of each work. We've identified these editors earlier in Section 3.1, but we will see them a little more in depth now.

3.4.1 3D View

The 3D View is where we do much of the work on modeling and scene creation. This editor is big and wide enough, but Blender has powerful tools to deal with everything we need to do in the 3D View. It's probably the editor we will spend more time with and, because of that, we need to know as much as possible about it. On a first and quick view at this editor, we can see we're dealing with something like a deep space with a grid floor and probably the famous Cube if we're in Blender's default scene, as shown in Figure 3.8. But this editor, like others, is comprised of different kinds of elements, as we already know, like a *Header* and a couple of panels; for example, the *Transform Panel* and *Tool Shelf* panel. We are going to check everything in depth so that we have a clear idea about where we are and what we are talking about.

1. *3D Viewport*: This is the big space with the grid on the floor where the actual objects reside. We can build our scene, modeling our objects or rigging our characters there.

2. *Header*: This contains very important information and, if I may say so, important buttons in the way of shortcuts making our workflow much more productive. Once we know and get used to shortcuts, we don't use frequently the elements placed in this header but sometimes it's still easier and faster to select a specific option from these elements rather than typing the shortcut commands. Some of the elements, the 3D View header contains, may change depending on the mode we are working on.

a. *Editor type selector*: This button pops up a list of the different editor types that we can switch to.

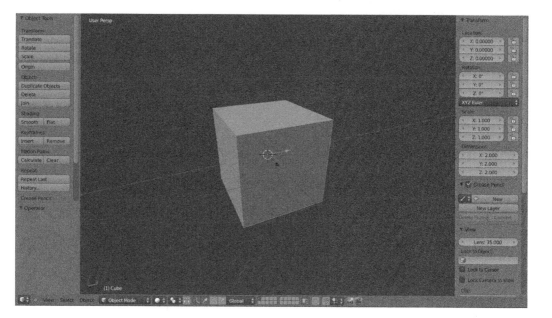

FIGURE 3.8   3D View Editor. The picture shows the editor in the *Object Mode* that determines the different options displayed in the header.

b. *Hide menus*: This is a small – (minus) button close to the Editor type selector that shows or hides the pulldown menus.

c. *Pulldown menus*: This contains relevant options for 3D View management depending on the mode we are in.

   i. *Object Mode*: While in this mode we have *View*, *Select*, and *Object* menus.

   ii. *Edit Mode*: While in this mode we have *View*, *Select*, and *Mesh* menus.

   iii. *Sculpt Mode*: While in this mode we have *View*, *Sculpt*, *Brush*, and *Hide/Mask*.

   iv. *Vertex Paint*: While in this mode we have *View*, *Paint*, and *Brush*.

   v. *Texture Paint*: While in this mode we have *View* and *Brush*.

   vi. *Weight Paint*: While in this mode we have *View*, *Weights*, and *Brush*.

d. *Mode selector*: This helps to switch between possible modes. Available modes in the 3D View are as described in the previous point *2c*.

e. *Draw mode*: Also known as *Viewport shading*, it determines how we see objects in our 3D View. Possible options are *Texture*, *Solid*, *Wireframe*, or *Bounding box*.

f. *Pivot Point*: This modifies the object pivot point, also called the *transformation center*, on the 3D viewport. It's only visible while in *Edit* or *Object Mode*.

g. *Transform Manipulators*: We can manipulate actions like *Scale* or *Rotate* thanks to these manipulators in the same way that we can make all of these in specific axes orientation. This is also possible by keyboard shortcuts, of course. These manipulators are only visible while in *Edit* or *Object Mode*.

h. *Layers*: The Blender layers are such that they can remain visible even as we move objects between them. This is important to understand to set render settings in the right way for successful rendering. The layer selector is visible in all modes except *Edit Mode*.

i. *Lock to Scene*: This option is visible in all modes except *Edit Mode*.

j. *Proportional editing object mode*: This is only visible in the *Edit* and *Object Modes*.

k. *Snap*: This controls the snapping tools that help in the modeling or transformation stage. It's only visible in the *Edit* or *Object Modes*.

l. *Open GL render active viewport*: This is usually used for previews and quick views of what we are working on. This option is visible in all modes.

3. *Tool Shelf panel*: This is the panel on the left that we can open or collapse by pressing the T key or using the small + (plus) button. It contains very useful operators to manage the required actions. *Object tools*, *Mesh tools*, *Brushes*, and more are located there depending on the mode we are in.

4. *Transformation panel*: This is the panel on the right that we can open or collapse by pressing the N key or using the small + (plus) button. *Transform* properties and coords, *Grease Pencil*, *Display*, or *Transform orientations* are some of the features located in this panel.

3.4.2 Timeline

Working in animation projects requires us to adjust to specific timelines, not in a business context, but in an artistic one. Each scene is conceived to adjust to that timeline that is usually fixed by the project storyboard. We have in Blender an editor to help in such circumstances. The Timeline editor, as in Figure 3.9, is usually at the bottom of the Blender workspace layout and is very useful in providing information regarding our scene. We can get important information on frames or seconds our scene is composed of, active keyframes for any specific object, the start and the end of the current scene, or addition of markers for a better comprehension of our developed scene.

FIGURE 3.9 Timeline. We can get a lot of information from our scene, use the playback options, or just stick to predefined timelines in production. In complex animation films, it is usual to use markers within the Timeline editor.

We may also control our animation by using the playback controls in the Timeline editor.

1. *Header*:

   a. *Editor type selector*: This button pops up with a list of the different editor types that we can switch to.

   b. *Pulldown menus*: These contain important options to operate with our animation. It's common for all the different modes. Available options are *View*, *Marker*, *Frame*, and *Playback*.

   c. *Preview range*: This is a small clock-like icons that help to bring some light to the current range for our scene.

   d. *Start*: This refers to the first frame of the range.

   e. *End*: This refers to the end frame of the range.

   f. *Current frame*: This is the number of frames we are manipulating at a determined moment. Changing its value moves the current frame line, also called *time cursor*, within the Timeline editor.

   g. *Playback buttons*: We can manage our animation scenes with these playback buttons. Available options are *Jump to first/last frame of range*, *Jump to next/previous keyframe*, *Play reverse*, *Play normal*, and *Stop/pause* when any of the play buttons are clicked.

3.4.3 Graphic Editor

The Graphic Editor, as in Figure 3.10, formerly known as IPO editor, deals with interpolation of keyframes using the well known F-Curves.

1. *Channel Box*: This is the area on the left side and contains the list of channels and everything that is linked to animation data; that is, anything assigned to keyframes. We can filter what we can visualize by enabling or disabling the small checkboxes.

2. *Header*:

   a. *Editor type selector*: This pops up a list of the different editor types that we can switch to.

   b. *Hide menus*: The small − (minus) button helps to hide the pulldown menus.

   c. *Pulldown menus*: This contains very useful options for markers, channels, or key administration. It's common for the different modes we can work in the Graphic Editor. Available options are *View*, *Select*, *Marker*, *Channel*, and *Key*.

   d. *Mode selector*: This helps switch between possible modes. In the Graphic Editor, we can work in *Drivers* and *F-Curve Editor* modes.

   e. *Channels' visibility*: We can decide here if we want to display channels for selected objects and data or also display channels for objects that are not visible. If Drivers

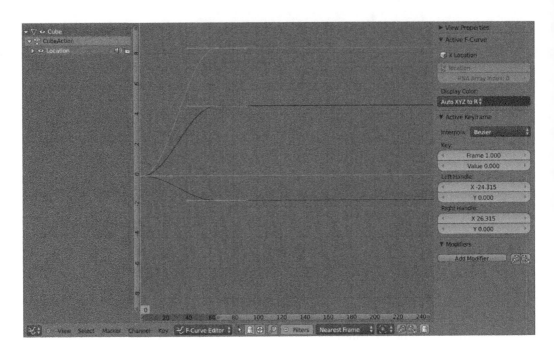

FIGURE 3.10 Graphic Editor.

mode is selected, then we also have an option to show only drivers that are disabled or have errors.

f. *Match F-Curve name*: This is an option to display those F-Curves that match the search text that is our input. By clicking on the lens-like icon, an input field, where we can enter our text, is automatically displayed.

g. *Filters*: If we enable this button, Blender offers us the possibility of filtering the curves we want to display according to the data type; that is, we can set the data type we want to display as scene-related animation data or world-related animation data, among others.

h. *Auto snap*: This allows us to manage the snap settings. Options available are *Nearest Marker*, *Nearest Frame*, *Time Step*, and *No Auto-Snap*.

i. *Pivot Center*: This is used for rotating or scaling. The available options are *Individual Centers*, *2D Cursor*, and *Bounding Box Center*.

j. *Copy/Paste keyframes*: These options are useful to copy/paste keyframes to the copy/paste buffer. It's also possible to do this with the shortcuts Ctrl+C and Ctrl+V.

k. *Create snapshot or Ghost*: Creates a background aid F-Curve for the selected one.

3.4.4 DopeSheet

This editor is used to find out how a scene is structured. We can check everything that is happening in the scene using this editor. The dopesheet lists all actions or keys within the

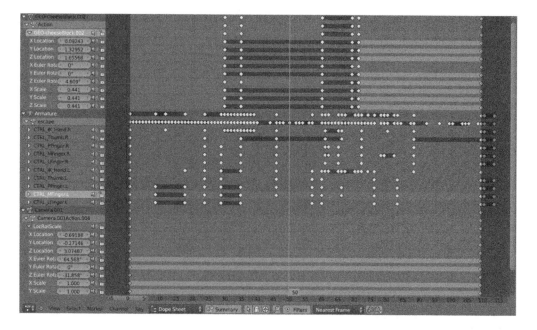

FIGURE 3.11 DopeSheet used in one of the scenes of the Platform Michelangelo Studio project *RAT bProficiency*. We can see the left column with animation channels and their respective keyframes stored in the Dope closed-up Sheet main editor. It is also interesting to notice a tree-like list of the whole animated data in the scene while in DopeSheet mode.

current scene, so animators can check their position in the timeframe, their length, and their relation to any other internal elements as shown in Figure 3.11.

There are four interesting modes in the dope closed-up sheet, and each one is used specifically in very different contexts.

1. *Dope closed-up Sheet*: This is used to edit and manage multiple actions by manipulating keyframes. All objects animated in the scene are listed here with their respective keyframes.

2. *Action Editor*: This is used to edit and manage actions by manipulating keyframes. It is used to manipulate a single action at a time.

3. *Grease Pencil*: All our sketches are edited with the grease pencil. Also keyframes are used to structure motion in a timeframe.

   a. *Header*:

      i. *Editor type selector*: This pops up a list of the different editor types that we can switch to.

      ii. *Pull-down menu*: This contains important options to manage the action strips. The available options for DopeSheet mode are *View*, *Select*, *Marker*, *Channel*, and *Key*. The available options for Grease Pencil mode are the switches *Key* to *Frame*.

iii. *Context selector*: We can use the drop-down list to select the right mode. The available options are *Dope closed-up Sheet*, *Action Editor*, and *Grease Pencil*.

iv. *Display summary*: This displays the additional summary line.

v. *Channels filtering*: These are some buttons to filter the elements we want to display. However, this is not available for Grease Pencil mode. The available options are *Display only selected*, *Show hidden*, and *Show only errors*.

vi. *Browse action*: This feature helps to select the action we want to display. We also have the option to create or delete such action, although only for Action Editor mode.

vii. *Copy and Paste keyframes*: These are a couple of buttons to copy and paste keyframes within the editor.

b. *Track tree*: This is the left column where the channels with actions are listed. This tree contains elements that we may expand or collapse to show information like transformation axis and such. The list is dynamically updated according to the mode we are in.

c. *Main editor*: This is where all the keyframes are located. When working on any channel containing animated data, strips and dots represent the action itself. We can deal with those keyframes and adapt to the horizontal keyframe scale. We also have a current frame line telling us where the active frame we are working on is.

3.4.5 NLA Editor

To avoid the hard work of manipulating or fixing animations using the keyframe method, we can use the NLA editor to make it user-friendly. We can manage a lot of interesting properties in our animations, tracks, and strips, to reorganize and fix everything we want in an easy manner. Figure 3.12 represents the NLA editor with a single animation track and strip.

1. *Header*:

a. *Editor type selector*: This pops up a list of the different editor types that we can switch to.

b. *Pull-down menu*: This contains important options to manage the animation strips. The available options are *View*, *Select*, *Marker*, *Edit*, and *Add*.

c. *Channels filtering*: We have three buttons to filter the NLA editor data we want to display. They are *Include channels related to selected objects and data*, *Include channels from objects and bones that are not visible*, and finally *Include animation data blocks with no NLA data*.

d. *Filters*: These show the options for whether channels related to certain types of data are included. By enabling this option, we have several other suboptions being

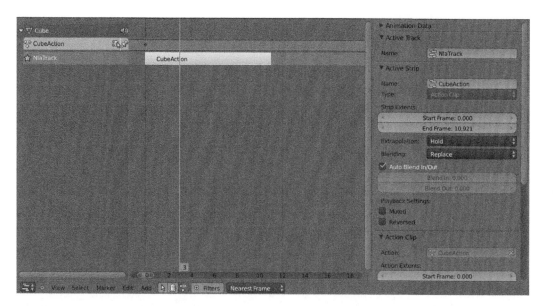

FIGURE 3.12 NLA Editor.

displayed, such as elements related to animation data on *Scene*, *World*, *Node*, *Object level*, *Mesh*, *Material*, *Lamp*, *Texture*, and *Camera*.

  e. *Time snap*: This helps us to Snap to actual frames and seconds. The available options are *Nearest Marker*, *Nearest Frame*, *Time Step*, and *No Auto-Snap*.

2. *Tracks*: The left panel is where we can manage our animation tracks like we deal with the outline elements. We can organize our animation tracks and strips easily from within this panel.

3. *Strips editor*: This is where the actual animation strips are placed and we can adjust, snap them to build our animation project.

4. *Animation Data*: The right panel, accessible with the N key, if hidden by default, is where we can manage all our track/strip data properties and customize the animation in order to get the final expected result.

3.4.6 UV/Image Editor

This editor is usually used to visualize rendered images or to deal with the UV unwrap technique to apply external textures to our objects.

We will see more about UV in Chapter 8.

3.4.7 Video Sequence Editor

Blender is a powerful tool. Although we are aware of it, not too many people know that Blender has its own editor to work on and manipulate video streaming and that we can combine the compositing nodes to work on both images or video tracks so the final movie is

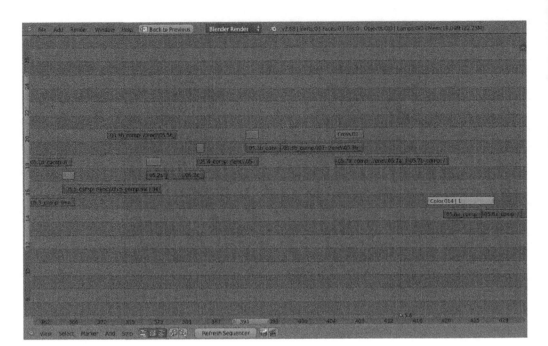

FIGURE 3.13 Video Sequence Editor.

obtained after assembling the video strips within the Video Sequence Editor as shown in Figure 3.13.

Many studios produce their final postproduction on external editors and assemble the final movie in really expensive software. We can't compare the VSE in Blender with such specific applications. Anyway, the VSE is powerful enough to suit the needs of small and medium studios that might use this editor for very different purposes like making animatics, composing rough timelines, applying effects to determined scenes, or assembling small projects.

1. *Header*:

   a. *Editor type selector*: This pops up a list of the different editor types that we can switch to.

   b. *Pull-down menu*: This contains important options to manage the strips. Available options are *View*, *Select*, *Marker*, *Add*, and *Strip*.

   c. *Type of Sequencer View*: We can select between three types of views. Depending on the selected view, we have available different options. The available views are *Sequencer*, *Preview*, and *Both*.

2. *Stripes*: This is the editor where we can add and manage the strips. We have them separated by channels and use the same horizontal rule as other editors, incorporating the timeline at the bottom, where we may control where the strips start and where they end.

3.4.8 Text Editor

It is not usual for 3D applications, but Blender contains an internal text editor as part of its editor types. It is very useful for scripting and coding within the Blender interface; at the same time, we can check our recent script in action with Alt+P keys that parses the text in the text buffer to the internal Python interpreter. It also comes with some useful plug-ins that help us to write classes or functions, word completion, or browse variables along the text. But there are many other useful reasons for getting the internal text editor within the Blender architecture; that is, taking notes for a to-do list for your project, scheduling your work, writing documentation, and so on. For example, imagine a rigger writing technical notes that the animator could check whenever he wants regarding the rigging specifications and use. Figure 3.14 represents the text editor with a Python file open.

1. *Text buffer*: This is where we write the text itself. Like any other editor; it's empty by default waiting for us to type and input our text. This text buffer is empty and doesn't allow you to type anything until you open a file or make a new file with the *New* button.

2. *Header*:

   a. *Editor type selector*: This pops up a list of the different editor types that we can switch to.

   b. *Pulldown menus*: This contains specific information and options for text management like format, templates, copy and paste, save, and more.

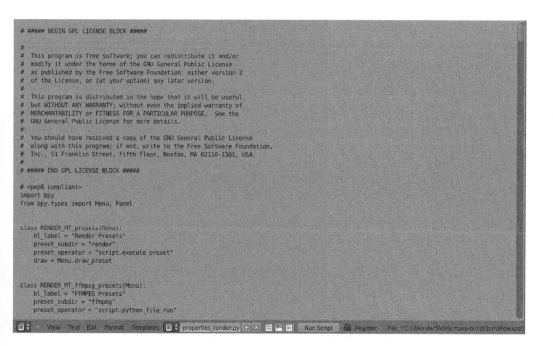

FIGURE 3.14 Text Editor.

    i. *Default*: By default, the available options for the pulldown menu are *View*, *Text*, and *Templates*.

    ii. *Create or Open Text*: When we create a new text or we open a text block, the available options for this menu are *View*, *Text*, *Edit*, *Format*, and *Templates*.

c. *Text Id block textbox*: We can select the text file we want to edit by browsing with the text Id block browser. A list of all our open files in buffer is displayed. Near this is the textbox which we can use to modify or input a new file name together with + (plus) and x (ex) buttons.

d. *Display options*: We have three buttons to enable or disable *Line number* column on the left of the text, *Word-wrap* horizontally, and *Syntax highlight*, which is useful for scripting.

e. *Run script*: This button is an alias of the Alt+P shortcut and basically executes the text buffer script we already have parsing it to the built-in Python interpreter. There is an option close to it to *Register* the script as a module on loading, so we don't need to load the script everytime we load Blender. If checked, Blender will load it automatically, for which our script should be a Python script.

3.4.9 Node Editor

When we need to post process or add any of the post effects to our renders, as in Figure 3.15, we need to deal with the Node editor, where we can use the *Nodes* for refining and texturing the material so that we improve the final composition. Here we give the final touch to the animation or render adding very different kinds of effects, settings, and values that determine the final output. That is directly related to the render time that Blender lets you spend for each still, because for complex projects with complex node trees, the render time increases as more resources are required for processing.

1. *Header*:

a. *Editor type selector*: This pops up a list of the different editor types that we can switch to.

b. *Pulldown menu*: This contains relevant options to manage the ongoing rendered frame. The available options are *View*, *Select*, *Add*, and *Node*.

c. *Node tree type*: We can switch between three types to display our node tree, like *Shader nodes*, *Texture nodes*, and *Compositing nodes*:

    i. In *Shader nodes* mode, we have a few other options being displayed like *Material datablock to be linked*.

    ii. In *Texture nodes* mode, we have options like *Texture datablock to be linked*, and the *Type of data* to take the texture from displayed with *Object*, *World*, and *Brush* as available options.

FIGURE 3.15 Node Editor. We can make the final postproduction composition updates and effects with a node tree within the Node Editor. This image represents the node tree for the project codenamed *Mushroom*.

    d. *Use Nodes*: This enables the compositing node tree.

    e. *Free Unused*: This frees nodes that are not being used during the compositing process.

    f. *Backdrop*: This uses the active Viewer node as the background for the current compositing; for example, in Figure 3.15, it enables display of the landscape background.

    g. *Channels*: These are the channels that are used to draw, namely *RGB*, *RGB and Alpha*, *Alpha*, and more.

    h. *Snap to*: This is the type of element to snap node to. The available options are *Node X/Y*, *Node Y*, *Node X*, and *Increment, Copy, and paste nodes*

  2. *Node board*: We'd add here the kind of nodes we need at any time or combine them to obtain the desired result. Here we can also group nodes and check the result of this combination in real time if the *Use Nodes* and *Backdrop* options are enabled on this editor header.

3.4.10 Logic Editor

This editor is the one dealing with all the gaming features Blender includes. It works with each game object, so they store a number of logical components usually called *Logic Bricks*

FIGURE 3.16 Logic Editor.

that guides directly the behavior of the objects in the scenes in the same way they do to others. Figure 3.16 represents the Logic editor by default.

1. *Header*:

   a. *Editor type selector*: This pops up a list of the different editor types that we can switch to.

   b. *Pulldown menu*: This contains specific information and options for views and deal with logic bricks. The available options are *View* and *Add*, the latest one where we can work with *Actuators*, *Controllers*, and *Sensors*.

2. *Logic Bricks*: Blender incorporates some prebuilt functions as blocks, also called bricks, that combine to create the logic of the game; that is, the way we control our main character, physics, or game targets. We found three kinds of logic bricks: *Sensors*, *Controllers*, and *Actuators*.

   a. *Sensors*: If we look in the Blender wiki, sensors are described as primitive event listeners, which are triggered by specific events such as collision, a key press, or mouse movement. That is a good definition in theory, but in other words, sensors are those elements Blender calls, when we execute any action as mentioned earlier, mouse movements. The sensors parse to Controllers anything that we make.

   b. *Controllers*: The controllers read the sensor output to execute actuators that are connected, if conditions are fine.

   c. *Actuators*: These are the logic bricks working with the game simulation directly.

3. *Properties panel*: In the Logic Editor, properties are those elements accessing data values for the whole game or for particular objects.

3.4.11 Properties Editor

The properties editor is the one that stores different panels for different contexts. Those panels contain the specific options for each context.

In Blender, we have several contexts available and we can switch between them depending on the object we have selected in 3D view. The available contexts are *Render*, *Render Layers*, *Scene*, *World*, *Object*, *Object Constraints*, *Modifiers*, *Object data*, *Material*, *Texture*, *Particle*, and *Physics* by default (Figure 3.17).

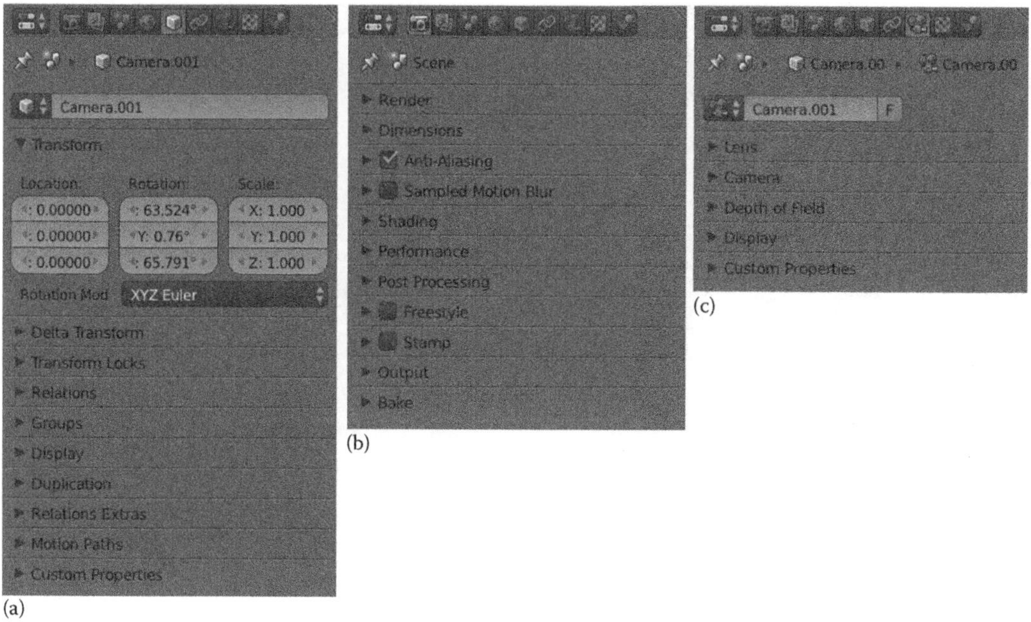

(a)

(b)

(c)

FIGURE 3.17 Properties Editor stores different panels with different options depending on the context that is determined by the type of object selected in the 3D view. The picture represents the Object context (a), the Render context (b), and the Object Data context (c).

There are some other contexts depending on the type of selected object like *Bone* and *Bone Constraints*, if we are working with bones and armatures.

3.4.12 Outliner

Some projects contain a lot of data, objects, datablocks, or scenes and keeping it organized is not an easy task. Blender has the Outliner Editor, that helps us to navigate through all the elements that our ongoing Blender session contains. With the Outliner, we can organize and programme our work, as shown in Figure 3.18; for example, view the current data tree, select or deselect objects, hide or show elements, make objects unselectable, allow objects to be rendered, delete objects, and more.

1. *Editor type selector*: This pops up a list of the different editor types that we can switch to.

2. *Pull-down menu*: This contains important options to work with Blender's objects and data. The available options are *View* and *Search*.

3. *Type of information to display*: This allows us to filter the outliner display to show different objects, datablocks, or specific data. The available options are *All Scenes*, *Current Scene*, *Visible Layers*, *Selected*, *Active*, *Same Types*, *Groups*, *Libraries*, *Sequence*, *Datablocks*, *User Preferences*, and *Key Maps*.

4. *Live Search Filtering*: This input is really useful to filter and fetch, within the Outliner, for the string we input.

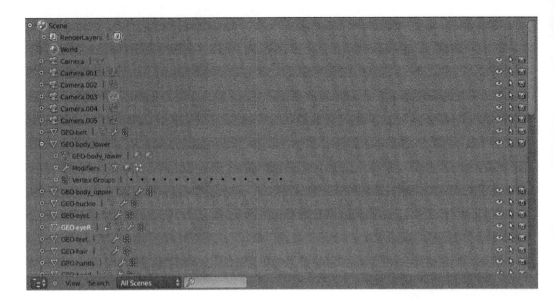

FIGURE 3.18 Outliner.

3.4.13 User Preferences

Like any other software, Blender can be customized to match users' needs using the User Preferences editor as shown in Figure 3.19. There we can modify options for very different purposes like interface, add-ons, files, or system options. Modifying these settings will result in how Blender works. The available options are *Interface*, *Editing*, *Input*, *Add-Ons*, *Themes*, *File*, and *System*.

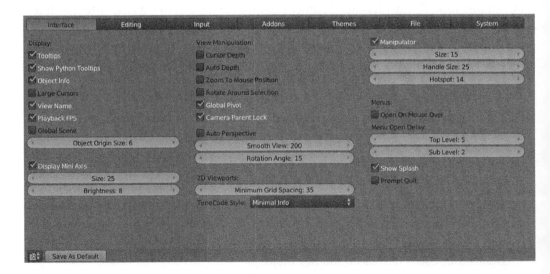

FIGURE 3.19 User Preferences. We can configure our Blender settings from this editor. Modifying these settings will result in a change in Blender's behavior.

1. *Header*: The User Preferences editor's Header is pretty simple and only contains the *Save As Default* that makes the current file the default .blend file.

2. *Options*: We can modify Blender's settings in seven different areas.

   a. *Interface*: Here we can configure how to display UI elements and their behavior. We have the chance to modify options for *Display*, *View Manipulation*, *Auto Perspective*, *2D Viewport*, *Manipulators*, or *Menus*. For example, we can enable/disable if we want Blender to show the splash screen or if we want to display the Tooltips.

   b. *Editing*: In this panel, we can configure how some tools will react to our inputs; for example, enable Auto Keyframing or make new objects enter edit mode by default when we create them. As we see, configuring these options will determine how we work with Blender, that is, how Blender reacts to our inputs. Some options are *Link material to*, *Undo steps*, *Grease Pencil*, *Keyframing*, or *Duplicate data*.

   c. *Add-ons*: Blender add-ons are simply features that are not enabled in Blender by default, but the user might enable and use them within his working sessions. There are a lot of add-ons available not only in each Blender release but also over the net. Add-ons are available in different areas of Blender like *Animation*, *Game Engine*, *Objects*, *Render*, and more. Many of the add-ons are simply Python scripts written by users and incorporated within the Blender trunk code. Each user is able to write his own add-on script and make it available by installing it on this panel.

   d. *Themes*: If we want to modify Blender appearance and colors, we can modify the Blender theme and make it our own. We can modify every aspect of the user interface here with regard to the colors; for example, in 3D View we may modify color for active object edges, the selected vertex, the active bones, and everything we want. As before, we are able to modify everything in color for each of the Blender editors.

   e. *File*: It is also possible to modify settings for the file managing system, so we may set a temporary folder, configure relative paths, set default fonts location, or decide where we want our render output by default. We can also configure here the number of saved versions we want, compress the file if we want to, and do more.

3.4.14 Info Window

In Blender, the *Info window* is like any other editor; however, it only contains the header where Blender stores important and useful information and options to control our Blender' sessions, as shown in Figure 3.20.

FIGURE 3.20 Info Window.

1. *Editor type selector*: This pops up a list of the different editor types that we can switch to.

2. *Pulldown menu*: This contains important info and options for control of Blender and user experience. Available options are *File, Add, Render, Window*, and *Help*.

3. *Select workspace layout*: This feature offers a drop-down menu with the different built-in layouts available as in Section 3.3.3. We may add or delete new layouts if desired.

4. *Select scene*: This is a drop-down selector with all our available scenes so that we can switch from one to another as required. We may add or delete scenes in our current Blender session from within this widget as we saw in Section 3.3.4.

5. *Engine for rendering*: This is the drop-down menu to select the render engine we want to use in the current Blender session. Available engines are *Blender Render, Blender Game*, and *Cycles Render*.

6. *Render progression bar*: While rendering, Blender shows a progression bar close to the *Engine to use for rendering* the drop-down menu. This bar shows the progress in the status of the current render process.

7. *File info*: The Info window also stores useful and important info for the current file relative to our scene and objects. So we have info like *Blender version, number of vertices* or *faces* or our meshes, *number of objects* and *lamps*, and probably the *amount of memory* our file consumes. All this info is important in order to know if we are going out of our hardware limits.

3.4.15 File Browser

The File Browser editor deals with file managing and operations like *fetch and open* or *save* and folders' structure such as *create folder*. Figure 3.21 represents the File Browse editor by default.

By default, the File Browser editor contains the following:

1. *Header*:

   a. *Editor type selector*: This pops up a list of the different editor types that we can switch to.

   b. *Move between folders*: This widget contains four buttons that allows us to move between folders on the disk. They are *Move to previous folder, Move to next folder, Move to parent directory*, and *Refresh the file list*.

   c. *Create new directory*: This is a button to generate a folder in the current selected path. A confirmation message will appear after clicking this button and once confirmed we will be able to apply a name to the recently created directory.

   d. *Display mode for the file list*: This is a set of three buttons that sets the display mode for the elements within the current selected path. The modes available are *Display*

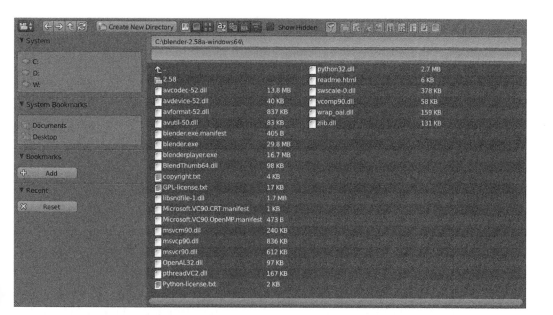

FIGURE 3.21   File Browser.

as short list where Blender shows just the file or folder name and size on disk (only for files), *Display as detailed list* where Blender shows all those in the previous one plus the modification date, and finally, *Display as thumbnails* that makes Blender show the folder structure with bigger icons and file names below.

e. *Sort by*: This allows us to sort the directory elements *alphabetically*, or by *extension*, *modification date, time*, and *size*.

f. *Show hidden*: This enables or disables the option to make hidden files within the directory visible.

g. *File filtering*: This funnel-like icon enables the option of filtering directory elements showing them according to several criteria. The available options are *show folders*, *.blend files*, *.blend1, .blend2, etc.*, *files*, *images*, *movies*, *script files*, *font files*, *sound files*, and *text files*. We can combine and select as many filters as we want, so, for example, we can filter to list only folders and .blend files in the current directory.

2. *Side panel*: This panel contains relevant options depending on the action we want to execute; that is, there are different tabs depending on whether we are saving or opening a file.

a. *If opening a file*: The file browser editor's side panel contains tabs for *System, System bookmarks, Bookmarks, Recent*, and *Open Blender File*.

b. *If saving a file*: The file browser editor's side panel contains tabs for *System, System bookmarks, Bookmarks, Recent*, and *Save Blender File*.

i. *System*: This contains a list of available drives that we have to navigate within.

ii. *System bookmarks*: This includes default system favorite folders for easy access.

iii. *Bookmarks*: We have the option to add new bookmarks to access our projects easily. Just navigate to that folder and click the *Add* button. We can delete bookmarks in the same way by clicking the x (cross) button.

iv. *Recent*: This shows a list of the recently accessed directories.

v. *Open blender file*: This allows us to deal with some important options before loading any blender (.blend) file and is visible when we select the *Open file* option either from the Info Window editor or by pressing Ctrl+O keys. *Load UI* allows us to load the workspace layout in the file because Blender saves that layout into the .blend file. Another option is the *Trusted source* that is useful when we are not sure if the file we are loading is safe or not.

vi. *Save blender file*: This deals with options for saving our session into the .blend file by selecting *Save as* from either the Info Window editor or by pressing Ctrl+Shift+S keys. *Compress* allows us to compress the saved file. *Remap relative* is useful to remap relative paths while saving in a different directory. *Save copy* makes a copy of the current system. *Legacy mesh format* is a bit complex and we deal with it later.

3. *File browser and folder navigation:* We have here a list of all files and folders in the current directory. We can see the current directory path in the top input field close to the *Open Blender File* button. The input below shows the selected file name close to the icons – (minus) and + (plus) and *Cancel*. The latest version closes the File Browser editor returning to the previous Blender workspace.

3.4.16 Console

To directly use Python with Blender, we can use the Console editor. It manages our Python commands directly over the Blender's core architecture. We can launch the Console editor by selecting from the *editor type selector* or using a keyboard shortcut by pressing Shift+F4. Figure 3.22 represents Console editor by default.

1. *Header*:

a. *Editor type selector*: This pops up a list of the different editor types that we can switch to.

b. *Pulldown menu*: We can manage some features and settings for the console editor. The available options are those of *Console*.

c. *Autocomplete*: This is accessible by pressing the button or just using Ctrl+Spacebar. Basically it suggests any expression and tries to autocomplete depending on the already typed characters; for example, typing *bpy* and enabling autocomplete option gives us the chance to use some of the bpy built-in modules.

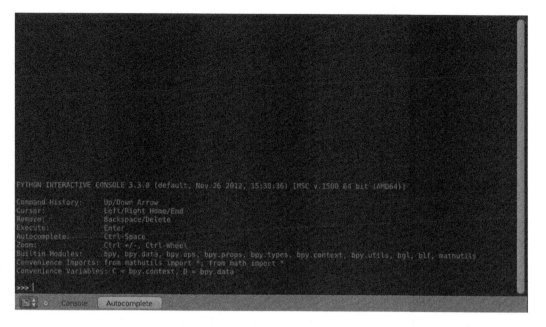

```
PYTHON INTERACTIVE CONSOLE 3.3.0 (default, Nov 26 2012, 15:38:36) [MSC v.1500 64 bit (AMD64)]

Command History:       Up/Down Arrow
Cursor:                Left/Right Home/End
Remove:                Backspace/Delete
Execute:               Enter
Autocomplete:          Ctrl-Space
Zoom:                  Ctrl +/-, Ctrl-Wheel
Builtin Modules:       bpy, bpy.data, bpy.ops, bpy.props, bpy.types, bpy.context, bpy.utils, bgl, blf, mathutils
Convenience Imports:   from mathutils import *, from math import *
Convenience Variables: C = bpy.context, D = bpy.data

>>> |
```

FIGURE 3.22 Console.

2. *Console display*: All results from our Python commands input will be the output in the console display. It's currently color mode enabled, so it helps us in the scripting process. Since Blender 2.5, Python 3.x has been accepted. Console displays the command prompt, that is, where we write our commands, in the way of ">>>" symbols.

3.5 MODES AND CONTEXT

We can not only display different options in Blender depending on the mode we are in but also filter such options according to the context we are working in. In Blender, we can select the context we want to be working in from the *Properties Editor*, which shows the *Context buttons* as shown in Figure 3.23.

The different context types Blender allows us to work with are

1. *Render*: Everything related to rendering of our scene is located in this panel. We can configure a variety of settings affecting the final render result. Here we can decide if we need to render our scene like an animation generating a motion picture or merely as a static still.

FIGURE 3.23 Context buttons. We can switch the context we are working in from these buttons. Each context displays its own options and features.

We can modify the dimensions of the final result or the range of frames for the animation. We can also decide on the quality of our render by applying anti-aliasing or enabling compositing with nodes.

Some of the panels located in such context are *Render, Layers, Dimensions, Anti-Aliasing, Sampled Motion Blur, Shading, Performance, Post Processing, Stamp, Output,* and *Bake*.

2. *Scene*: From here we can modify general settings related to the scene like change the metrics, simplify subdivision to streamline computer processes, or even modify gravity, which is specially useful for simulations projects.

Some of the panels located in such a context are *Scene, Audio, Units, Keying Set, Gravity, Simplify,* and *Color Management*.

3. *World*: Our scene will also be affected by the settings we can modify in the World context. Here we find settings like the type of color we want for the horizon while we are in 3D View, enabling ambient occlusion, modifying the environment lighting, or applying indirect lighting and enabling a kind of fog denominated *mist*.

Some of the panels located in such a context are *World, Ambient Occlusion, Environment Lighting, Indirect Lighting, Gather, Mist,* and *Stars*.

4. *Object*: All those aspects that allow us to modify the appearance of our objects, primitives, or models, are located in the object context. Here we can modify our object's name, change its transformation properties, that is, *Location, Rotation,* and *Scale*. We also may lock such properties to avoid the object being translated, scaled, or rotated. Another interesting feature is that we can move our objects between layers or organize them in groups within this context.

Some of the panels located in such a context are *Transform, Delta Transform, Transform Locks, Relations, Groups, Display, Duplication, Relations Extras,* and *Motion Paths*.

5. *Constraints*: This is a very important context because it determines the relationship between our objects and how they operate between them and the environment. Constraints are just tools that modify our objects' behavior and sometimes enable some kind of relationship between them.

We find four big categories of constraints according to its purpose. They are *Motion Tracking, Transform, Tracking,* and *Relationship*. There are constraints that allow us to copy location, rotation, or scale and others to limit location, rotation, scale, or distance. Some are merely there to force our object to track another one if the latter modifies its transform properties.

a. *Motion Tracking*: *Camera Solver, Object Solver,* and *Follow Track*.

b. *Transform*: *Copy Location, Copy Rotation, Copy Scale, Copy Transform, Limit Distance, Limit Location, Limit Rotation, Limit Scale, Maintain Volume,* and *Transformation*.

c. *Tracking*: *Clamp To, Damped Track, Inverse Kinematics, Locked Track, Spline IK, Stretch To*, and *Track To*.

d. *Relationship*: *Action, Child Of, Floor, Follow Path, Pivot, Rigid Body Joint, Script*, and *Shrinkwrap*.

6. *Modifiers*: Even as constraints affect the behavior of our objects, modifiers change the appearance of our objects. There are four categories of modifiers depending on their purpose. They are *Modify, Generate, Deform*, and *Simulate*.

Some modifiers change the aspect of our objects by applying deformation like Armatures or Lattices. Others are used to generate new objects by using the first one as the base, like Mirror, Array, Bevel, Solidify, or the famous Subdivision Surface. Our objects may be targets of simulations and physics too, because of which we find modifiers like Cloth, Collision, Fluid Simulation, Particle System, Smoke, or Soft Body.

a. *Modify*: *UV Project, Vertex Weight Edit, Vertex Weight Mix*, and *Vertex Weight Proximity*.

b. *Generate*: *Array, Bevel, Boolean, Build, Decimate, Edge Split, Mask, Mirror, Multiresolution, Remesh, Screw, Skin, Solidify, Subdivision Surface*, and *Triangulate*.

c. *Deform*: *Armature, Cast, Curve, Displace, Hook, Laplacian Smooth, Lattice, Mesh Deform, Shrinkwrap, Simple Deform, Smooth, Warp*, and *Wave*.

d. *Simulation*: *Cloth, Collision, Dynamic Paint, Explode, Fluid Simulation, Ocean, Particle Instance, Particle System, Smoke*, and *Soft Body*.

7. *Object Data*: This context focuses on modifying those properties related to our objects in Edit Mode. In fact, some of the panels located in this context are only available if we are in such a mode. From here we may add vertex groups, change the name of ObData, apply new shape keys, or add new UV maps.

Some of the panels located in such a context are *Normals, Texture Space, Vertex Groups, Shape Keys, UV Maps, Vertex Colors*, and *Geometry Data*.

8. *Materials*: Everything related to materials that we want to apply to our objects are here. In this context we can create our materials library that we can apply later to our objects. We can also modify all those parameters to get the material quality desired. From here we can modify color, intensity, and the kind of specular light and its intensity.

We also can modify the quantity of light emitted, the ambient light received by our objects, and the transparency or raytrace. From here we can also modify materials when our objects have applied a particles modifier. We can also select the kind of shadow projected and received or get rid of the shadows completely.

Some of the panels located in such a context are *Preview, Diffuse, Specular, Shading, Transparency, Mirror, Subsurface Scattering, Strand, Options*, and *Shadow*.

9. *Textures*: As in the previous context, here we can work with the kind of texture we want to add to our objects, the type of map we want to apply to such texture, and how many

influence should use. We can create new textures and add them to our library to use later in our objects and improve the quality of our work.

Some of the panels located in such a context are *Mapping* and *Influence*. Blender offers different kind of internal textures, also called procedural textures, namely, *Blend, Clouds, Distorted Noise, Environment Map, Image or Movie, Magic, Marble, Musgrave, Noise, Point Density, Stucci, Voronoi, Voxel Data, Wood*, and *Ocean*.

10. *Particles*: By default this is an empty context until a new particle system is added. We can then find parameters to modify such a system, because we can select between emitter and hair. Some parameters that will affect our particle system are the number of emissions, physics, children, as for example, if we want to render emissors, velocity, or if we want to apply such a particle system to the whole object, or just to any vertex group. The particle system context incorporates a very interesting panel called Force Field Settings where we can apply internal forces like Wind or Turbulence, for example.

Some of the panels located in such a context for the Emitter particles are *Emission, Cache, Velocity, Rotation, Physics, Render, Display, Children, Field Weights, Force Field Settings*, and *Vertex Groups*.

Some of the panels located in such context for the Hair particles are *Emission, Hair dynamics, Render, Display, Childrens, Field Weights, Force Field Settings*, and *Vertex Groups*.

11. *Physics*.

3.6 INTERNATIONALIZATION

Blender has been updated to support international languages for both the interface and tooltips. Even though the default language is English, we can enable our preferred language from the User Preferences editor under the System tab as shown in Figure 3.24. If we enable it, Blender shows three different settings:

1. *Language*: We can select our language here.

2. *Interface*: If we want Blender's user interface showing buttons and menus in our preferred language, we have to enable this option.

3. *Tooltips*: As before, enabling this option shows all Blender's Tooltips in our preferred language.

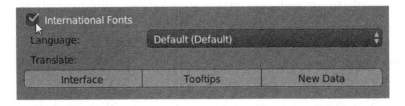

FIGURE 3.24 Internationalization options. We can switch to another language from the User Preferences editor.

## CHAPTER 4

Blender in a Digital Studio Pipeline

BEFORE WE START ENUMERATING the reasons why Blender is a 3D suite that could suit any animation studio requirement, we need to know how those studios work and what are the different stages of any project.

Every kind of studio—big or small or home based—has several standard stages. That doesn't mean all studios work in the same way, using the same production process.

A very important thing to take into consideration is that big studios have a larger number of people working in their films, and the projects are usually different in size and quality, though the last point about quality is not always true.

It has been proven that there are a fair number of open movies of good quality developed with Blender to demonstrate that small projects—we should probably call them modest projects—can be developed with the same professionalism as the big studios without huge infrastructure, executive producers, and funds.

We know that Blender has already been used for years in a professional way, for example, in commercials. There are a lot of incredible professional commercials that have been developed using Blender.

In the same way, there are many open movies developed with this 3D creation suite, as demonstrated by the Blender Foundation and Blender Institute funded open movies or the ones developed by private studios or those incorporating Blender in their pipeline at a particular point as shown in Figure 4.1.

This open movie was the first to give us a clear idea on how to develop a 3D film. What happens inside any of the big and famous animation studios is usually a mystery but nowadays, thanks to the open source concept, we can understand each of the specific areas a 3D film is composed of.

We already know how to set up our disk to store everything and how the different teams work together in modeling, lighting, and compositing, for example.

FIGURE 4.1 Orange studio at the Blender Institute. The resulting open movie *Elephants Dream* become the first open movie developed entirely using Blender.

And this has resulted in the big studios opening their doors and letting us know how they develop their products, and the different stages and processes to finally create the magic. It's common nowadays to learn about it on their own websites where they describe all these processes in production.

Anyway, as mentioned earlier, we can find some common stages in any 3D film production independent of the studio and the size of the project. The different stages we find in 3D film development are

1. Script writing

2. Storyboarding

3. Art conceptualization

4. Modeling

5. Rigging

6. Choosing the surface

7. Deciding the layout

8. Character animation

9. Producing effects

10. Postproduction

Actually, Blender is commonly used in production stages such as modeling, rigging, animation, and more, but it's less common to use Blender for preproduction or postproduction purposes. However, we'll see right now that it's also possible to do this and sometimes even recommended.

4.1 USING BLENDER FOR PREPRODUCTION TASKS

In animation studios, the preproduction stage is the one where the project is in a very initial stage with rough ideas, concepts, and things to develop. It's normal to have many meetings with the project crew and create teams for different purposes.

We can argue about what's good and what's bad in comparing big and small studios. For example, having to organize teams and contents in an extremely super production is not an easy task and maybe small studios cooperate better with fewer members in the team organizing roles.

At the same time, production is, logically, slower in small studios than in big animation studios, if we talk about projects of the same size. It is always a good idea to have everything organized, not only for big productions but also for small ones. It's highly recommended to have organized a clear idea on the project timeline, and at the same time, it's important to keep organized the project structure on the disk.

This, though it seems the logical thing to do, is not always possible. We can't have everything under control in a film production. Sometimes there are delays in development, sometimes we need to modify a specific character, or directly get rid of determined scenes.

That is an inevitable consequence of film productions being artistic creations. Things could change independently when we think we have everything under control.

Because of this, it's also common to work together with spreadsheets and calendars. It's very important in a very well organized project to know how much time is spent by each department and how much time any team has left to complete the stuff. This makes the whole project stick to deadlines and executive producers are usually pushing to get things done within that scheduled deadline.

Spreadsheets are usually used to store as many details as possible, so different departments have useful information to develop their parts of the project. Some of the information we store in those breakup are scene number, scene name, shot number, shot type, description, frames, duration, use of environment or props, use of physics, dialog, ambience, or even render engine to be used, and the render time as shown in Figure 4.2.

As mentioned earlier, it's also common to use a schedule sheet so that the project is organized in the calendar determining the production length as shown in Figure 4.3. Developing a good schedule is a very important task, but that doesn't mean tasks are merely scheduled with no reason. It has to be done by thinking carefully about what the film needs, the available team skills, and the amount of funds the project has. It's also common to develop different schedule graphics to take care of delays in production.

Anyway, what we want to know is how Blender can deal with this preproduction stage and with things like writing the script, developing our storyboard, or creating the concept art, for example.

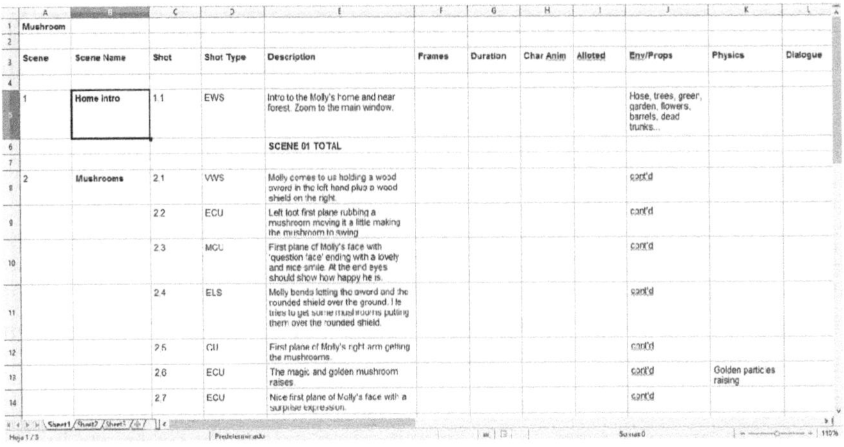

Scene	Scene Name	Shot	Shot Type	Description	Frames	Duration	Char Anim	Alloted	Env/Props	Physics	Dialogue
1	Home intro	1.1	EWS	Intro to the Molly's home and near forest. Zoom to the main window.					Hose, trees, greer, garden, flowers, barrels, dead trunks...		
				SCENE 01 TOTAL							
2	Mushrooms	2.1	VWS	Molly comes to us holding a wood sword in the left hand plus a wood shield on the right.					cont'd		
		2.2	ECU	Left foot first plane rubbing a mushroom moving it a little making the mushroom to swing					cont'd		
		2.3	MCU	First plane of Molly's face with 'question face' ending with a lovely and nice smile. At the end eyes should show how happy he is.					cont'd		
		2.4	ELS	Molly bends letting the sword and the rounded shield over the ground. He tries to get some mushrooms putting them over the rounded shield.					cont'd		
		2.5	CU	First plane of Molly's right arm getting the mushrooms.					cont'd		
		2.6	ECU	The magic and golden mushroom raises.					cont'd	Golden partic es raising	
		2.7	ECU	Nice first plane of Molly's face with a surprise expression.					cont'd		

FIGURE 4.2 Mushroom project breakup. We can use spreadsheets to develop the project breakup. This gives a lot of information for the different departments.

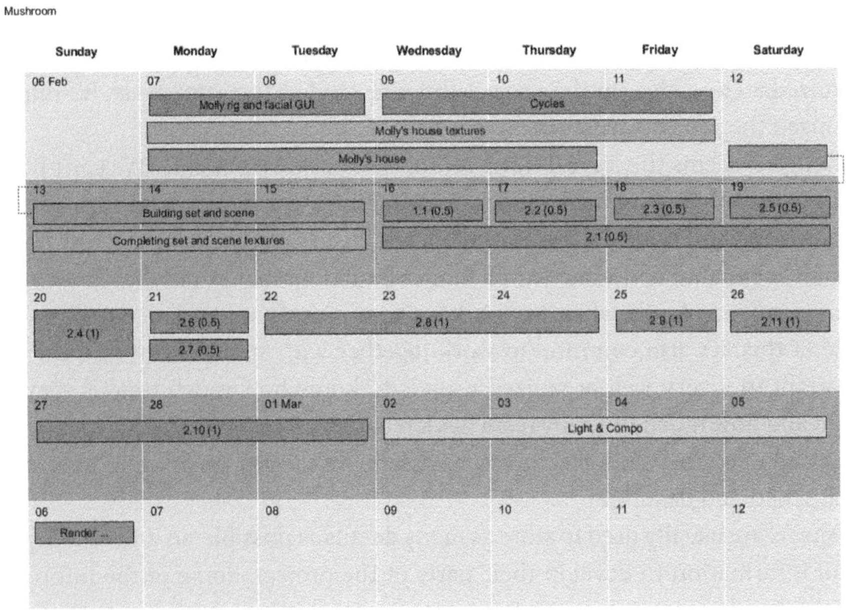

FIGURE 4.3 **(See color insert.)** Schedule graphic determining the project stages in the calendar. Picture represents the schedule document for the Mushroom project.

4.1.1 Developing the Script with Blender

Writing the script is one of the first things when developing animation projects, at least having a rough set of ideas is really important before the machine starts working. For that, writers have a lot of applications to work with depending on the platform and operating system they are running but we'll see how we can do it with Blender too.

As we already know, Blender incorporates a *Text Editor* that is supposed to be used to run Python scripts within the Blender architecture, but we also said that this editor suits other

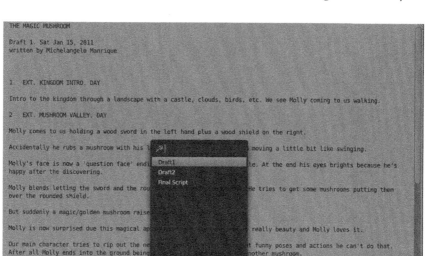

FIGURE 4.4 Script written within Blender. We can also write our script using Blender's Text Editor, which suits our needs perfectly.

requirements in our projects and one could be the writing of our project script. It's not crazy to have a .*blend* file with our script written in Blender, as shown in Figure 4.4.

4.1.2 Using the Video Sequence Editor to Build the Storyboard

Once we have the story script in any manner, we will start working on our storyboard. It's true that Blender doesn't support painting 2D like other editors such as GIMP or MyPaint, for example, or at least not at the same level; so we'll need to develop our sketches there. But what we can do is to build our storyboard, and start playing with timeline and layouts, using the Video Sequence Editor within Blender. We can compose, add or delete sketches, and adapt our storyboard to the purpose of our project and we can also check our script that was written earlier with the Text Editor.

4.1.3 Creating Concept Art

Every animation project requires a lot of work in concept art, so artists recreate what we have in our script and storyboard in their drawings and pictures. A lot of references, models, and inspirational concepts that will be used in the production are developed by artists in these concept art 2D sketches.

It's normal to use painting software to develop the concept art, and we already know that Blender is not a tool for such kind of painting. But what can we do regarding concept art in Blender? Well, we can use Blender as the base for concept art sketches; that is, we can develop layout structures and objects or build our primitive scene with Blender's primitive objects and then retouch and paint it with external tools to feature the final concept art sketch.

This is a practice that is used so artists can play with the scene compositing in space layout, disposition, measures, and more, making the concept art sketch more accurate to the final shot, as shown in Figure 4.5.

FIGURE 4.5 Concept art primitives. We can get the primitives of concept art using Blender and then repaint with external tools.

But, painting software is not always required. It's also usual to develop the whole concept art in a traditional way, using paper and ink or any other technique. The fact is that the days of concept art creation are really stressful because it's common to fill everything with drawings, ideas, concepts, and more. Everything in the studio is covered by a lot of potential ideas as shown in Figure 4.6.

Not all ideas go to the final film of course. There are a lot of them that simply don't go further for very different reasons but anyway, each one of them helps in clarifying the idea of the film. After the concept art is created, we have a clear idea what we have in the film and what we don't have appearing in it (Figure 4.7).

4.2 USING BLENDER FOR POSTPRODUCTION TASKS

It's usual that once studios have the production almost ready, they fix or add final bits to the compositing and it's common to use external applications for things such as adding effects, fix compositing lights, or making the final composition with video and audio editors.

FIGURE 4.6 *Elephants Dream* project. The picture shows a desk full of artwork and concept art for the movie.

FIGURE 4.7 **(See color insert.)** Omega stop motion project. Directed by Eva Franz and Andy Goralczyk, this is an awesome stop motion movie developed using Blender. The picture represents the concept art developed for the movie.

Blender has all we need to make this with no need to export or work in external applications for that. We'll see postproduction features later in this book but it's interesting to know at this point that such things are possible with Blender.

As we can see, Blender suits almost everything any studio needs to successfully develop any animation project, from preproduction tasks to production work and finally postproduction tasks.

4.3 ORGANIZE THE PROJECT IN DISK

It's also important for any studio to have a clear idea on how the project folder in the disk is organized. For that, it's strongly recommended to follow some guidelines and naming conventions, as shown in Figure 4.8. And this is so, because in large projects, the number of files, tests, animatics, mattes, and more is huge so it is easy to lose anything or expend valuable production time in messy directories and folders or incomprehensible file names.

At the same time, it's a very good idea to track everything with version control systems. Nowadays, it's really common for animation studios to collaborate with each other from very different locations thanks to the Internet.

This relationship is not possible if they don't work under version control systems such as git, subversion, mercurial, or any other out there. The time spent in re-factoring or re-modeling a whole scene is valuable in money in professional productions so using backups to previous revisions makes the difference between success and breakdown.

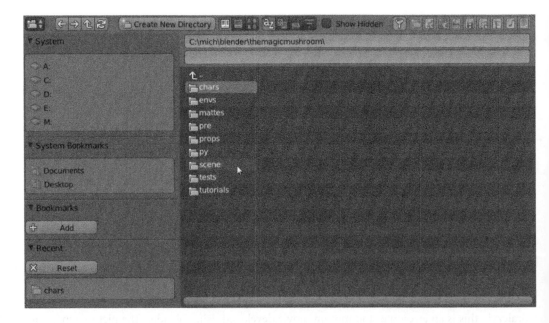

FIGURE 4.8 **(See color insert.)** Project's folder structure. Having a clean and organized project folder helps in productivity. It is strongly recommended to apply a project naming convention to avoid mistakes and messy project structure on disk.

A good folder structure could be as follows:

1. *chars*: The folder contains all our project's character models using naming conventions; that is, it's a good rule of thumb to have *bunnymodel.blend* for our bunny model and *bunnyrig.blend* for our bunny rig in separate files. This folder usually contains a textures folder where all textures used in our models are placed.

2. *envs*: This is for everything related to the environment and is usually where we store objects, building sets, and scenarios. Everything that won't be animated in the scene is here. Like the *chars*, it might contain a textures folder where all our objects' textures are located.

3. *mattes*: This folder usually contains 2D paintings used in backgrounds. Think on mattes like those backgrounds used for theatrical plays.

4. *pre*: In times of the *Lighthouse Animation Studio* and the *Mushroom* codenamed project we were using this folder to store everything related to preproduction, such as script and storyboard or breakdown and schedule sheets.

5. *props*: This is the folder for the known *properties* that are basically those objects we will animate in our project. This folder might also contain a textures folder.

6. *py*: The folder to store all our Python scripts that we might be loading later in our project.

7. *scene*: This is an important folder because we store here the whole scenes tree of our project. For very large projects, we need to set up a clean structure here.

8. *tests*: For all our tests and animatics or render tests.

9. *tutorials*: When we are developing an open source project, it's common to launch our project with some written or video tutorials.

10. *production*: For postproduction purposes and to store all final shots and compositing.

Blender currently offers many open movie workshops where we can learn not only technical aspects like modeling or texturing but also how to organize projects as shown in Figure 4.9.

One of the most interesting things of open movies is that they include almost everything used in film production, that is, from concept art pictures to 3D models, riggings, complete set of scenes, and so on.

This also gives us an idea of how is it all organized by the different teams, not only on disk but also in the production breakdown.

4.4 BLENDER AND THE OPEN MOVIES

The open movies is a concept that has become popular in last few years. The idea is to create a film with a wide range of people from different places and then release the whole content as open source under any of the current open source licenses.

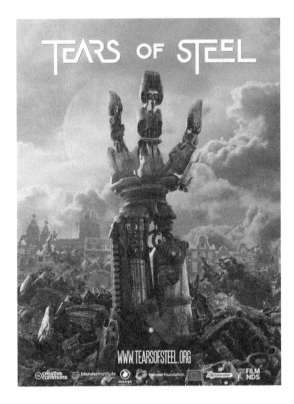

FIGURE 4.9 **(See color insert.)** *Tears of Steel* DVD box. Blender released not only the movie but also a whole open movie workshop containing all files used in the 3D film production.

The Blender Foundation started in 2006 with the very first open movie project. The usual period of work for open movies developed in the Blender Foundation is about 6–12 months where artists are invited to the Blender Institute and coordinated as teams for the different stages of the film production.

With such a small number of artists it's common to see each one working in several different disciplines. This is something that does not happen in big studios where it's not usual to work in any area other than what you were contracted for.

The final open movie product is released by the Blender Foundation in DVD or downloadable format. First, a preorder campaign looking for donations and funds is launched, so the project's costs are supported and the film is completed.

Nowadays, there are other ways to get funds in order to develop artistic content. A very well-known project, the Tube open movie, uses a kickstarter platform in order to obtain the required amount of money for its development.

So, for example, the Tube project started with a goal of $40,233. The first Blender Foundation open movie, *Elephants Dream* cost $100,000 to produce. The recently produced *Sintel* cost $400,000–$500,000. As expected, the amount of money an open movie costs depends on very different things like the length of the movie, the number of people in the teams, or added elements that raise the production expenses.

As we see, it's not free as in *free beer* to develop a film but we don't want to say that money is everything in a film. We want to think that there should be something more. Obviously, it helps in film production but let's get rid of this thought now and focus on the artistic one.

At the moment, the Blender Foundation has released four open movie projects and each one has been used to improve the Blender features and pipeline.

1. *Elephants Dream*: 2006. Codenamed the Orange project. This project needed the whole animation system refactored in the same way and the render engine needed a whole recode. But the great improvement Blender got from this project is the node-based compositor. Directed by Bassam Kurdali and produced by Ton Roosendaal.

2. *Big Buck Bunny*: 2008. Codenamed the Peach project, we have to talk about the great improvement in the particles system because of the requirement for furry characters. Directed by Sacha Goedegebure and produced by Ton Roosendaal.

3. *Sintel*: 2010. Codenamed the Durian project, this was a very ambitious and epic project that finally resulted in a 15 min short film. The main improvements were to test the stability, illumination rendering, or testing tools like sculpting of the refactored 2.5 version. Directed by Colin Levy and produced by Ton Roosendaal.

4. *Tears of Steel*: 2012. Codenamed the Mango project, this time the Blender Foundation developed a film with real actors in order to test Blender in vfx and realistic rendering. This film is based on a sci-fi theme recorded in Amsterdam. The use of green screen and motion track was introduced for visual effects. Directed by Ian Hubert and produced by Ton Roosendaal.

At the moment of authoring this book, the latest open movie project announced by the Blender Foundation was codenamed Gooseberry. It's intended to be a feature film developed by the Blender Institute and small studios around the world together.

As we see it's a very interesting idea that makes it easy for small studios to contribute to feature films and that demonstrates that Blender could be used in the pipeline of current studios.

We can then say that open movies are not only a way of producing 3D films but also a way to share knowledge. They are a way to contribute to other people sharing the hard work developed by an enthusiastic team. This becomes an interesting knowledge for other people improving their skills, creating better and committed artists, and making a more competitive market.

## CHAPTER 5

Modeling Your Main Character

WITHOUT DOUBT, ONE OF the most important points when developing an animation film is related to the main character design. It's mandatory that this design matches all the requirements in the film's preproduction meetings.

The main character in a film will be the one maintaining a straight forward relationship with the viewer both visually and sentimentally.

Because of that, animation studios have more than one 3D departments working on the project, but one art department where all the first sketches, backgrounds, environments, ideas, color tests, and everything regarding the visual aspect of the film are recreated with digital or traditional painting techniques.

Animation studios spend a lot of time of the preproduction stage developing all these details, where the artists don't stop developing sketches and tests that will be studied and approved later so they can go directly to the production team, making all the 3D work necessary to adapt those ideas to the final expected product.

Once the production team have something to work with, let's say the main character, one of the first things to do is to model everything. All sketches and tests should be moved from 2D to the 3D environment, in our case using Blender, of course.

The resulting model is not always exactly as the original idea developed by the creative art team because like any other task in a film production, everything evolves and new ideas and changes are incorporated at the same time that others are rejected.

Anyway, in very ambitious productions developed by big studios this rarely happens because the preproduction time is huge in such cases and everything needs to be clear when production starts to avoid delays in production, resulting in waste of time and money.

In small studios, modifying some ideas during production time is much more common, the project evolves at the same time as the ideas come; however, this is a very risky production method because if the project falls into the incorporation of new ideas with no control, the production time exceeds the expected one and each change requires time to develop and introduce, maybe resulting in an absolute failure and abandoning of the project.

In Blender, modeling our main character or any other kind of object or scene is a very intuitive process thanks to the built-in tools and the workspace where the mouse and keyboard peripherals interrelate to help us and speed up our work. Regarding that, the Blender community have something like a slogan, *use Blender with your left hand in the keyboard and your right hand on the mouse*, and we will see their reasons.

The design or model of our main character will depend on the kind of story we are developing, because the final result will vary depending on each case. We also have to take care of an important thing, that is to think about the next department using our recently developed model.

That means that when we are developing a model, object, or scene, this will automatically go to the next stage in the production chain, in our case the rigging department where they will apply the armature and bones to be used later by the animation team.

As mentioned earlier, from the business point of view, the time spent in any film production costs money. Each aspect of the film is studied before starting the production. They test production time and possible delays and finally producers will supply and invest enough money to start film production. If the productive time is delayed for any reason, the budget increases and this might make the investors retire from the project.

From a creative point of view, each error of the creative art team harms the work of the next department, and this means waste of time and money trying to fix those technical issues. But, what does it mean if we are talking about modeling with Blender?

Easy. While modeling a character, we have to take care of important things like how we develop the mesh, topology, proportions, and how to distribute vertices and edges so the rigging team can make a proper rig that the animation team could use without trouble.

An example of a mistake in this stage was recorded in one of our first projects in Platform Michelangelo Studio, codenamed RAT bProficiency, where we didn't complete the model of our main character by distributing vertices and edges as it should have been. The result was we had trouble in animating hands, where we developed a completely wrong topology as shown in Figure 5.1.

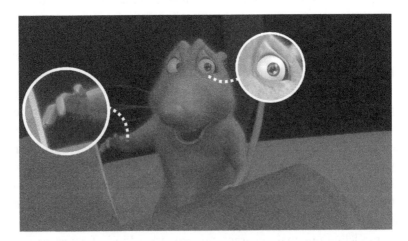

FIGURE 5.1 A wrong model will create trouble in the following stages of production, hurting the final result. In the picture, we see some of those modeling issues that will become bigger in the animation of hands and eyes.

FIGURE 5.2 Different types of characters. The top picture represents a mechanical character whereas the bottom one has a very much organic and toon-styled character.

With this in mind, again, good results are usually the result of very good preproduction work as we have already mentioned. This means we must ensure we have in mind a character that suits the idea we want to transmit in our project (Figure 5.2).

Some examples of different ideas when developing characters are the following:

1. *Action*: This is the mechanical part.
   Character: We design our character with a rigid body, some tubes, and lights, making it look technical and ensuring all moving parts are well designed to avoid future overlapping.

2. *Action*: This is the Toon part.
   Character: We design our character to allow for a soft body—do not confuse this with the dynamic soft bodies in Blender—to make it elastic and funny. We ensure those parts that stretch are well designed to avoid unstable behavior during animation.

FIGURE 5.3 **(See color insert.)** Developing a convincing character is not always easy. The picture represents the main character for *Tube* open movie. Notice that it suits perfectly the project concept, giving credibility to the film and increasing the viewer interest for this awesome film.

This seems to be a matter of common sense but is just here where people fail. A not-so-well designed character makes the whole production fail as well. Production requires hard work in specific areas to go to the next improving it and making it look as it should do.

Again, when a piece of the chain fails, then the production is not a success. Because of that, it is very important to take some time developing this model in the preproduction stage. If our project is a homemade one and we have no time frame for it, then we're lucky, because we can modify it as many times as we need because a successful animation requires a successful model to animate, but we currently have the most appreciated value in any production, time.

We must remember that a good animation is as good as the mesh allows. Having a well-designed character and a right model or mesh makes life easier while working in other areas.

It adds proficiency to our project and ensures good results. Riggers are usually supervising the modeling work to be sure they will be provided with models with enough quality to develop their rigging that automatically increases possibilities for animators (Figure 5.3).

5.1 MODELING IN BLENDER

We have several ways for modeling. Blender allows us to use the traditional method of *extrude*, where we are making and adapting faces and vertices to the desired topology.

In the same way, we build our character using sculpting tools, where we modify the volume to finally get our character from the primitive block.

FIGURE 5.4   This picture represents the difference between Object, on the left, and Mesh, on the right.

Another method is to use other tools such as curves, but depending on the character, this method might not help to achieve the desired result, so it is commonly used to model objects and props.

We are going to cover here the extrusion method in the same way as we'll talk about some of the most important modifiers that help in our character's development. We should make clear that Blender allows modeling using meshes, objects, curves, surfaces, text objects, meta objects, or groups of objects.

First of all, we need to understand the difference between mesh and object, as shown in Figure 5.4. This difference is not always clear, especially so for beginners, although it is a common topic in dedicated forums.

In Blender, there are different types of objects such as meshes, curves, surfaces, meta objects, text, armatures, empties, cameras, lamps, and force fields. These objects are usually available where Blender is in Object Mode, as we had mentioned in Chapter 3. What we need to study now is the first kind of object called *Mesh*.

A mesh is, basically, the object's structure composed of faces, vertices, and edges that can be edited with the editing tools within Blender; that is, a mesh is the object itself but in *Edit Mode* we can modify its topology.

As an example, we can think about a block of plasteline on the table, where if nobody modifies it, we have a block of plasteline in object mode. We can move or translate this block and we still are in object mode, but if we start modifying or deforming it like adding more plasteline or modifying its topology we'd be in edit mode then.

5.2 MODIFIERS

The purpose of modifiers while modeling is to help and accelerate the process so modelers don't have to deal with tedious operations. What modifiers do is to display and render the object in a different way without affecting the basic topology. We can think

FIGURE 5.5 We can select the modifier from the *Add Modifier* dropdown menu. The list of modifiers contains four types or groups of modifiers depending on the purpose of its use. Basically *Modify*, *Generate*, *Deform*, and *Simulate* are the main groups where modifiers are located.

about modifiers like visual effects we apply to objects to alter their visualization but not their topology.

In Blender, we have four types or groups of modifiers depending on their function or the generated effect as shown in Figure 5.5:

- *Modify*: They are a group of modifiers affecting the object data. They differ from Deform because the latter affects the object shape exclusively. Some of the modifiers found here are *Mesh Cache*, *UV Project*, *UV Wrap*, and *Vertex Weight*.

- *Generate*: As the name implies, they are modifiers affecting or altering the geometry of the object. They are so named because they generate a new geometry. Some of the modifiers found here are *Array*, *Bevel*, *Boolean*, *Build*, *Decimate*, *Edge Split*, *Mask*, *Mirror*, *Multiresolution*, *Remesh*, *Screw*, *Skin*, *Solidify*, *Subdivision Surface*, and *Triangulate*.

- *Deform*: These types of modifiers only affect objects' shape. Some of the modifiers found here are *Armature*, *Cast*, *Curve*, *Displace*, *Hook*, *Laplacian Smooth*, *Lattice*, *Mesh Deform*, *Shrinkwrap*, *Simple Deform*, *Smooth*, *Warp*, and *Wave*.

- *Simulate*: This is usually auto generated in the modifiers' panel when we add a Particle System or we play with Physics. Some of the modifiers found here are *Cloth*, *Collision*, *Explode*, *Fluid*, *Particle Instance*, *Particle System*, *Smoke*, *Soft Body*, *Dynamic Paint*, and *Ocean*.

When we add modifiers, they are stored in what is called a *modifier stack*. We have to take care of the order of modifiers in this modifier stack because this order affects the final result.

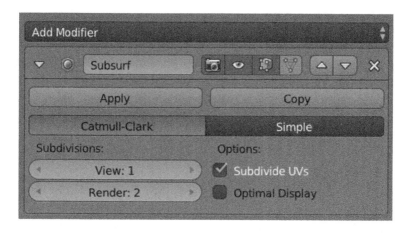

FIGURE 5.6 **(See color insert.)** The modifier panel contains some common elements shared by all kinds of modifier types, but also specific buttons and properties. The picture represents the Subdivision Surface modifier.

Probably the most common example is that applying a Subdivision Surface modifier in the first place and a Mirror in the second place gives a different result from applying a Mirror modifier in the first place and a Subdivision Surface later.

What is the significance of all these options within the modifier panels? Well, each modifier might have its own options depending on the purpose of the modifier effect. But, we can talk about some common parts shared between the modifier panels as shown in Figure 5.6.

The elements that a modifier panel is composed of are as follows:

- *Header*: In the modifier panel header, we find important icons that we can use to collapse the panel, change modifier name, or display filter to use this modifier while rendering in realtime or in Edit Mode. We also have some buttons to move the modifier over the stack or to delete the modifier from it.

- *Apply/Copy buttons*: The Apply button confirms the modifier's action making it real to the object. The Copy button just duplicates the modifier in the stack with the same settings. The latter option is especially useful if we need to apply another similar modifier to the object by simply changing a couple of settings.

- *Modifier settings*: These settings are specific to each modifier and might contain different options, buttons, and inputs depending on the purpose of the modifier.

It is important to know that all modifiers are not always available. They are listed only under certain circumstances like the object type. That means that we can add a modifier to the stack by using the dropdown menu in *Add Modifier*, but the list of available modifiers is automatically updated according to the selected object type.

5.3 MAKING PROPS

Usually, a normal scene is composed of different kinds of objects; so, in order to successfully complete a whole scene animation, studios usually set some differences between three types of elements: Characters, Properties, and Environments.

They can all be part of the same scene together, of course, but combined in a very different manner depending on the purpose of the scene or the project sketch. At the end of the day, they usually follow some criteria.

1. *Characters*: These are the primary elements in the scene usually. They do the actions playing with props in the scene environment. They feel emotions or they are the ones changing the events in the story.

    Studios spend much of the preproduction time and money trying to find a perfect and suitable character, because it's the one with which the spectator will identify or the one the viewer will hate, depending on the story. Concept art is very important at this point as shown in Figure 5.7.

FIGURE 5.7 Concept art for characters in the Blender Foundation Peach project. It is evident that character concepts evolve from the beginning sketches to the final concept. Adapting personality and appearance is very important to obtain the desired result.

FIGURE 5.8 **(See color insert.)** Some of the props used in the *Big Buck Bunny* open movie. All those elements are part of the animation process because at any moment they can require animation. In other words, they interact with characters somehow.

Geometry, topology, and appearance are, of course, very important but building the personality of the character is one of the most important tasks when developing any character.

2. *Properties*: In the animation business, we call those objects props that are involved in the action we are developing such as elements our characters get, give, use, or play with as shown in Figure 5.8.

   In some old cartoons like Hanna–Barbera's original animations, they are easily recognizable because they usually use a shading very different from the background plates. I mean in the original, to differentiate from remastered ones.

   So, for example, in a table you easily recognize the element Fred Flintstone has in his hands because the shading of the object itself is very different from the surrounding elements even if they are of the same family, say books, and they are on the table too. I'm personally fascinated by this peculiarity of the old animation process.

3. *Environments*: These are elements that compose the foreground or background scene but they are mostly nonanimated objects but not necessarily motionless, as we will see later.

In this chapter, we cover the Properties elements. If we have a look at the previous list, it's the usual hierarchy of character, props, and environment but we can switch its elements in projects and productions.

That simply depends on the story or the scene objectives. Zooming along a landscape is a well-known introduction and resource where the environment gets importance in the scene and probably is the only element in the scene itself, as we know from *Big Buck Bunny* produced by the Blender Institute.

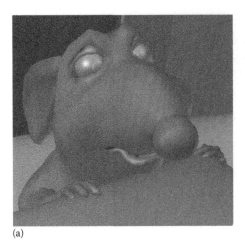

(a)   (b)

FIGURE 5.9 Character and props relationship. Relationship between character and properties should be as real as possible avoiding overlapping or wrong positioning: (a) represents a normal relationship but (b) represents an overlapping one. Look at the cheese block.

Another example could be an object like a ball moving down a staircase, as you may remember from the scene in *The Changeling* by Peter Medak, 1980, where the ball becomes the prop., also called property, that is the main element in the scene. We can say that the ball is almost the main character of the scene.

Making props is also a hard job because they play with characters in the most common cases and where they don't they become the most important element of the scene. When props and characters establish a close relationship, then it needs to be as true as possible.

Credible relationship is possible only if props and characters are at the same level of details, for example, using the same or similar shading and lights levels and contact between both elements is as close as possible without overlapping as shown in Figures 5.9 and 5.10.

Imagine any character you know, say *Sintel* from Blender Institute's Durian project, in the scene where she takes Scales, the baby dragon, in her arms. Both, the girl character and baby dragon need to have a credible shading and lighting compositing and contact between both elements should be as real as possible avoiding overlapping or artifacts as shown in Figure 5.11.

Now we know basic concepts about properties, we are going to make a simple exercise with a single Glass to show how to model some kind of properties in the same way we continue learning more about Blender's modeling features.

Modeling a glass is really easy for several reasons. We can do it manually, extruding and modeling from primitives or just play with *Curves* and *Modifiers* that Blender supports really well, making it in just a couple of steps.

The latter method is the one used in most animation studios working under several production times and getting the final object faster and looking more professional. So now we see another reason for making Blender the tool for animation studios.

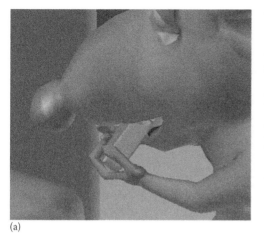

(a)   (b)

FIGURE 5.10 Character and props relationship. Relationship between character and properties should be as real as possible avoiding overlapping or wrong positioning: (a) represents a normal relationship but (b) represents a wrong relationship with overlapping. Look at the fingers.

FIGURE 5.11 Sintel and Scales relationship. The Blender crew got to create a convincing relationship between both characters. As we see, relationship between objects in a scene must be real, not only between props and characters, but also between characters and environment.

First, we add a new *Bezier Curve* using the process we already know by using the *Add Menu* panel in either of the two ways we have discussed. Then we go to *Right View* by pressing 3 Key in Numpad and rotate the curve by pressing R key and enter −90 after that and press Enter key to confirm. We should ensure we are in *Ortho View*. Then we go to *Front View* by pressing 1 Key and move the curve a little bit on the X axis. To make it, we just press G key to grab the curve and X key to tell Blender the axis we want to move along. Then, we move the curve a little bit more to the right.

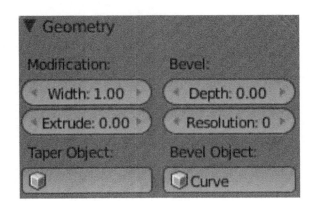

FIGURE 5.12 Geometry Panel for curve object. Bevel Object option receives the instruction of using the Curve object to modify the mesh according to changes made in that object.

Now we add a new object. This time a *Circle Curve*. To make it, we just go to *Add* panel by pressing Shift+A key and add a *Curve → Circle*. There is no need to change the view if we are still in Front View, and we should be. Now we will assign, or link, the previous Curve to the Curve Circle object; so, modifying the previous one will modify the second too.

With Circle Curve selected, we go to the Object Data button in the Property Panel. We click on the icon that looks like a curve. There should be a panel inside titled Geometry and a Bevel Object, an input option. We will use the first curve we have added at the beginning. So we select that one and type *Curve*; if all is fine, it should appear in a floating menu after clicking the input option, then just select it as shown in Figure 5.12 so we have an object like the one shown in Figure 5.13.

Now we have to select the Curve object, check the Outliner Editor in case of doubts, so we can modify it as we do with any other mesh. Then we go to *Edit Mode* with Tab Key to use the editing operators we are familiar with. The *extrude, translate,* and *rotate* operators should be enough to get something similar to the object shown in Figure 5.14. Once we do this, we can see that Circle Curve, left object in the picture, modifies the mesh automatically when we modify the Curve, which is the right object in the picture.

FIGURE 5.13 Bevel Object applied to Circle Curve. Circle Curve after the Bevel Object option application. Modifying the Curve Object will modify the Circle Curve object.

FIGURE 5.14 Bevel Object result. Circle Curve after the Bevel Object option and the Curve editing. Left object takes the form of the right one thanks to the Bevel Object operation.

We have to remember that our left object in Figure 5.14 is still a curve, Circle Curve to be specific. To convert it into a mesh to apply shading, textures, and so on, we need to use another operator. In Object Mode, we have to select the Circle Curve object, again the left one in the picture, or the cup look-alike and press Alt+C Key. The *Convert* menu appears. Here, we can convert objects in two different ways:

1. Curve from Mesh/Text

2. Mesh from Curve/Meta/Surf/Text

We need the second method to convert the Curve into a Mesh. We tell Blender we want to convert our Curve into a Mesh. The result will be to have an object with vertices, edges, and faces that we have modeled with a simple curve instead of extruding it from basic primitives.

This is a common technique used for symmetrical objects such as glasses, cups, crockery, and so on. Then, once we have converted our curve into a mesh we should ensure that the Object Data in the Property Editor is now in Mesh properties instead of Curve properties. And if we go to Edit Mode we will see the cup now as a mesh, as we mentioned earlier, with vertices, faces, and edges (Figure 5.15).

In one of the first projects we made in Platform Michelangelo Studio, later the homemade studio Lighthouse Animation, codenamed *RAT bProficiency*, we used this method to model cups, glasses, and dishes and it was really easy to have them ready in a couple of modeling sessions.

This technique allowed us to speed up our production time so we could invest much more time in other stages such as animation. Why we didn't do it and released the project without refining animation is another story.

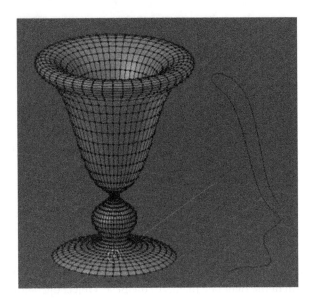

FIGURE 5.15 **(See color insert.)** Convert to Mesh from Curve. Circle Curve after the Convert to Mesh from Curve operator. We get access to this by selecting the Curve to convert and pressing Alt+C Key.

Anyway, as can be seen, this technique is really powerful, and there is no need to model these kinds of objects using the *Mirror* and *Extrude* method, which requires special care and details (Figure 5.16).

As mentioned earlier, props will be important stuff in the animation result because they will be used by characters to play with or they become the most important element in the

FIGURE 5.16 **(See color insert.)** RAT bProficiency. First project developed by former Platform Michelangelo Studio was an educational resource for Blender teaching, releasing its production files using the GPL License. This project was also mentioned in my Blender Foundation Certification.

FIGURE 5.17 **(See color insert.)** *The Doctor Show*. We can see the relationship between the props and the character must be as refined as possible. In this case, the Blender constraints help while animating the swords at the same time as our character's hands.

scene when there is no character; so it's important to pay attention to detail when we develop them and, as we did with our character, take the time to develop them in sketches or concept art drawings.

Maybe the most clear definition of property in animation business is that the object has a direct relation to the character itself, because that character gets the property on its hands; so the relationship between the property object and the character's hand should be completely credible.

In another project from Platform Michelangelo Studio, codenamed *Gecko* later released as *The Doctor Show* we had a kind of small monster as the main character and in the first episode, he gets a couple of swords in his hands. Every time he moves his hands, the swords, the property objects, in essence, should make the same movement.

What we need to understand right now is that developing a solid relationship between props and characters is not only a matter of good modeling, but also achieving as perfect an animation as possible. This can be achieved thanks to the Blender constraints as we will see in the animation chapter (Figure 5.17).

5.4 BUILDING THE ENVIRONMENT OF THE SCENE

The environment of the scene is everything that builds the world surrounding the scene. It's really easy to understand if we think of it as something made of elements that do not require animation. They are just there to complete the scene helping to create the feeling we want to produce in the viewer.

Sometimes, because of the nature of nonanimated objects, we tend to forget their importance. We don't spend the same time developing such elements like the time we spend on

FIGURE 5.18 **(See color insert.)** The paranoia of the *Elephants Dream* open movie perfectly suits the world developed by the Blender Institute crew. Characters and environment keep viewers attention within the story.

the character's development. This is an error because we need our characters in a world that completes the feeling between the scene and the viewer. The environment is very important in order to get catch the viewer's attention as shown in Figure 5.18.

Good productions have a great team working on environment development. Backgrounds, colors, materials, textures, and lights, everything should match whatever production wants to transmit to the viewer. The quality of the final production results directly from the relationship of all those elements. We don't want to see a super character in a really crappy environment. We can lose all interest in the story simply because both don't match.

The environment development is usually the result of preproduction meetings where the team talks about localizations, structure, volumes, appearance, or ambience. This, like any other aspect of the animation movies, is taken into consideration by the concept art artists. For very big productions, a large number of sketches are done for that. They don't want to miss anything about the environment of the scenes. Everything should be in the right place. Everything should look good. And everything should match the story background as shown in Figure 5.19.

5.5 TOPOLOGY SOLUTIONS

The following pictures represent different solutions to different tasks. We see interesting solutions in topology for modeling eyelids, mouth, hands, and more.

As mentioned earlier, having a well-developed model will help to succeed in the next stage. Sometimes we find different solutions for a problem while modeling our characters but to get the best possible solutions is a very important skill for people in modeling (Figures 5.20 through 5.26).

FIGURE 5.19   **(See color insert.)** David Revoy's sketches for the Blender Foundation's Durian project. The environment of the *Sintel* open movie perfectly matches the story and its characters.

FIGURE 5.20 **(See color insert.)** Topology example, notice the loops around the mouth and eyes.

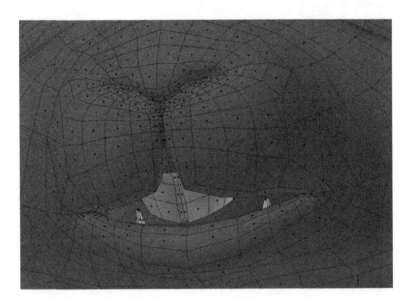

FIGURE 5.21 **(See color insert.)** Topology example, notice the loops and faces building the mouth.

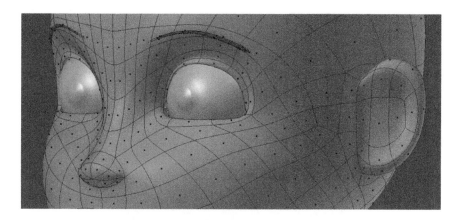

FIGURE 5.22 Example of easy topology for toony character.

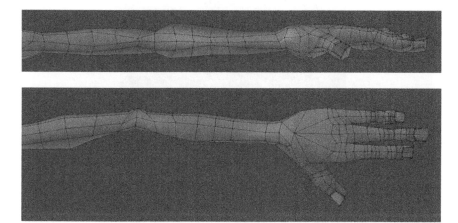

FIGURE 5.23 Example of Macandy topology for fingers.

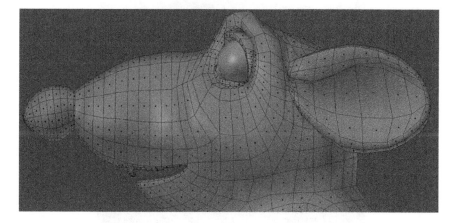

FIGURE 5.24 Another example of topology for Platform Michelangelo's RAT bProficiency project. Notice the loops for nose and eyes. Also, the ears are a nice example of the use of Blender loops.

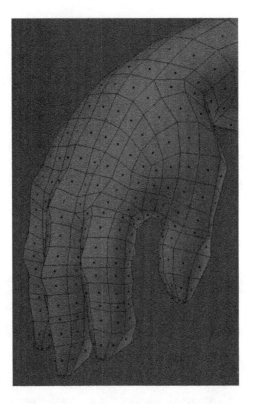

FIGURE 5.25 Nice example of topology for hands. From BI's *Peach* project and chinchilla character.

FIGURE 5.26 Another example of loops used in legs.

## CHAPTER 6

Applying Materials to Our Objects

W HEN WE TALK ABOUT materials we think about colors. This topic surely needs a whole book to help us understand how wrong we are if we think about materials in this way.

The process to apply materials in Blender is also known as Shading a model. Blender has a powerful shading system really able to manipulate objects' colors in the most suitable way for our project. Working together with textures, shading is also a kind of science so avoid trying to understand all shading parameters at the beginning. We look at the basics here to apply materials to our models without apparent complications so that the model appears as we would like it to.

There are different ways to apply materials; it depends on whether we want to apply a material to the whole object or just part of it, say vertex groups alone.

We can apply materials to the surface of our objects in different ways, by using the *Material* button in the *Properties editor* and then add and modify new materials' settings. Another way might be by using the *Nodes*. The latter is less common at least for beginners.

Talking about the first method, we add new materials using the traditional method. We first select the object we want to apply the new material to. To do it we must be sure we are in Object Mode and then go to the Properties panel and select the Material button as shown in Figure 6.1.

Once we have selected the Material property, we should see an empty container with plus and minus buttons close to it. The plus button is to add a new material property to the object and the minus one is just the inverse. By clicking on the button for adding a new material property we create an empty *material* for our object as shown in Figure 6.2.

If we want to apply a real material to the recently created slot, we need to click on New button below. After adding a new material we then have a single material working for our model. This makes available different new tabs with lots of properties. Trying to know everything at one go will be a mistake, because of that, I will introduce some basic operators that suit our basic requirements at the moment. We really don't need to know the whole of Blender's material system at this point.

FIGURE 6.1 Material button located in the Properties Editor panel. This makes us work in the right context to apply materials to our objects.

FIGURE 6.2 The new empty material linked to our object.

It's also possible to expand the drop-down list where we have something like a library with all the materials used in our current scene. We can reuse any of our recently made materials on any other object in the scene.

As mentioned earlier, we have now different panels such as *Preview*, *Diffuse*, *Specular*, *Shading*, *Transparency*, *Mirror*, *Subsurface Scattering*, *Strand*, *Options*, *Shadow*, and *Custom Properties* as shown in Figure 6.18 later in the chapter.

The materials' properties panel is given here for a quick overview:

1. *Preview*: How the material appears

2. *Diffuse*: What color to apply

3. *Specular*: What specular brightness the object shows

4. *Shading*: How the color works in the scene environment

5. *Transparency*: How to make the objects look like transparent objects

6. *Mirror*: How to apply a reflective effect like mirrors

7. *Subsurface scattering*: How to use values to apply like different skin levels

8. *Strand*: How to use values to play with particles and strands, say green

9. *Options*: How to use values to play with the material itself

10. *Shadow*: How the material works with shadows

11. *Custom Properties*: How to add new and custom user's properties

So, going back to our object, we have added a material to it. To modify the color, we just need to go to Diffuse panel and click over the color to open the *Color Picker*.

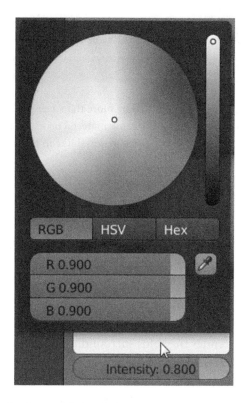

FIGURE 6.3 Diffuse is easily changeable by clicking in the color bar and picking a new color from the Picker Color. The vertical bar is just for darker/lighter Diffuse. Moving the mouse out of the Color Picker after choosing the right color will close it automatically.

After selecting the one we desire, our Preview panel should update automatically as shown in Figure 6.3.

Now our object should have the same color as the one selected in Diffuse. The Intensity slider in the Diffuse Panel makes the color intensity increase/decrease making it looking vivid/darker, respectively. Values here go from 0.000 (darker) to 1.000 (vivid).

Blender shading is really complex and it is directly related to the render engine. Depending on the render engine, we might have different results. Blender shading also allows us to work with textures we can link to materials making it even more complex to understand. As mentioned earlier, explaining all the shading functionalities is not the purpose of this book, because the subject is so vast it deserves a whole book to talk about relations between materials, textures, lighting, and render engine simulation.

We have to take care of the selected render engine because results may vary a lot depending on if we are using the Blender Internal engine or the Cycles one. They both process the scene information in very different ways and the required settings are completely different from each other.

FIGURE 6.4 We can see that material is not used by more than a single user in the top picture. However, when we duplicate the object or assign the same material or we click on that number to make it single, we can see the number of users sharing this material like in the picture at the bottom.

However, going back to our recently created material, we can see four different types of render format:

1. *Surface*: This is the basic type applying the material as a single plate over the objects' surface.

2. *Wire*: This applies the material to the wireframe of the object and renders only its edges.

3. *Volume*: This is specially used to render clouds or smoke.

4. *Halos*: This is used to render the halos surrounding the objects' vertex.

We have said we can reuse materials, but we must know something about this option. First, if we have an object with an applied material and we duplicate the object, then we probably think we are also duplicating the same material in our library. That's wrong, we are telling Blender that material is used by two users, in other words *objects*.

This is easily recognizable because of the small button showing the number of users using the active material as shown in Figure 6.4.

As mentioned earlier, there is also the option of applying materials to some faces or vertex groups of the object instead of applying it over the whole object. Using the same principles we can deal with it really easily.

First, we need to add a new material for the whole object, as we did earlier. Once we have our object using the new material with the surface render type, we must add a new material by using the plus icon and clicking the *New* button as we did before.

A new material is deployed probably labeled *Material.001*. Once we select the diffuse color we want to apply to the vertices group we need to go to the 3D View and enter *Edit Mode*. We just need to select those vertices or faces we want to apply the new material and then click on the Assign button just below our materials library as shown in Figure 6.5.

When reusing materials in more than a single user, we should take care as modifying the shared material in any object will result in modified materials in any other object sharing the same material. So, in order to make small or bigger modifications in any of the shared materials, we must remember to free it as we already know.

Select the object you want to modify the material for and click on the button where it mentions the number of users sharing the same material. This number will be reduced by one unit and you can now be sure that the material you are going to modify won't affect others.

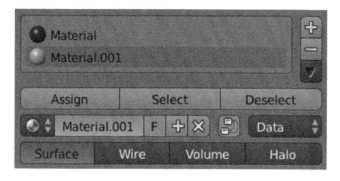

FIGURE 6.5 This method allows us to apply different materials to the same object. The Assign button is only deployed if we are in Edit Mode.

6.1 PREVIEW

We have a quick-preview visualization about how the material will look. This is an approximate idea though because, as mentioned earlier, this will change once the render engine processes all the elements required. Anyway, we might have a good approach to the final result in this preview.

We can select between different shapes so we can preview as close as possible to our object. For example, if we are applying this material to a sphere, it's much more interesting to preview with the sphere selected than the plane. The same is true with all other preview types:

1. Plane

2. Sphere

3. Cube

4. Monkey or Suzanne

5. Strand

6. Sphere with Sky

6.2 DIFFUSE

If we don't want to complicate it too much, we can say that diffuse should be handled like the color to apply to the object. We can think about the basis of shading where all other parameters do affect, but it's a good approach to obtain the result of the desired material based on the color as shown in Figure 6.6.

If we play with the intensity value then we will have the same color being modified in brightness getting darker or more vivid results.

We can also select in this panel the type of shader from the *Diffuse Shader Model* dropdown list. This will determine the aspect of the material and each one of the available values is useful for specific purposes.

FIGURE 6.6   Diffuse panel. We set up the base color of the material here. This will be improved later by modifying different settings.

- Lambert, Blender's default shader
- Oren–Nayar
- Toon
- Minnaert
- Fresnel

6.3 SPECULAR

We can see a kind of brightness in all objects. That is the specular brightness. We have taken into consideration the fact that specular brightness is strictly related to the point of view.

Like in the Diffuse panel, we can pick up a color for the specular brightness and we can play with its intensity too. That is a lower intensity results in a less-appreciable specular brightness and a higher value resulting in a vivid and strong specular brightness as shown in Figure 6.7.

Again, like in the Diffuse panel, we have a drop-down list where we can select the *Specular Shader Model* from the available values:

- CookTorr, Blender's default
- Phong
- Blinn
- Toon
- WardIso

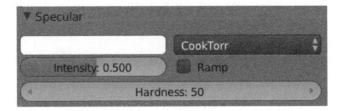

FIGURE 6.7   Specular panel. Here, we can modify all values to work with specular property.

We can see another interesting property too. The Hardness slider allows us to determine the size the specular brightness will have. So, a lower value in this property results in a very small specular brightness and a higher value results in a bigger specular brightness projected over the object.

We notice that Specular and Diffuse panels share an option called *Ramp*. We can use this property when we need the material being modified to have its base color blend into another depending on the results we are looking for.

It's easy to understand if we think of it like the typical gradient color in other applications. We can not only play with ramp values to obtain the desired gradient color but also to play with textures so they are applied according to the ramp values. Available properties for Ramp features are as follows:

- *Add/Delete*: We are able to add or delete stop strips on the colorband.

- *Flip*: This is particularly useful if we want to flip the whole colorband without the need for moving the stop strips.

- *Active color stop*: We can select the active stop strip to play with either this button or click directly over the color stop.

- *Interpolation*: Determines the relationship between the color stop strips. Available values are *Linear, Cardinal, Ease, B-Spline*, and *Constant*.

- *Colorband*: This is the visual representation of the gradient result.

- *Position*: This is the actual position of the color stop. We can refine its position by modifying this integer.

- *Color*: This sets the color for the current stop strip. This determines the gradient of the final result.

- *Input*: This tells us how is the ramp mapped on the object's surface. Available values are *Shader, Energy, Normal*, and *Result*.

- *Blend*: This tells us how the ramp is applied to the diffuse color or the specular shader. Available values are *Mix, Add, Multiple, Subtract, Screen, Divide, Difference, Darken, Lighten, Overlay, Dodge, Burn, Hue, Saturation, Value, Color, Soft Light*, and *Linear Light*.

- *Factor*: This, simply put, determines the amount of color ramp applied. In other words, we can think about it like alpha. Less factor results in a transparent color ramp and higher values result in a totally opaque color ramp (Figure 6.8).

6.4 SHADING

The shading panel is the one where we can set those properties affecting relationship between material and scene or strictly speaking, the environment, as shown in Figure 6.9.

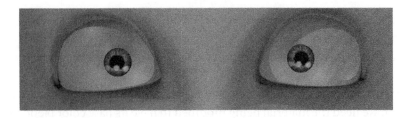

FIGURE 6.8   Probably the most common use of the specular is to simulate the brightness in the eyes.

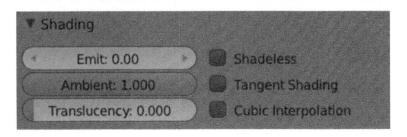

FIGURE 6.9   Shading panel.

- *Emit*: It's basically the amount of light the current material emits to the environment.

- *Ambient*: This is the amount of ambient color the material receives from the environment.

- *Translucency*: This determines the amount of shading the material receives on the back side.

- *Shadeless*: This material has to be enabled or disabled to make it nonsensitive to light or shadows.

- *Tangent Shading*: We can enable this option if we want to obtain anisotropic shading effects.

- *Cubic Interpolation*: This option improves the transition between the lighted and shaded zones.

6.5 TRANSPARENCY

Like any other computer graphic imaging application, Blender has the ability to apply transparency to its shaded objects. To make materials using the transparency process, we just need to enable the *Render material as transparent* checkbox close to the Transparency panel title as shown in Figure 6.10.

This allows us to play with some interesting options and properties that Blender shows up within the same panel. The first thing we need to know is that we have three methods to use for rendering transparency. We can select one from the three buttons *Mask, Z Transparency,* and *Raytrace*.

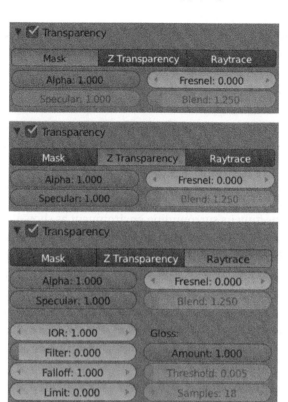

FIGURE 6.10 Transparency panel with different possibilities. The top one uses the Mask feature. The middle one uses the Z Transparency one and the bottom picture uses the Raytrace feature. Notice the raytrace-specific properties.

- *Mask*: This simply masks the background. We can't modify Specular values in this method.

- *Z Transparency*: A bit more complex than Mask, this uses the alpha buffer for transparent faces. Here also we can play with the Specular value.

- *Raytrace*: This is too complex to understand but basically uses raytracing to calculate refractions. When using this mode, we have very technical options to play with, like Index of Refraction, Falloff, Limit, and Gloss, for example. The final result of the material will be determined by a mix of all those properties.

The Transparency panel also shares some common properties, like Alpha, Specular, and Fresnel.

The Alpha value determines the level of transparency of the material. So, higher values, near 1.0, will give a totally opaque material and lower values near 0.0 result in a very transparent material.

The Specular slider works in the same way but just for the specular value. Here it's interesting to understand that if we are in the Mask method, we can't set up a completely transparent material and a shiny specular, but we can get that result if we are in the Z Transparency method.

For example, we set the Alpha slider at 0.0 and the Specular value at 1.0. Then we switch between Mask and Z Transparency methods. The result will be a completely transparent material while in the Mask method, and a shiny sparkle while in the Z Transparency method.

6.6 MIRROR

In Blender, the mirror effect is simulated using raytracing. This algorithm can be used to simulate a material reflecting its surrounding environment as shown in Figure 6.11.

Like the Transparency, the Mirror effect can be enabled by the *Enable raytraced reflections* checkbox near the Mirror panel title. Then, we have some options available.

First of all, we must know that the amount of mirror reflection is determined by the *Reflectivity* value. The higher the value is set, the higher is the resulting mirror effect.

We can also set a color for the mirrored effect. Usually, a mirror object will reflect colors similar to the ones surrounding it but sometimes the color reflected is not the same. Because of that, we have the option of selecting the color we want the mirror effect to reflect in the context by picking one from the color picker.

There is also an interesting option called Fresnel, working together with the Blend slider. This option controls how reflective material is dependent on the Blend factor. This is usually used to make a proportional relation between those areas of the material to be reflective and those nonreflective.

For the Mirror effect, we must take care of the value of Depth. This sets the number of bounds the reflection is processed. Higher values could increase the render time. This value should be taken into consideration depending on the number of reflective objects we have in the scene.

We also have to know that reflected rays are also result of the Maximum Distance value. Those being of higher value they are determined by the Fade to option, usually *Sky* or *Material*.

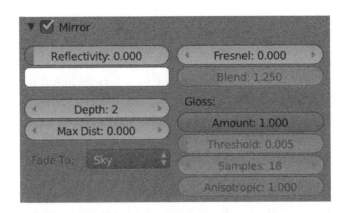

FIGURE 6.11 Mirror panel.

Finally, we have the Gloss properties where we can play with some values to make a realistic reflection. The Gloss basically results in a flat or grainy surface and combining their properties together the Mirror ones to obtain the desired reflection is something that could take time.

If we want the best result, we need to consider all the factors involved. Visual results are time consuming while processing. Obviously, getting the most professional result while working on raytracing is directly related to the power of the machine we are working on. Anyway, as stated earlier, finding the balance between everything, performance and visuals, is the big task while working with mirrored materials.

6.7 SUBSURFACE SCATTERING

This is really useful for those material compounds at various levels. Quite often, all objects are not simply compounded by a single color or in other words, by a single-color level, so the light has to bounce between every level of skin being processed to get the final skin material.

This effect is specially used for human or animal skins, fruits, and basically a lot of organic and inorganic materials. The Subsurface Scattering is always used to achieve the level of realism desired. Professional results are only possible when using the Subsurface Scattering properties.

Like the Transparency and Mirror panels, the Subsurface Scattering can be enabled by clicking the *Enable diffuse subsurface scattering effect* checkbox near the Subsurface Scattering panel title. Again, some options are then available to us.

We notice first when enabling the Subsurface Scattering that it is a preset selector. Blender offers us some prebuilt presets to be used quickly. They are according to the purpose of the preset and set the basic properties for us, that is, *IOR*, *Scale*, and *Color*. This doesn't mean we have everything done when selecting a preset; we still need to modify some values to make it look the way we want it. We are able to add or delete presets from this panel too (Figures 6.12 and 6.13).

FIGURE 6.12 Subsurface Scattering panel.

FIGURE 6.13 Great example of subsurface scattering for rendering at blenderworkshop. (From www.wordpress.com.)

6.8 STRAND

When we play with strands in Blender, we refer to Hair particles system that might be used to simulate hair or green, for example. In Blender, there are two different types of strand methods. The strand panel contains interesting options so, we can simulate our particles in a such detail as we need, as shown in Figure 6.14.

First of all we see a very important option called Size, where we have Root, Tip, and Minimum. These will determine the size of the strands, so we can make fat or thin strands

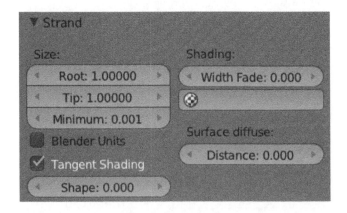

FIGURE 6.14 Strand panel.

FIGURE 6.15 Awesome example of Blender strands use. The *Big Buck Bunny* was a step forward in strands and fur.

by modifying the root or tip options. A very important option is the Blender units, where we use Blender to enable the strands using the Blender units instead of pixels value.

The aspect of the strands will also be determined by the combination of Tangent Shading and the Shape input value. With that, we tell Blender to use the direction of strands as normals (Figure 6.15).

6.9 OPTIONS

With this panel, we determine how material will be applied in the rendered scene. It contains different options to alter the appearance of the material and includes some added features that modify the final render.

Some of the checkboxes we find here are *Traceable*, *Full Oversampling*, *Sky*, *Use Mist*, *Invert Z Depth*, *Face Textures*, *Face Textures Alpha*, *Vertex Color Paint*, *Vertex Color Light*, *Object Color*, and *UV Project* as shown in Figure 6.16.

Their names are very representative of what they do, for instance, Traceable allows material to be included in the raytracing, Sky helps to render material with sky background, or Use Mist enables the option Mist in the World context.

A very interesting option is the Light Group one. Here, we can tell Blender to limit lighting to a predefined group of lamps.

6.10 SHADOW

This panel, obviously, deals with the relationship between material and shadows; basically, how shadow affects the material. Technically speaking, the shadows appearing in any scene are calculated by very different parameters like objects' shape, lighting, materials, and more as shown in Figure 6.9.

We see here some options like Receive, Receive transparent, Cast Only, and Shadows only. We might exercise control at this point to decide if we want this material to receive shadows,

FIGURE 6.16   **(See color insert.)** Options panel.

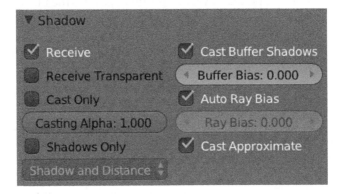

FIGURE 6.17   **(See color insert.)** Shadow panel.

if we want the object to be invisible and only cast a shadow, and if we want to apply an alpha value (Figures 6.17 and 6.18).

Notice that we can manage what we want to do with shadows and with how material affects those shadows within this panel. This is very important in order to obtain realistic and interesting renders.

FIGURE 6.18 **(See color insert.)** After adding a new material, we have different panels to play with. Depending on the results we want for our model, we shall play with the operators of those panels, so, if we want our object to look like a transparent one, we just need to activate the Transparency panel and play with operators inside.

## CHAPTER 7

Blender Internal Textures

WE ALREADY KNOW ABOUT how to apply materials to objects, but sometimes that is not enough to obtain the desired result. Well, we can say that there can be no professional result if we don't combine the material with textures. However small the project is, we have to know how to apply textures to materials in order to improve the final look.

A texture is a simple image or pattern that is applied to the surface of the object and usually combined with the material. This process is commonly called *mapping* by studios.

The good thing about textures is they might affect almost everything, not only color but also specular, transparency, and reflection, and they are available not only to work with materials but also to apply a kind of property to sculpting or painting methods.

We first need to know where the texture options are placed in the Blender's user interface. We need to go to the Texture button within the Properties editor so some texture panels are displayed for us as shown in Figure 7.1. The available panels are *Texture datablock*, *Mapping*, and *Influence* by default, but when we have any texture created within our library, we also have *Preview*, *Colors*, and specific texture options panel as shown in Figure 7.2.

The first thing we see when we are in the Textures context is that we can work with three kind of textures, namely, *World*, *Material*, and *Other Data*:

- *World*: Texture is applied to the world. This requires that the option Blend Sky from the World context is enabled.

- *Material*: This affects the selected object and is combined with the material the object surface has applied.

- *Other Data*: We have the option to create a Brush and a Brush Mask texture here.

We must understand one thing now. Independent of the type of texture created, we must know that all textures we create are being saved in a library, so they are available for choice even when we are in any other context. For example, if we create a texture using the Material type, we will have this texture available for use if we are, say, in Sculpt Mode, or if we want to use the same texture for the World type.

FIGURE 7.1 Texture button located in the Properties Editor panel. This makes us work in the right context to apply textures to our objects.

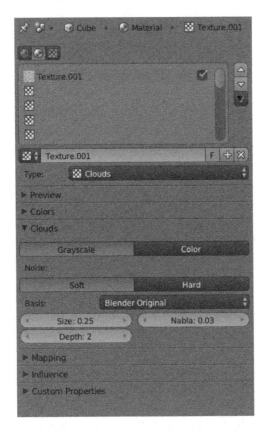

FIGURE 7.2 Panels for the recently created Clouds texture. Notice we have some common panels over the whole texture types and specific panels depending on the selected texture.

Because the most interesting texture for us is the Material one, from the point of view of the animation studios' productions, we will start with that type of texture. The first thing we must think about is that textures are like layers we add to the base material to complete its properties until we get the object surface to look close to reality. Even if we don't look for photo reality in our project, the thing is that almost every studios' productions use textures in addition to base materials in order to improve the quality of rendered scenes.

By default we have an empty texture datablock, so we need to create a new texture item so we can start working on applying that texture to the object surface. Remember we're talking now about Material type of texture. For the latest Blender releases, an empty texture slot is generated automatically, but it has no texture type associated by default. If necessary,

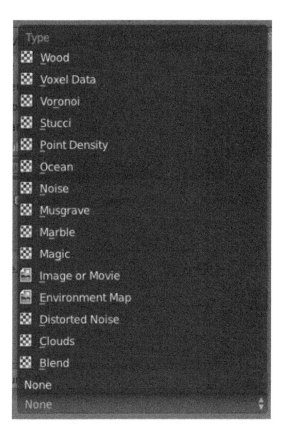

FIGURE 7.3 List of available texture types. Each one will show different custom panel properties in the texture context.

we will get rid of it and create a new one, so we understand the whole process of creating new textures.

In order to create a new texture slot, we must click the New button. This will make a new texture slot within the texture datablock. Here we can move the texture slot up and down, we can modify the texture name, make it single user like we can do with materials, and save even if it has no users associated with it or simply delete it.

The most interesting feature here is the Texture type drop-down list where we can select the kind of texture we want to use already as shown in Figure 7.3:

- *Wood*: As its name indicates it's usually used to simulate wood or any other ring-based texture. Like the Marble texture, we can determine the strip band wave with the *Sine*, *Saw*, and *Tri* options. In this case, we also can select the type of bands we want the texture to simulate; the available options are *Bands*, *Rings*, *Band Noise*, and *Ring Noise*. Once we have this, we can choose the texture to have a *Soft* or *Hard Noise* base option.

- *Voronoi*: It's a very particular texture, commonly used to simulate metal and organic shades. The first thing we need to do is to select the algorithm to use for Distance Metric.

The available options are *Minkowski, Minkowski 4, Minkowski 1/2, Chebychev, Manhattan, Distance Squared,* and *Actual Distance.* We can play later with the Feature Weights to adjust the final appearance.

- *Stucci:* This is definitely the most interesting for creating grainy surfaces like walls, asphalt, fruits, and so on. We can adjust the type with *Plastic, Wall in,* and *Wall out* options. This will determine the aspect of the texture. Then, we can adjust the Noise by selecting *Soft* or *Hard* and the Noise base to combine. As usual in textures, we also can adjust the *Size* and *Turbulence.*

- *Noise:* This is a true generated noise that is not Perlin. That means it's totally different for each frame. This might end in artifacts while rendering the animation.

- *Musgrave:* This is an interesting texture type. Commonly used to simulate organics, it can be practically used for everything. We can select from different Musgrave texture bases like Hetero Terrain, fBM, Hybrid Multifractal, Ridged Multifractal, and Multifractal. This texture is combined with the Noise base option by selecting one from the drop-down menu. The available options are *Cell Noise, Voronoi Crackle, Voronoi F2-F1, Voronoi F1, Voronoi F2, Voronoi F3, Voronoi F4, Improved Perlin, Original Perlin,* and *Blender Original.*

- *Marble:* As its name indicates, it's usually used to simulate marble or fire. We have the option to modify the strip bands with the *Sin, Saw,* or *Tri* options and make them *Soft, Sharp,* or *Sharper* at the same time by combining these parameters. We also can combine it with a Noise either Soft or Hard by applying a Noise base from the drop-down menu. We can adjust the final look with *Size, Turbulence, Depth,* and *Nabla* options. We can play with a lot of properties while using this texture, and a minimal change determines a completely different texture. Some available parameters are *Dimension, Lacunarity, Octaves, Offset, Intensity,* and *Gain.* As usual with textures, we can also adjust *Size* and *Nabla.*

- *Magic:* This is not a commonly used texture. Maybe if you want to apply some kind of interference to the film, you can use this. The available options to adjust are *Depth* and *Turbulence.*

- *Distorted Noise:* This texture type takes the selected Noise Base and applies a Noise Distortion obtaining a mixed one. We can control and modify parameters from Distortion, Size, and Nabla to obtain very different results. The available options for both the Noise drop-down menus are *Cell Noise, Voronoi Crackle, Voronoi F2-F1, Voronoi F1, Voronoi F2, Voronoi F3, Voronoi F4, Improved Perlin, Original Perlin,* and *Blender Original.*

- *Clouds:* Using this texture is like using the Perlin noise. We can select the algorithm that determines the final appearance of the texture. We can do that from the Noise Basis drop-down list where available options are *Cell Noise, Voronoi Crackle, Voronoi F2-F1, Voronoi F1, Voronoi F2, Voronoi F3, Voronoi F4, Improved Perlin, Original Perlin,* and *Blender Original.* We also have some other options to play with like make the clouds texture appear in grayscale or color and make it soft or hard. Parameters like Size, Depth, and Nabla will determine the final look of the texture.

- *Blend*: This texture type is the most commonly used. It's used to blend textures between them or to apply gradient effects. We can tweak the direction of the texture progression with the Horizontal and Vertical buttons. The available progressions for this texture type are *Radial, Quadratic sphere, Spherical, Diagonal, Easing, Quadratic*, and *Linear*.

7.1 PREVIEW

This panel like the material preview one provides a first visual picture of the appearance of the texture. The visualized result is a very first impression of its appearance, we must remember that Blender render has a lot of procedural parameters to take into account. Anyway, this is a good start in order to obtain a previsualization of our selected texture.

Here we can combine this previsualization with Material to know how the texture is applied to the current Material.

If we are previsualizing the texture using any of the Texture or Both option we have a Show Alpha checkbox we might enable so the alpha channel is also previsualized (Figure 7.4).

7.2 COLORS

This panel is specially useful if we want to apply or modify colors of the new texture. For that, we can activate the checkbox Ramp. We are already aware how the ramp properties work and how to manipulate the stop strips.

We can modify color with the values of *Brightness, Contrast*, and *Saturation* as shown in Figure 7.5.

7.3 MAPPING

When we talk about mapping a texture, we are looking at how we want it to affect the object. We can modify such a texture to appear exactly as we need it in projection, size, or

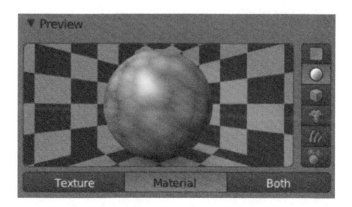

FIGURE 7.4 Texture Preview panel within the texture context. It is the very first attempt to get the texture type displayed.

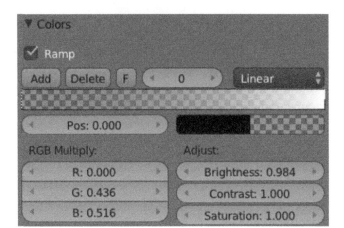

FIGURE 7.5 We can modify values like Brightness, Contrast, or Saturation of the texture but also apply or modify a new ramp color.

coordinates. The mapping panel is commonly used to adapt the texture to our object surface modifying parameters such the ones mentioned earlier.

For example, we can select the Texture Coordinates depending on Blender's built-in options, so we can select between *Tangent, Stress, Reflection, Normal, Window, Strand/Particle, UV, Generated, Object*, or *Global*.

In the same way, we can modify the Mapping Projection applied to the texture, depending on if we want to project our texture as *Sphere, Tube, Cube*, or simply *Flat*.

As mentioned earlier, we can play with those parameters but in the same way we can apply or limit the texture to being used in combination with the three axes X, Y, and Z.

There are two very interesting options too in this panel. The Offset for the X, Y, and Z locations and the Size for X, Y, and Z. Playing with those values, we can also make our texture move within the object surface and scale it to finally being adapted to our needs (Figure 7.6).

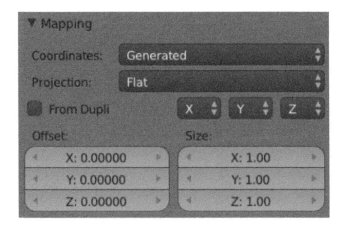

FIGURE 7.6 The mapping panel allows us to adjust our texture to our needs in size, offset, and projection. Depending on our needs, we need to play with all these values to obtain the desired result.

7.4 INFLUENCE

The Influence panel splits some properties into different groups. In short, we can modify different properties for Diffuse, Shading, Specular, and Geometry. We can enable or disable these properties and modify their values.

For Diffuse, we have properties like *Intensity, Color, Alpha*, and *Translucency*. These are basically properties to modify the amount of texture applied to such specific diffuse-related properties.

For the Shading group, we have properties like *Ambient, Emit, Mirror*, and *Ray Mirror*. They are basically properties affecting the amount of texture applied to such specific shading-related properties.

For Specular group, we have properties like *Intensity, Color*, and *Hardness*. They are properties affecting the amount of texture applied to such specific specular-related properties.

For Geometry, we have properties like *Normal, Wrap*, and *Displace*. These are properties affecting the amount of texture applied to such specific geometry-related properties.

We have in this panel a very important option, Blend Type. That determines the mode used to apply the texture. We have several options here such as *Linear Light, Soft Light, Color, Value, Saturation, Hue, Lighten, Darken, Divide, Difference, Overlay, Screen, Multiply, Subtract, Add*, or *Mix* (Figure 7.7).

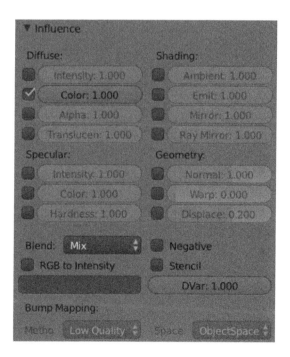

FIGURE 7.7 Blender's influence panel. We can modify the final look of our materials by playing and combining the different options.

## CHAPTER 8

UV Unwrap and External Textures

T HE UNWRAPPING TECHNIQUE IS commonly used in each film production. But we won't discuss it like a big tutorial. We'll explain in short, what unwrapping is and why studios use this technique, say for complete character textures.

In fact, it's a really important technique for mapping textures because what it does is to build a plain shape of our object's topology so that it might be modified and repainted to adapt the new texture to the same object's topology. It's easy if you think of it like origami (Figure 8.1).

8.1 UNWRAPPING A MESH

Before starting to unwrap our objects, we need to be sure we don't need to modify their topology. Well that is not crucial, but it would save time because then we would have to rewrap the new changes made in the object's topology.

To wrap our objects we need to mark our edges as seams. That will tell Blender from where we want to break our object in order to create the plain shape. Once we have the object with our seams marked, we are able to go to UV/Image Editor where our unwrapped object should appear.

We should see some different points that corresponds to the vertex in the recently wrapped mesh. Consequently, we will also see the edges and the faces, but now everything is flat. Our object looks flat on the UV/Image Editor.

The UV is so complex that we won't see it in depth. We just need to know that almost every 3D film we watch has an incredible work of wrapping to apply external textures, sometimes to develop a completely new look, sometimes to paint and refine specific aspects of the object's original texture, and sometimes to add layers of details so the final appearance suits the required needs.

FIGURE 8.1 Some textures used in *Big Buck Bunny* open movie for the chinchilla character.

8.2 UV LAYOUTS

Usually, UV maps are generated so we can use a couple of them in the same object, for example, for texture, specular, or bump maps. But, sometimes, we also need to translate a specific UV map to another mesh.

It's easily done in Blender with the Shift key and by selecting the mesh containing the UV map we want to transfer. Then, go to *Object menu > Make Links > Join as UVs*. When we do this we have a mesh with a UV applied that matches the original mesh UV map.

This is the easy way, of course. Talking about UV, we have some other complex things to take into consideration, like the multiple UV layouts. So imagine we have or we want several UV layouts for different parts of any object. We could make new UV layouts using the New button from the UV Maps panel within the Mesh (Object Data) Properties context as shown in Figure 8.2. This is useful, as mentioned earlier, when some UV maps are required for the same mesh but we have to take care when we need to unwrap the same face several

FIGURE 8.2 UV Maps panel within the Object Data Properties context. We can use this panel to add or delete UV layers.

times because the result will be determined by the combination of the alpha values of those UV layers.

Sometimes copying UV layouts from one mesh to another is very useful, especially in those cases where we need to restore something because of an issue. Anyway, we should take special care in deleting UV maps because this option deletes everything related to the unwrapping linked to the selected mesh.

As mentioned earlier, we could create new UV maps using the New button, but also delete UV layers taking special care that everything related to the unwrapped mesh will be deleted too. From this panel, we could modify the UV map to anything more comprehensible like *UV Skin* or *UV Face*.

In the same way, we can enable or disable the UV layer from the rendering process using the small camera icon close to the UV Map name.

8.3 EDITING UVS

Editing the UV maps is a bit difficult at least for the very beginners but nothing we could not manage in a couple of training sessions. More complexity comes if we don't have enough knowledge of the UV wrapping feature.

At the moment, we have some basic knowledge of what the UV maps are and why they are so important for any film production. But how can we edit the UV maps within Blender?

This is probably a very huge topic that might deserve a whole book. In fact, there are some interesting publications out there on this.

Once we have our seams marked and the UV map generated, we need to accommodate our vertices and islands. The size of the UV faces might vary from a single pixel to a very wide size. Anyway, we need to adjust our points so we can convert it to anything we could paint so we can use it as texture.

We have some interesting operators to play with the UV regions:

- *Border Select*: We can use the B key to use something like a box lasso to select our points.

- *Select or Deselect All*: As we already know, we can select or deselect all with the A key.

- *Linked UVs*: With the combination of Ctrl+L keys, we can select everything that is part of the current UV map.

- *Pin UVs*: This is really useful to avoid the UV maps moving meanwhile we are making any unwrap action. This is accessible by using the combination of Shift+P keys.

- *Border Select Pinned*: We can use the Shift+B keys to select only the pinned UV points.

- *Unlink Selection*: We can use this feature to cut the selected points from the current map. This is only applicable to those points that conform to a whole face. We can do this using the combination of Alt+L keys.

When editing UVs, there is a very interesting and important option, namely, the Sync Selection. When we enable this option, which is located in the UV/Image Editor header, we are able to visualize in this editor everything we select in the 3D view.

That means that if, for example, we have some faces of our object in the 3D view selected, they are also selected and visualized in the UV/Image editor. This is a very important feature because it allows us to have an accurate control over the recently unwrapped map with enough knowledge of which parts correspond to the object in 3D view as shown in Figure 8.3.

When we are in the opposite case, with the Sync Selection disabled, only those faces selected are visualized in the UV/Image editor. Notice the edges or vertices are not visualized in this mode unless we switch to that mode in the header of the UV/Image editor as shown in Figure 8.4.

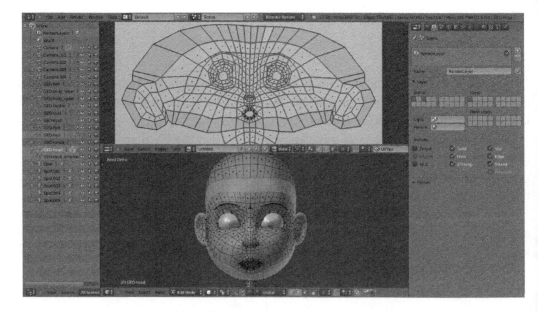

FIGURE 8.3 Unwrapping from the Mushroom project. With Sync Selection enabled, we can visualize the selected vertices, faces, or edges automatically in the wrapped model within the UV/Image editor.

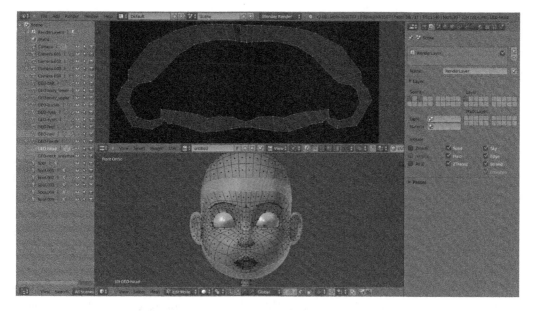

FIGURE 8.4 Unwrapping from the Mushroom project. With Sync Selection disabled, we only visualize in the UV/Image editor those elements selected in the 3D view.

Available selection modes are *Vertex*, *Edges*, *Faces*, or *Islands*.

We also have a small selection menu where we could manage everything our maps share, it's called the Sticky Selection Mode. The available modes are *Shared Vertex*, where we can visualize the vertex shared; *Shared Location*, where we can visualize the UVs sharing location; and *Disabled* that disables the Sticky Selection mode.

A peculiar thing we should have in mind is that Sync Selection doesn't work as we expect in all cases. For example, if we select Edges, it will work like when using the Shared Vertex mode but if we select Faces, then this feature works like in Disabled Stick Selection mode.

But what can we do with UVs? Just use the select feature?

Well, we can also manipulate UVs like any other object, so we can translate, rotate, or scale. We also are able to show or hide like we could do with any normal object using the H key. The UVs can also be locked in any of the X and Y axis.

As we see, the UVs behave like any other kind of object so we can manipulate it over the UV/Image editor like if it was a desktop.

Another interesting element in the UV/Image editor is the Pivot Point. This determines the behavior of the cursor with respect to the selected elements together at the center. The available options for the Pivot Point option are *Bounding Box Center*, *Median Point*, and *2D Cursor Location*.

In the UV/Image editor header, we also have a Proportional Editing. This is an interesting feature that works in the same way as the 3D editor. With this feature, we can control the elements surrounding the selection in a smooth way so that moving a specific vertex within a specific range by Proportional Editing will affect those surrounding vertices (Figure 8.5).

FIGURE 8.5 UV/Image editor header that contains almost everything we need to manage a wrapping session.

The Snap feature works in the same way as it does in 3D view, but we have to take care that it works only if we snap to UVs and not to pixels.

For the snap feature, we could find more options if we go to the Snap submenu within the header. The available options are *Snap Pixels* that moves the selection to the nearest pixel if an image is loaded, *Snap to Cursor* that moves selection to the 2D cursor position and *Snap to Adjacent Unselected* that moves the selection to the close adjacent unselected element.

What if we can weld or align UVs elements? Well, what the W1 makes is to weld, in other words, move selected elements to their average position, but the Align, W2, W3, and W4 line up the selected UV elements on the X or Y axis.

It is also interesting that we can Mirror the elements that compound a UV map. And we can do it, as expected, in the X and Y axes. This is basically done as we do in the 3D view by combining the Ctrl+M key and then entering X or Y key for the axis.

In the same way that we can split and cut elements in our UVs, we also can join or stitch UVs sharing vertices. We can modify the parameters for stitching by adjusting options like Limit and Limit Distance.

But what we can't forget is the Minimize Stretch tool that helps us relax the UVs element angles. Applying this feature makes the UVs appear smooth and a bit relaxed as mentioned earlier.

We previously talked about enabling a lock for some elements in the UVs but the practical way to use is to use the Pinning feature. This is really useful sometimes because it keeps some elements without altering its location.

We can use this feature using the P key to pin selected elements or Alt+P keys to unpin those selected elements.

There are plenty of examples for the Pinning feature, but probably the analogy with the Mirror Modifier is the most effective to understand how powerful this feature can be.

When we are editing a symmetrical object in 3D view using the Mirror modifier, we have some vertices in the mirror axis that can be shared by both sides, the original and the mirrored one. If we enable the option to pin those vertices, then they will share the place and stay in the same location.

With this in mind, imagine how useful this feature can be if we use it with live unwrap, where the work is visualized automatically (Figure 8.6).

8.4 OPTIMIZE THE UV MAP

The usual process to unwrap a mesh is to use the Seams marks. But this is not enough to keep it clear and this isn't a warranty of success either. We have to make some changes to the recently unwrapped mesh like Modify orientation of the UV map, arrange that map, or stitch several maps together.

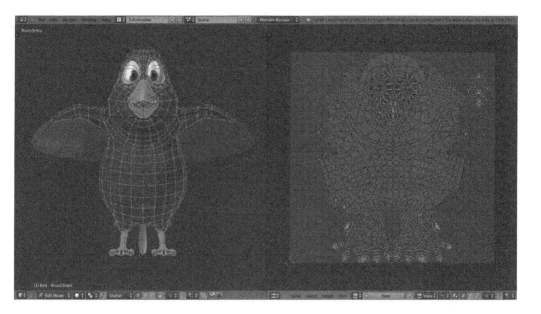

FIGURE 8.6 Bird wrapped from the *Big Buck Bunny* open movie developed by the Blender Foundation.

Sometimes, we need to add more faces or vertices to our unwrapped mesh. This could end in a kind of trouble, so even Blender adds those new elements to the UV map automatically.

This was discussed earlier in this chapter, but again, if possible we have to try to start our unwrap process once we reckon the mesh is as complete as possible, trying to avoid adding new faces or vertices when the unwrap process has started (Figure 8.7).

8.5 COMBINE UV MAPS

When working on unwrapped meshes it's very common to have a very high percentage of the job done but we always have parts of the unwrapped map that don't suit the expected result ending in a very messy organization of islands, edges, or vertices.

In such cases, we need to clean up the corrupted zones so they look fine and clean and the UV texture is applied correctly.

A first step to success in these cases is to separate elements to unwrap. That is, make each one a separate UV map. If we make it in this way we ensure we are unwrapping the mesh using the right solution for each case.

Once we have the different pieces unwrapped, then we can check that we have all those different UV maps as part of the same UV Texture map so we can finally make the entire UV map using the stitch feature discussed earlier.

To complete the task, we need to arrange and stitch the different UVs. One of the most interesting operators while working in this kind of work is the Average Island Scale that creates all islands so that they are on the same scale more or less. This is a great help as generalizing and resizing the islands to the same scale ensures a smooth appearance. We can use this feature with the combination of Ctrl+A keys.

FIGURE 8.7 The chinchilla character from the Blender Institute's project. Notice how we have some parts of the model selected say by using vertex group and it is automatically visualized in the UVs within the UV/Image editor.

Now that we have our islands looking approximately the same size, we can use the Pack Islands feature to let them fill up almost the whole UV space. It's a very efficient feature making logical use of the available UV space so the generated UV map makes use of it.

To avoid UVs going outside of the UV range, we can enable the Constrain to Image Bound option.

8.6 REFINE LAYOUT

Once we have applied a UV map texture to our characters, we then have the option to refine it if more detail is required at some point. But sometimes we realize that we don't have enough space in pixels to achieve the desired level of details.

A common solution is to scale the UV map to a specific point where we need more details. But then, we should be careful because what we do will provide the same detail to any other zone of UV texture even to those zones with less visibility in the final film production.

We are talking about using UV textures and what we have to think about is how powerful is the machine on which we are developing or the one where we will render our film. Then we talk about memory again. We are manipulating images and this requires computation memory and resources.

So, how can we manage this memory in a responsive way? By reusing resources. So we can share some UV textures in very different objects and then modify or alter another UV map with those different elements. A very practical example is to use a generic UV texture for the skin in arms, hands, legs, and such elements so the loaded images don't jeopardize the machine resources.

8.7 APPLYING IMAGES

We already have talked about this. The final reason to use UV textures is to apply such external, usually painted, textures to our characters. What we should know about UV maps in Blender is how to export UV layout images and how to apply textures.

The export process is useful because sometimes the team working in the unwrap process is not the same as the team painting those textures. So, the export option is really useful in such cases.

In Blender, we can export our UVs using the Save UV Face Layout option located in *UVs > Save UV Face Layout* menu. We have the option to save our UVs in very different formats. The available export options are as follows:

- *All UVs*: If this option is not enabled, then only the selected UV faces will be exported.

- *Modified*: This option exports the UVs from the modified mesh.

- *Format*: We can select from among the available formats seen before.

- *Size*: We can select the size of the image in pixels.

- *Fill Opacity*: We can export our outlined image using an opacity factor or a transparent one.

We have to take care to have all our edges and islands within the boundary of the UVs space before exporting it as an image. Otherwise, everything outside that boundary will not be generated and exported.

Then we have our outlined model in a plain 2D image so the artistic team is able to edit and paint texture according to requirements or following the Concept art guidelines.

Once we have our texture painted, we can apply it back to the UVs layout.

Here, we have to say that Blender incorporates an interactive view so we can check automatically what we do in the UV/Image editor directly over our character model in the 3D view. For that we can switch the viewport shading option to *Textured*.

Right now we have everything in place but we have to tell Blender to enable the UVs in the render processing. There are a few ways in which this can be done. Use UV Coordinates and set up a texture using its UV coordinates.

We can do this in the Texture properties context by selecting an image as texture type. Then in the mapping panel we can choose the UV from the Coordinates menu and select the UV layer we want to use.

An option is to select the Color property in the Influence panel in the same way as the Use Alpha property in case our texture is using the alpha channel.

We are able to load or save images within the UV editor. We have to take care of this when we are working in a film production because if we are editing the .blend file and we are

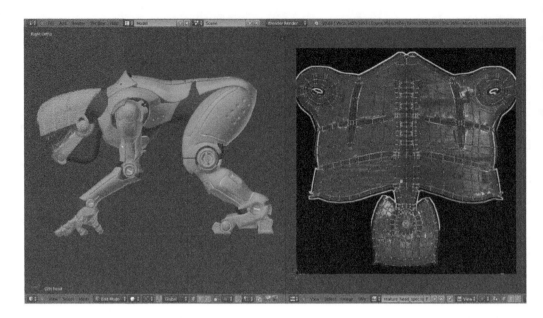

FIGURE 8.8 The creature character for Creatures Factory open movie. Notice different UV maps in the picture just corresponding to the head where a specular texture was applied.

already modifying the UV texture with an external tool, we have to remember to Reload the texture before saving the .blend file again.

In the same way, we should take care about moving the texture between folders because we need to tell Blender where the file has been moved to.

To keep this clean is even more important where the unwrap process and texture painting are in different departments. Working both teams in separate environments makes things complex, so a clear organization and a strong communication are vital for success (Figure 8.8).

In such cases, remember Blender incorporates a text editor where we could add notes, to-do lists, or messages to any specific team regarding guidelines to follow or simply track the latest changes made to such a file.

When we want to generate a new image, Blender shows us some options:

1. *Image name*: As expected, apply a name to the generated image.

2. *Width and Height*: We can also set the width and height in pixels.

3. *Color*: It creates a solid color for a solid image.

4. *Alpha*: It adds an alpha channel to the generated image.

5. *Generated Type*: This is for the type of image to generate. The available values are *UV Grid*, *Color Grid*, *Blank*, and *32 bit*.

In the same way, we can save our image to any of the external formats supported. This works like any other software and we have the options of *Save*, *Save as*, and *Save as Copy*.

There is also an interesting option that Blender supports. We can pack images within the .blend file. That means the current UVs are packed into the file. But what does the packing mean?

If we pack our images inside Blender, then in any case the file is modified in the future, the images will not be auto repacked, so the old versions of the images will be still available. To update, we have to repack or reload images.

FIGURE 1.1 The Wind is Changing by Andy Goralczyk, 2006. Awesome rendering demonstrating how powerful Blender can be in the right hands. This still is an awesome render from 6 years ago. I can assure you that Blender has improved even more in its latest releases, so can you reach the limits?

FIGURE 1.2 Gorilla by Everett Gunther. Interesting use of Blender's particle system.

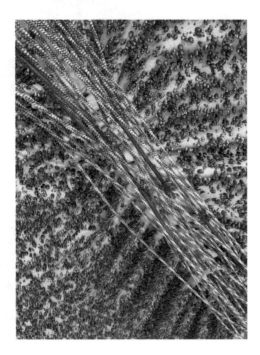

FIGURE 1.3 Contractile Ring simulation by BioBlender. Here, we see how Blender is used in scientific projects.

FIGURE 1.4 *Big Buck Bunny* project developed by the Blender Institute. The open movies developed by the BI represent a great example of Blender used for film production.

FIGURE 1.5 *Tears of Steel* is another great example not only for Blender used in animation films but also for vfx projects.

FIGURE 1.6 *Sintel* became a very ambitious project for the Blender Foundation and served as an important test for new awesome features added to Blender's code.

FIGURE 1.7 *Tube*, an open movie developed by Bassam Kurdali and urchn.org.

FIGURE 1.8 *Ara's Tale*, a movie developed by Martin Lubich.

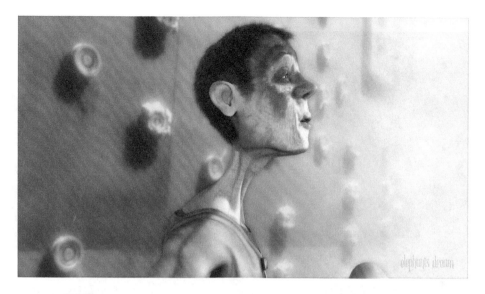

FIGURE 2.1 *Project Orange* resulted in *Elephants Dream,* the first open movie developed by the Blender Foundation.

FIGURE 2.2 Project Peach resulted in the *Big Buck Bunny* movie developed by the Blender Foundation as a result of which Blender was improved to end up with the 2.46 version.

FIGURE 2.3 Project Apricot was the first game developed by the Blender Foundation to be run within Blender Game Engine and resulted in the development of Blender 2.48.

FIGURE 2.4 Project Durian represented a step forward in Blender development. With the new 2.5 redesign proposal, the *Sintel* movie ended up with the Blender appearance as we see it now.

FIGURE 2.5 Project Mango, titled *Tears of Steel*, was a vfx and realistic rendering project using both real and cgi developments. The Blender Foundation developed this vfx movie involving real human actors together with visual effects developed entirely with Blender and resulting in the development and improvement of the most recent Blender versions.

Mushroom

Sunday	Monday	Tuesday	Wednesday	Thursday	Friday	Saturday
06 Feb	07	08	09	10	11	12
	Molly rig and facial GUI		Molly's house textures	Cycles		
			Molly's house			
13	14	15	16	17	18	19
	Building set and scene		1.1 (0.5)	2.2 (0.5)	2.3 (0.5)	2.5 (0.5)
	Completing set and scene textures			2.1 (0.5)		
20	21	22	23	24	25	26
2.4 (1)	2.6 (0.5)	2.8 (1)			2.9 (1)	2.11 (1)
	2.7 (0.5)					
27	28	01 Mar	02	03	04	05
	2.10 (1)			Light & Compo		
06	07	08	09	10	11	12
Render ...						

FIGURE 4.3 Schedule graphic determining the project stages in the calendar. Picture represents the schedule document for the Mushroom project.

FIGURE 4.7 Omega stop motion project. Directed by Eva Franz and Andy Goralczyk, this is an awesome stop motion movie developed using Blender. The picture represents the concept art developed for the movie.

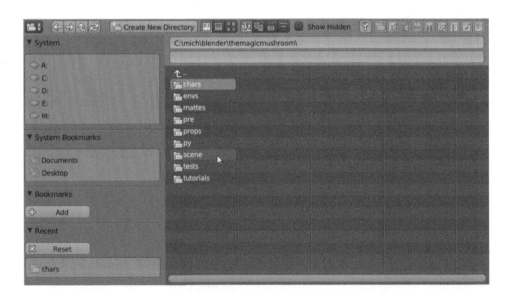

FIGURE 4.8 Project's folder structure. Having a clean and organized project folder helps in productivity. It is strongly recommended to apply a project naming convention to avoid mistakes and messy project structure on disk.

FIGURE 4.9 *Tears of Steel* DVD box. Blender released not only the movie but also a whole open movie workshop containing all files used in the 3D film production.

FIGURE 5.3 Developing a convincing character is not always easy. The picture represents the main character for *Tube* open movie. Notice that it suits perfectly the project concept, giving credibility to the film and increasing the viewer interest for this awesome film.

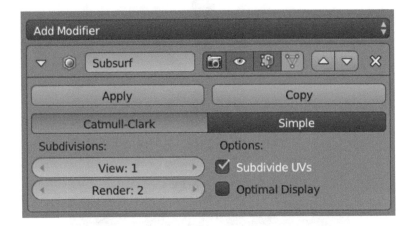

FIGURE 5.6 The modifier panel contains some common elements shared by all kinds of modifier types, but also specific buttons and properties. The picture represents the Subdivision Surface modifier.

FIGURE 5.8 Some of the props used in the *Big Buck Bunny* open movie. All those elements are part of the animation process because at any moment they can require animation. In other words, they interact with characters somehow.

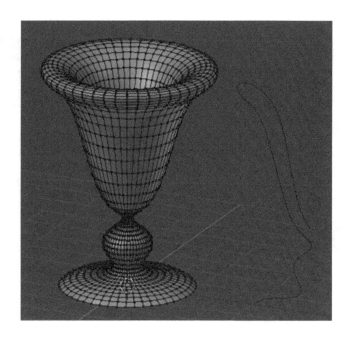

FIGURE 5.15 Convert to Mesh from Curve. Circle Curve after the Convert to Mesh from Curve operator. We get access to this by selecting the Curve to convert and pressing Alt+C Key.

FIGURE 5.16 RAT bProficiency. First project developed by former Platform Michelangelo Studio was an educational resource for Blender teaching, releasing its production files using the GPL License. This project was also mentioned in my Blender Foundation Certification.

FIGURE 5.17 *The Doctor Show*. We can see the relationship between the props and the character must be as refined as possible. In this case, the Blender constraints help while animating the swords at the same time as our character's hands.

FIGURE 5.18 The paranoia of the *Elephants Dream* open movie perfectly suits the world developed by the Blender Institute crew. Characters and environment keep viewers attention within the story.

FIGURE 5.19 David Revoy's sketches for the Blender Foundation's Durian project. The environment of the *Sintel* open movie perfectly matches the story and its characters.

FIGURE 5.20 Topology example, notice the loops around the mouth and eyes.

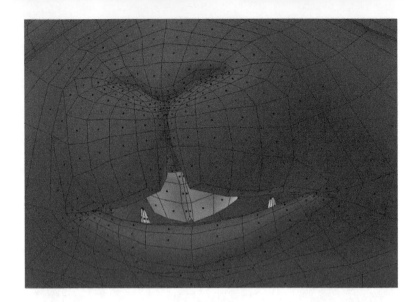

FIGURE 5.21 Topology example, notice the loops and faces building the mouth.

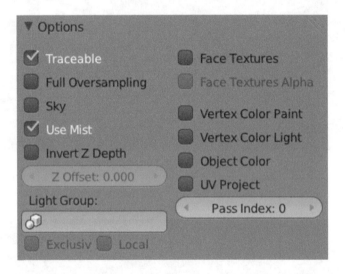

FIGURE 6.16 Options panel.

FIGURE 6.17 Shadow panel.

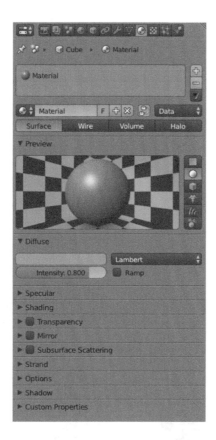

FIGURE 6.18 After adding a new material, we have different panels to play with. Depending on the results we want for our model, we shall play with the operators of those panels, so, if we want our object to look like a transparent one, we just need to activate the Transparency panel and play with operators inside.

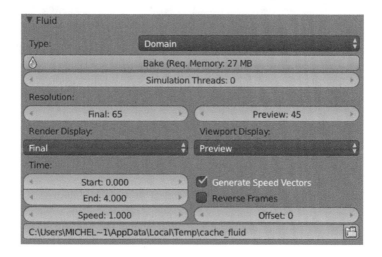

FIGURE 13.36 Fluid Domain type.

FIGURE 14.18 This picture represents an example of FreeStyle render result. Notice the toon style that Blender is capable of achieving using this feature.

## CHAPTER 9

Introduction to Rigging

Armatures and Bones

W HEN WE SEE CHARACTERS and objects moving in an animation movie, it doesn't mean they are all using an Armature, that is, it is not mandatory all objects have to pass the Rig process.

We may animate any kind of object by adding a couple of keyframes modifying its location over the scene and we will get our object going from point A to point B on the scene within a determined timeframe.

There are different techniques in animation that we will cover later in this chapter, but rigging is one of the most important tasks in animation movies.

As we discussed in the previous chapter, a good model is necessary if we want to achieve good results, because the rigger will need to apply an Armature, or skeleton that will be manipulated later by the animation crew so they are able to apply deformations resulting in poses making the final animation possible.

The complexity of a very good rig varies depending on the project and the final result expected. In very important projects, the number of bones that compose the skeleton of the main characters is overwhelming. We must mention here that the rigging team usually shows the final skeleton with the minimum manipulators needed, keeping those secondary bones or helpers hidden in layers.

A very good rigging not only consists of using the necessary bones and applying the right constraints but also organize it in layers, keeping it clean, and adding widgets and manipulators to keep it as organized as possible as shown in Figure 9.1.

The *rigger* job is related to very technical aspects and closely related to maths and programming because many times the rigger must resolve artifacts issues or any other kind of malfunction in the model and it's there where the rigger starts a very technical process of research.

In the same way, an advanced knowledge of constraints is basic for the development of this job because that will determine the workflow, not only for the rigger but also for the final result.

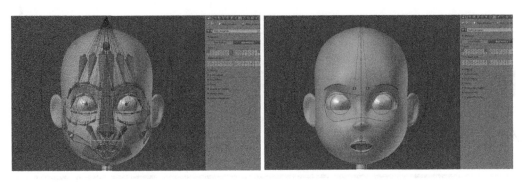

FIGURE 9.1 The final rigging must be structured and organized in layers so that we can show or hide bones, widgets, and manipulators easily, avoiding chaos in the animation process.

FIGURE 9.2 Scene of the Pixar's *Bugs* movie where we can think about the reuse of the armatures on a group of similar characters, instead of developing a specific one for each character.

Many times, we reuse armatures and it's very important we keep this in mind when we need to use similar armatures on the same type of characters, for example, in a group scene as shown in Figure 9.2.

In a typical work day of a studio's rigger, we find the following tasks to be done:

- The rigger gets the model.

- The rigger starts a study about how to develop the armature, probably on paper first.

- When the rigger has anything to start with, the first bones are generated, making children and parents follow a naming convention.

- The rigger adapts bones to the mesh by making sure the bones are aligned with the edges and vertices of the model so that the deformations are smooth.

- The rigger applies constraints like copy location, rotation or scale, IK, track, or any other needed to get the bone working as expected.

- The rigger applies the skeleton to the model and redefines to avoid possible issues, usually using Weight Paint.

- The rigger organizes different groups of bones using colors and layers.

- The rigger makes widgets for easy manipulation.

Next, we will see in depth how to work with Armatures in Blender. Without doubt, work in Blender on our own skeleton is bound to be an exciting experience, and we will see how Blender's versatility suits any animation studio requirements for this kind of job.

9.1 THE ARMATURE OBJECT

As discussed, the Armature object is like any other kind of object, say mesh, lamp, or empty, for example. Like them, the object Armature shares some common properties with other Blender objects. To name some examples, it has a center and a determined location and rotation or scale properties that may be modified. To modify, they should be in Edit Mode, might be reused and linked in different scenes or files, and might be animated like any other Blender object.

At this point, we must understand that when we say that it might be animated like any other Blender object we refer to the set of bones forming the armature like unique object. In order to use the armature and make the poses manipulating the bones, we must be in *Pose Mode*.

When a rigger makes an armature, he is making his first pose. That means every time we edit the armature in Edit mode we are modifying the so-called *rest position* or default position of the armature as shown in Figure 9.3.

We can access the Armature properties panel once we get it selected and we click on the Armature context icon within the Properties editor as shown in Figure 9.4, where we will see different panels to manipulate our Armature properties like apply name, manage layers, type of armature to show, or a library with poses and groups of bones.

Let's see the panels that show the properties of the object Armature:

1. *Armature name*: We can apply a custom name to our Armature by editing this input button. If we have some armatures in our scene, we are able to select them using the Outliner editor or using the small button on the left of the previous input button that will drop down a list with all available armatures in the scene.

2. *Skeleton*: In this panel, we might adapt our armature to different and useful options. We first tell Blender if we want our armature in Pose Position or Rest Position. That is the default and original position of the armature. In the same way, we can move and organize the bones in different layers, allowing a clear visualization and a better organized project. This option is specially useful, to organize bones depending on their nature, for example, widgets for head or arms, helpers, IK layers, drivers, and so on.

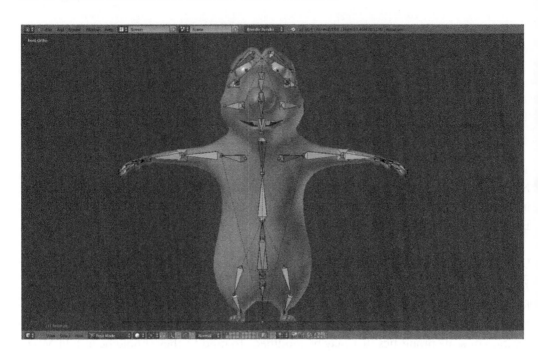

FIGURE 9.3 When we are making the armature in Edit Mode, we are modifying the so-called *rest position*. In the picture, we see that position by default in Pose Mode.

3. *Display*: We can select how we want Blender to show the armature, specifically the type of figure representing bones. We also can filter to show names, axes, shapes, colors, x-ray, and so on. The available figures are Octahedral, Stick, B-Bone, Envelope, or Wire. Each one has its pros and cons, and the decision about taking one over the rest is up to the rigger depending on his preferences and needs.

4. *Bone Groups*: A very important property helping riggers in their work is the separation of bones into different groups and apply different colors to these groups. This will make the armature comprehensible not only for the rigger himself but also the animation crew. An example could be a group of bones called *deformGroup* where we can place all those bones deforming the mesh and apply a black color to that group. We might add another group for *IKGroup* where we could place all those bones related to inverse kinematics and apply a yellow color to that group. In this way, the rigger's work is pretty dynamic because we can see which kind of bones we are manipulating with a single overview, in which group the bone is placed, and its nature and its purpose.

5. *Pose Library*: Blender allows us to store different poses in something called Pose Library; we can use any of the stored poses later in production. To add or delete poses from that library is really easy from this panel, in the same way as renaming poses. Blender also allows us to add more than a single library. That is specially useful to organize our libraries as different groups of poses, for example, a library called *Dancing* and another called *Running*.

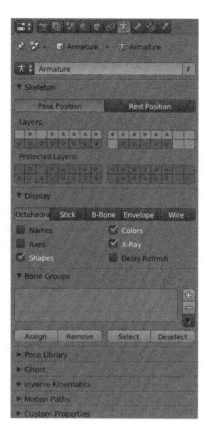

FIGURE 9.4 Properties of the Armature object are located in the Properties editor once we click the Armature context button.

6. *Inverse Kinematics*: This determines the type of IK solver used in the animation. Available options are *Standard* and *iTaSC*.

7. *Motion Paths*: We can use it to enable the option to visualize the motion paths our animated objects leave when they are animated. We can select the type of range between *Around Frame* and *In Range*. We can display both paths depending on the selected range or range of frames from the current one.

9.2 BONES

As discussed earlier, the bones are the elements that compose the armature object. This means that adding a single bone to our characters implies creating an armature object, even if it is composed of a single bone. Bones may be represented in diverse ways as we pointed out in Section 9.1. The Octahedral type is used by default, and we will use it as the basis to continue with this rigging adventure (Figure 9.5).

To manipulate bones correctly so we can complete our armature successfully we should know the elements that the bones are composed of.

FIGURE 9.5 Widgets are really useful for the animation crew. Using these widgets, there is no need to visualize complex armatures. It is kind of what you see is what you need paradigm.

1. *Start point*: This is also called *root* or *head*.

2. *Body*: It's the bone's core itself and may be modified and adapted in location, rotation, and scale.

3. *End point*: This is also called *tip* or *tail*.

At this point, there is something we need to know. Both the root and the tip may be manipulated independently, but they only allow modification of their location property. They can't be resized or rotated independently. On the other hand, the bone's body allows it to be escalated, rotated, or translated. It's also important to understand that we can extrude bones from an existing one and we must do this from the root or the tip of the previous bone.

It's important to check from where we are going to extrude new bones because the behavior might vary depending on whether it extrudes from root or tip. Usually, in a lot of riggings, the extruding action is done from the tip, because this creates a logical structure for the skeleton. But, we must remember that sometimes it's not useful for our purpose and then we need to extrude from root. It's up to us depending on our needs (Figure 9.6).

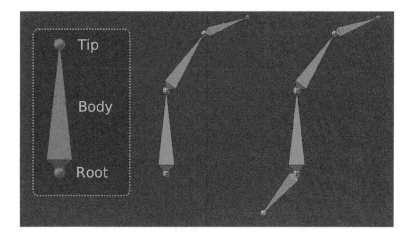

FIGURE 9.6 Bones' structure represented on the left, where we can see bones' elements like tip, body, and root. The two figures on the right represent an extruding exercise, one from the tip (middle) and one from the root (right).

We can access the bones' properties panels by selecting the Armature context with the bone-like button from the Properties editor. We will see all available options automatically where we might modify our bones' properties with such a transformation, lock axis, add relationships to groups, modify deformations, or change appearance and display (Figure 9.7).

Let's see the panels that the bones' properties provide:

1. *Bone Name*: We can apply a name to our bones from this input. During the rigging process, it's very important to follow a naming convention helping to locate bones in the armature tree. This keeps the structure clean and organized. By default, Blender adds the bones' name automatically, something like Bone.001 that in very large projects like the big animation studios ones, are not really useful, in fact, worse because it delays production. We will see later a proposal for naming conventions.

2. *Transform*: In Edit mode, we can manage the head, tail, and roll values from this panel. We can also lock the bone properties by enabling the Lock option.

3. *Relations*: We can move our bones to different layers. We can also modify their relationship or assign a new parent, connect to that parent, or make them independent. Here, we have the useful feature to add our bones to different predefined groups.

4. *Deform*: If this option is enabled, we are allowing our bones to deform geometry so we can apply values to factors like Envelope, or add segments and modify the influence ratio.

5. *Display*: This panel contains all options to modify our bones the way we want to see them. We can show or hide bones, like we can do in the Outliner editor. A very important property in this panel is that we can apply a custom widget. This means that we are able to apply any other shape to the bone so that bone is displayed with that shape

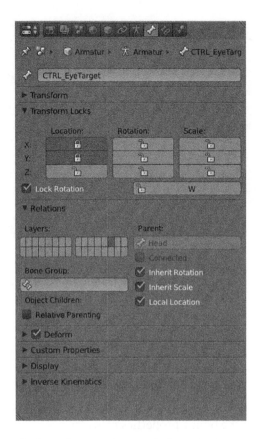

FIGURE 9.7   We can access the bones' properties panels from the Armature's context by clicking the bone-like icon in the Properties editor.

instead of the predefined bone shape like Octahedral, Stick, etc. This is really useful to create a widgets as manipulators that will help the animation crew in the animation process.

6. *Inverse Kinematics*: Once we know a lot of armatures and bones, we notice a very interesting property of the bones. They are composed of small segments making the bone very flexible in case we need that property. By default, a bone is composed of a single segment but we can modify that, as discussed to apply some flexibility to that bone. This allows us to play with the number of bones we need to introduce in our characters.

9.2.1 Bones' Segments

In cartoon animations, it's very easy to see some characters requiring this kind of property because in this animation style it's common to use the stretch and bounce resource by increasing the number of segments the bone is composed of. This technique comes from the first Walt Disney animations and you can see what we mean in any of the classical cartoons of that company.

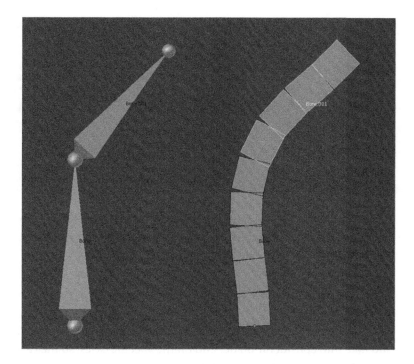

FIGURE 9.8   In the picture, the armature on the left uses bones with a single segment by default. On the right, the armature uses four segments per bone, so deformation and flexibility of the object are smooth.

We see an example in Figure 9.8. Notice the difference between add bones with a single segment and that when we raise the number of those segments. We notice, in the armature of the right, that the flexibility support when we increase the number of segments in each bone. Specifically, we can use four segments per bone.

This will allow us to deform our characters and objects smoothly, avoiding strange artifacts and reducing rigidity, making it look natural. If we need a practical example where the segments are really necessary, we could talk about the RAT bProficiency project where the segments are really necessary when we want to apply the rig to the character's tail. This element should be very flexible and should avoid any rigidity. We can solve that by adding as many bones as needed but we could be making the skeleton overly complex with the attached risk of making it less organized than expected. The perfect solution for this trouble is to add some bones to that character's tail and then apply the segments solution by increasing the number of segments per bone. In doing this, we make the character's tail deform smoothly and we have a clean and organized skeleton with less bones and better results as shown in Figure 9.9.

We can do this from the panel Deform within the Bones' properties context. We must mention here that working with B-bones we must be careful with the mode we are working on. If we work with B-bones in Edit mode, these bones will be displayed as any other bone in edit mode, that is like, rigid elements. However, if we switch to Object mode, we will notice that our bones are displayed as segments and how Blender automatically calculates

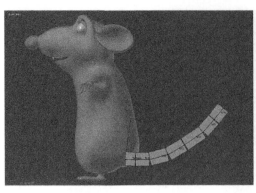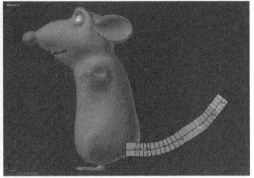

FIGURE 9.9   The picture on the left represents the number of bones added to the solution. The picture on the right represents the number of segments added to the solution. On the right, we increase the number of segments per bone and the result looks smooth and clever.

the deform curve depending on our bones' properties. Finally, if we are in Pose mode, we can deform and apply poses.

This means that segments are always present, we can see them even at a glance. The elements we should take into consideration depend on the specific cases, so the riggers must be careful with those elements requiring this solution.

9.2.2 Bones' Influence

Bones are grouped to complete the whole armature as we already know, but they should be applied to the object we want to deform in the manner that objects deform their original shape as we move bones. The principle of applying the skeleton to the object so it's affected by the change is called *Skinning* and we have different methods to apply it in Blender. We'll see now one that is commonly used in the studios.

To let our characters or objects to be deformed by our bones, we must link our bones to those objects, that is, basically, link our Armature. Blender needs to be able to recognize that a determined object has linked an armature and the bones composed in that armature are then allowed to deform our object depending on their influence.

Blender supports a couple of methods to link an armature to our objects. One is to add an Armature modifier to our object. The other one is to create a parent–child relationship between both object and armature.

We reckon the modifier Armature as the most interesting one to illustrate Blender skills. First, once we have our object and our armature, we must be sure to be in Object mode, then we select our object, and we go to the Modifiers context by clicking on the wrench-like icon in the Properties editor. There we find the Armature modifier and selecting it we have Blender showing all available properties for that context. We have some very interesting panels there; let's check the most interesting ones:

1. *Modifier name*: We supply a modifier name here, in our case the object that represents our armature. As discussed earlier, a single object might contain different armatures, so it's important to use a naming convention.

2. *Display type*: This is used as a filter where we enable the option to show or hide our modifier in different states. The available options are *Use modifier during render*, *Display modifier in realtime*, and *Use modifier while in Edit mode*.

3. *Move modifier panel*: These are basically two arrows, up and down, to move our modifier around others. It's important to take into consideration the order of the modifiers. Because Blender takes care of the modifier position in the tree, results may vary depending on that position. For example, applying a Mirror first and a Subdivision Surface later ends in a different result compared to applying a Subdivision Surface first and a Mirror later.

4. *Remove modifier*: This deletes or unlinks the modifier and the object. Basically, it breaks the relationship between both elements.

5. *Object*: This refers to the name we apply to our Armature as object. Here, we will tell Blender the object that should be used as armature is our recently created Armature.

6. *Bind To*: This is a method where we can bind the armature to any provided mesh and this can be done by enabling or disabling Vertex Groups or Bone Envelopes.

7. *Vertex Group name*: We might apply our modifier to vertices groups in specific objects instead of on the whole object itself. Sometimes, this is used to apply some effects to specific parts of meshes, so the modifier doesn't affect the rest of the vertices.

The second option is to apply our armature by establishing a parent–child relationship between object and armature. For that, we need to select our object in Object mode and pressing the Shift key we select our Armature. Then, we press Ctrl+P keys to use the parent feature.

The Set Parent pop-up menu appears asking us about the type of relationship we want to apply to both objects as shown in Figure 9.10, where we can select Armature Deform with envelope, for example.

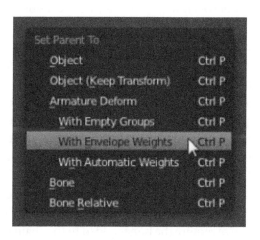

FIGURE 9.10 The Set Parent To pop-up menu allows us to select the type of relationship between two objects. Here, we select Armature Deform to make the armature deform the object.

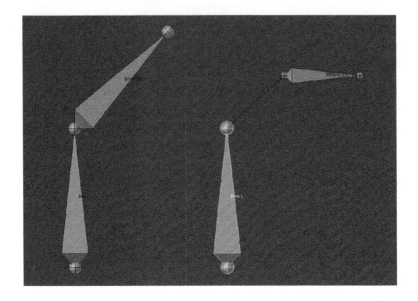

FIGURE 9.11 We see that Bone.001 is directly connected to its parent in the picture on the left. But the bone Bone.001.L is not directly connected showing a dotted line in the right picture.

Then, our armature is automatically linked to the object and each kind of deformation of our bones will affect that object. It must be said that the skinning method by applying a modifier Armature is very interesting and gives us more control over our rig. So, the parent–child method can be used for small tasks by animation studios like an auxiliary method.

As we can see, an armature is composed of a bone's chain that might or might not be connected between them. This implies that bones might or might not share contact between them. As shown in Figure 9.11, bones that keep contact in the parent–child relationship also share location for root and tip. That is, the tip for one bone is in the same place as the root of the other one. On the other hand, we have bones that have a parent–child relationship even when they have no contact between them. Instead, we see a dotted line between the tip of one bone and the root of the other one.

Sometimes, it's not necessary to keep the direct contact between bones; sometimes it's even necessary to break this contact, so we can enable or disable that with the *Connected* option located in the Relations panel.

In both cases, whether the bone is connected or not, we are able to tell Blender to avoid this bone inheriting the parent's rotation or scale from the same Relations panel. Disabling these options we make the child bone keep its own rotation or scale. In some animation styles, this is really important and to know our bones' chain offers these possibilities is important to understand the complexity of the rigging process.

We have seen how to create a simple bones' chain and how each bone keeps a parent–child relationship. There are some motivations in the rigging process to modify this relationship. This means that sometimes we require the bones added to the chain to be able to change their relationship and so we have to assign another parent to them. This is easily done in Blender and we have a few methods to do it.

FIGURE 9.12 Make Parent float panel. Here, we could modify the child–parent relationship and the option to make it connected or keep the offset between both bones.

We can use the Relations panel that we are familiar with. For that, in Edit mode, we select the child bone and then we insert the new parent bone name in the Parent input field.

Another way is by using keyboard shortcuts. In the same way we talked about linking objects and armatures, we should select the child bone in Edit mode, then by pressing Shift key we select the bone we want to be parent. To apply the relationship, we press Ctrl+P and then select if we want this relationship to be Connected or Keep Offset (disconnected) as shown in Figure 9.12.

As shown in Figure 9.13, now our bone displays an influence range that says the range could affect in a possible deformation. We can scale that influence range from the Pose mode. We select the bone and then press Alt+S.

It's important to know that if we are in Edit mode and the display type is Envelope, we can select the tip or root of our bone and scale so the influence range is proportionally scaled as shown in Figure 9.13.

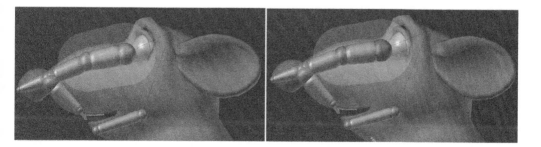

FIGURE 9.13 We can visualize Envelope mode so we know the influence range. That influcence range might be modified in Pose Mode, as seen in the left image. On the other hand, we can scale the tip and the root so the influence is proportionally scaled too like in the image on the right.

## CHAPTER 10

The Animation Process

A ND WE FINALLY COME to the hot point in any studio's animation project. Well, people consider this the most important stage in any film production, but as we already know from the previous chapters, every small task is important for a successful result.

We saw the importance of getting a good story, how a very good concept art makes it really interesting for viewer, and how a wrong model might end in future errors for riggers and, therefore, in the animation process.

It's completely normal that people who do not work in an animation studio's environment might think on these lines. At the end, the animation, the rendered motion is the visual contact between the product and the viewer.

We don't say this process is not important, not at all. We must understand at this point that the animation process is as important as the rigging or modeling ones with the attached risk than a very bad animation is visible to everyone at a glance.

Technically speaking, animation means to move any object or character or simply change their shape over time. But under this simple principle, we have very different ways we can use to animate any object. Here are three ways we can use:

1. Modifying the location, rotation, or scale of any object

2. Modifying the mesh by using, say, shape keys

3. Deforming the object via Armature, that is, using the rig attached to the object

In Blender we have three methods for animation:

1. *Key framing*: Poses are stored using single frames. This is a manual method because each frame might be moved in time changing its position so the animator can adjust them in a precise manner.

2. *Curves*: This method uses animation curves that give the animator a high degree of control of the movements. The animator manipulates something like graphics where the values stored in location, rotation, and scale are represented vertically while the timeline is represented horizontally.

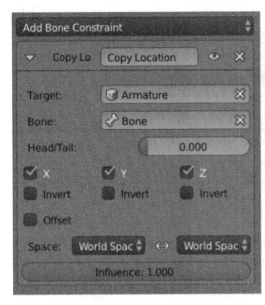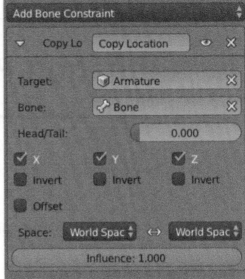

FIGURE 10.1 The picture represents how we can animate almost everything. In the picture, we have animated the Influence value of Copy Location constraint. We can see the default option in the left image, but notice the animated Influence option in the picture on the right. We just animated it by pressing the I key with the mouse over the option.

3. *Path*: They are just drawn in the 3D Viewer and then the object uses a constraint to follow that path according to some properties. This is not a very accurate method, but it's used frequently for specific purposes.

One of the most interesting improvements in the latest Blender releases is that almost everything can be animated. This is a really interesting point because we can animate whatever we want including property values, say Shader intensity, alpha values, and location coordinates. It's really simple by using the I key with the mouse over the property we want to animate as shown in Figure 10.1.

10.1 TIMELINE AND ANIMATICS

If we have to talk about animation, then we have to make some reference to the Timeline editor. We already know something about this editor from Section 3.4.2.

We know that Timeline is really important in production because we control there the actual length of the scene either in seconds or frames. We can visualize where the keyframes are, control the start and end of the scene shot, add or check for possible markers helping in production, playback the animation, and set all changes we need to get the expected result.

What we need to know is how important the so-called *animatics* are for any film production. There are several type of animatics, with more or less details, but what they basically do is to set an approach for the final scene in timeline words.

FIGURE 10.2 *Elephants Dream* open movie, codenamed Orange project. Animatics give us very important information about the scene length and resources consumption.

With animatics, we not only know if the scene is going as we expected and if it takes the time we want but we also know if animation is going to be as we desire. For that, we can use a very different type of animatics, as explained earlier, with more or less quality that depends on the purpose of the animatics.

For instance, if we want to know if our character goes from point A to point B in a credible timeline, we can make simple animatics of primitive objects moving from point A to point B, just as if our character were in place moving between these locations.

On the other hand, if we want to check a movement our character makes, say running or walking, then we need to make better animatics and just render the whole scene with very low quality and probably no colors and composition. In such cases, it's usual to render only the character movement, without added elements such as environment or any other thing, except those properties we want to check if any.

Animatics are really important and give us an idea on how the animation will look in timeline terms (Figure 10.2).

10.2 MARKERS

Another great solution helping animators is the use of markers that we might read from the Timeline. These markers are usually used to delimit actions or hot points. Animators should take into consideration, say where a specific character talks, the point the camera has to switch to, the point where some vehicle crashes, or anything else the animator should take care of.

Even though they are specially useful in the animation process, markers are not exclusive to the Timeline editor but may also be used in very different editors in Blender, like Graph Editor, Action Editor, or Dopesheet, each one for its own purpose, of course.

The beautiful thing is that the marker we make for specific frame is also visible in all other supporting markers. So, if we think we need to add a marker in Timeline at frame 10 because our character starts talking by phone, the same marker will appears in Action Editor at frame 10 so future production teams or any other member of the film crew is able to see that at this frame we have something interesting happening that should be taken into account.

10.3 KEYFRAMES

In animation, the keyframes are the golden egg. They form the basis of animation. In short, they store information about the value of specific data at determined frames (Figure 10.3).

Their use is really simple. We control animation by applying control points and manipulating the interpolation curve. For instance, if we want a wheel spinning, then we can use the following scheme:

1. *Control point 1:* A value of 0 at frame 0

2. *Control point 2:* A value of 20 at frame 20

In that example, we can visualize that the wheel has a value of 10 at frame 10, but what if we want the wheel having a value of 30 at frame 10 instead? Well, it's really simple, what we need is just add another control point at this frame:

1. *Control point 1:* A value of 0 at frame 0

2. *Control point 2:* A value of 30 at frame 10

3. *Control point 3:* A value of 20 at frame 20

To add keyframes, we just need to press the I key. Then, a pop-up menu appears with very different options as shown in Figure 10.4. We can select between add keyframes for *Location, Rotation* or *Scale, Location and Rotation, Location and Scale*, and so on.

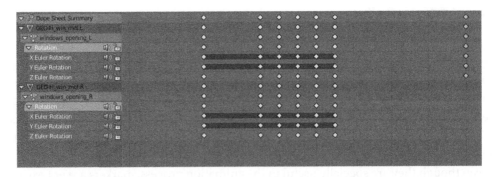

FIGURE 10.3 Keyframes example. The picture represents the stored keyframes for different objects. Notice the stored keyframes are related to Rotation.

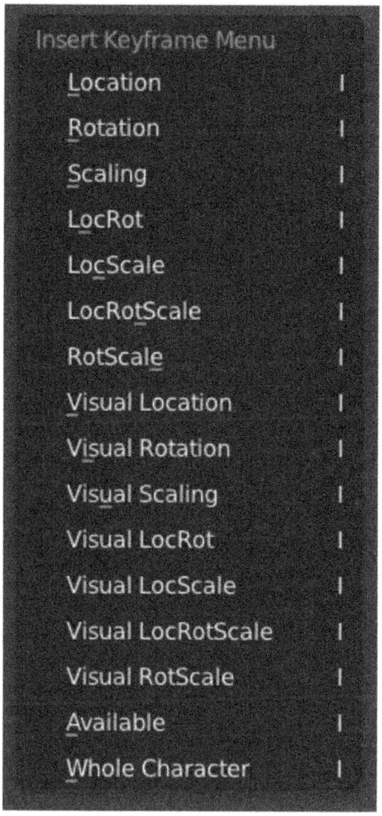

FIGURE 10.4 Insert keyframe menu. We can select the type of keyframe we want to store by pressing the I key and selecting the one we want from this pop-up menu.

As mentioned earlier, one of the most interesting updates in the latest Blender releases is the ability to animate almost everything. It's absolutely amazing to be able to animate properties by simply letting the cursor hover over the image and press the I key. At this moment, Blender makes a keyframe storing the information on this property. If we want to add another value then we can use the same technique to store another value at any other frame in the timeline, getting an animation of this property.

This is probably best illustrated with an example, so let's say we are in frame 1, we go to materials, let the mouse hover over diffuse, select the color blue, and then press the I key. We then go to frame 15, let the mouse hover over diffuse, select the color orange, and then press the I key. If we render that as animation, we'll see our object switching the color from blue to orange in just 15 frames, probably in less than 1 s depending on the frame rate settings.

In the previous example, what we have are just two control points which we can modify by the interpolation curve or by moving the respective keyframes in the Dopesheet editor.

This technique is really useful and speeds up the animation process but doesn't exclude the responsibility of taking care of such keyframes. When we add keyframes in this way, we cannot be totally sure how they are being stored in the whole animation structure and it's good to control and check everything is fine even if we use this technique.

10.4 TYPES OF ANIMATION

We can think about two types of animation. This is really important to know so we understand the animation process and how to develop specific animations in the right way. This doesn't mean they are not compatible with one another, because film productions usually mix both techniques depending on the requirements of the animated scene.

1. *Straight Ahead*: This animation type basically begins at the beginning and ends at the end. So easy!

2. *Pose to Pose*: This is a type of animation using a progressive refinement.

Obviously, the first type of animation, straight ahead, is subject to improvisation, can get out of hand easily, is hard to track progress of, and a bit messy if we compare with the second type. It's also harder to fix because we need to modify more keyframes manually if we need to fix specific values on any frame.

The second type of animation, pose to pose, looks planned and structured. In case we need to fix things it's rather easy because the use of control points where refinement is done with interpolation curves is an easy way to do it.

10.4.1 The Twelve Principles Developed at Disney

1. Squash and stretch

2. Anticipation

3. Staging

4. Straight and ahead, action, and Pose to Pose

5. Follow through and Overlapping action

6. Slow In and Slow Out

7. Arcs

8. Secondary action

9. Timing

10. Exaggeration

11. Solid drawing

12. Appeal

10.5 USING CONSTRAINTS IN ANIMATION

We can control our object properties using constraints. In fact, they apply some kind of limit or add specific values to these properties so the result is affected by these new rules. For instance, imagine applying a limit rotation to any specific bone within an armature.

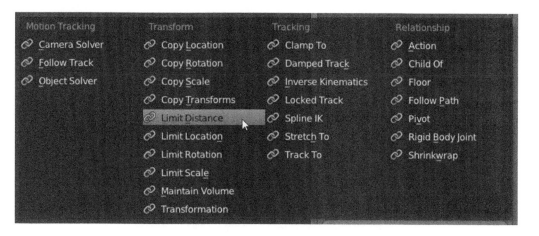

FIGURE 10.5   Different constraints available in different groups depending on the desired purpose.

In animation, we can use constraints for those elements that only allow constraints using targets. Without going into too much detail, it is enough to say, it's usual in animation studios to use these kind of constraints in animation projects. As mentioned earlier, imagine a bone with a constraint of *Copy rotation* from any other targeted bone.

In such a case, the owner of the constraints will copy rotation once the targeted bone modifies its own rotation. This is a kind of *indirect* constraints animation.

Constraints are accessible from the Properties editor by clicking the bone and chain-like icon, once we have a bone selected.

Then, an Add Bone Constraint selector appears in such a context as shown in Figure 10.5.

Blender provides us with four groups of constraints, grouped depending on the purpose.

- *Motion tracking*: Available constraints in this group are *Camera Solver*, *Follow Track*, and *Object Solver*.

- *Transform*: Available constraints in this group are *Copy Location*, *Copy Rotation*, *Copy Scale*, *Copy Transforms*, *Limit Distance*, *Limit Location*, *Limit Rotation*, *Limit Scale*, *Maintain Volume*, and *Transformation*.

- *Tracking*: Available constraints in this group are *Clamp To*, *Damped Track*, *Inverse Kinematics*, *Locked Track*, *Spline IK*, *Stretch To*, and *Track To*.

- *Relationship*: Available constraints in this group are *Action*, *Child Of*, *Floor*, *Follow Path*, *Pivot*, *Rigid Body Joint*, and *Shrinkwrap*.

10.6 SHAPE KEYS

The shape keys definitively provide us with an interesting method of refining deformations. It's common lately to see studios putting more and more work on the shape keys animation method.

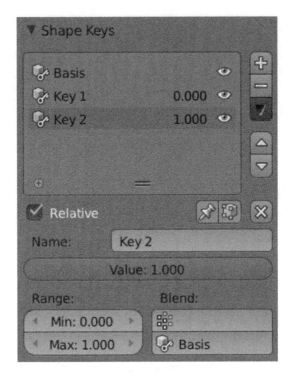

FIGURE 10.6 The shake keys panel stores the library of the different shapes we have added. Notice the options Relative and Value of influence.

If we talk about shape keys we have to mention facial deformation. Nowadays, we can't imagine facial expressions and animations without shape keys. Of course, any of the super productions in these days use a very complete facial rig (Figure 10.6). Without doubt they use a lot of constraints to make the rig work properly depending on the circumstances but we must be sure that they also use shape keys to refine deformations and speed up the animations.

In Blender, shape keys are used in some kind of objects like meshes, curves, or lattices but it's specially designed to deform object vertices so we can build new shapes ready to be used in a simply way.

Technically speaking, we can see two different types of shape keys, the Relative one, where the new shape key is applied based on the base one and the Absolute one, where the new shape key is relative to the previous and next one.

They are used for different purposes, so for instance, if we have made a facial animation using our armature and facial bones, we can refine the possible glitches with a shape key refining eyelids for example. In this case, we are using a relative shape key.

On the other hand, if we want to have a sphere object deforming its topology from sphere to cylinder and then to a cube, we can use the absolute shape keys, where it is based on the previous and next figures involving a lineal deformation over time (Figure 10.7).

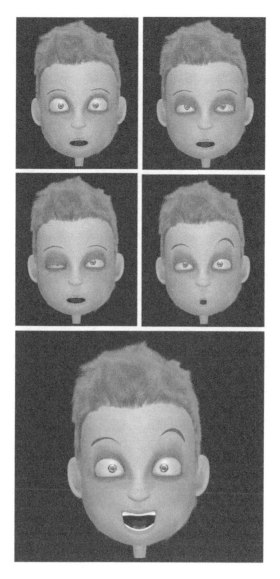

FIGURE 10.7 With shape keys, it's really easy to manipulate facial expressions in Blender. It's great to use this technique to refine poses fixing possible issues.

10.7 WALKCYCLE

Absolutely every animation project, if not all, has its own walkcycle. This depends on the level of the project. We don't refer to walkcycle as the animation process where any character seems to be walking.

Well, that is the most common meaning of the walkcycle but we can see walkcycle or simple cycles in more animations like mechanical or organic ones. So, for instance, a ball bouncing on the wall could be done with a *bouncecycle*. Same is applied for running or jumping, for example.

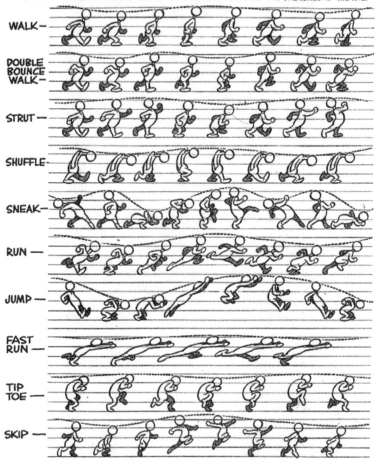

FIGURE 10.8   Interesting comparison between cycles. (From http://minyos.its.rmit.edu.au/.)

A basic walkcycle, talking about the process of any character walking, consists of 13 frames where we can visualize some acting like references. So we have called it *Two contact positions* or the *Middle Pose* but what we need to take care of are frames 13, 11, 7, 3, and 1. We will see that graphically (Figure 10.8).

## CHAPTER 11

Introduction to Lighting

IT MAY SEEM REDUNDANT if we say that lighting is a very important step in film production. But, again, we are not exaggerating when we say the lighting team is responsible for the success or failure of a project.

Again, this is so because building the lights for a film is really complex and its result is directly visible for the viewer. We can allow an unnoticed error in rigging or animation but visual errors in light, texturing, materials, and other similar areas will be very obvious to the viewers.

Lighting a film is a kind of art that requires some skills but is so rewarding at the end. We should be aware of this. We could have a great scene with very detailed characters and wonderful animation, but if lights are not managed in great detail, the whole project will be ruined.

We already know that every scene in Blender is affected by several laws and properties from materials, lights, textures, environment, and world settings. But what are the elements affecting lights in Blender?

1. *World:* The color of the ambience is very important to set the right lights.

2. *Ambient occlusion:* This option is necessary to give some realism to the scene.

3. *Indirect light:* Like in the real world, objects' color will be affected by surrounding objects' colors.

4. *Lamps:* Depending on the lamps setup, we will have very different results.

5. *Engine:* Obviously, depending on the render engine selected the whole result will vary, for example, from Blender Internal to Cycles.

We won't talk about the technical laws of lighting because this requires a lot of effort that is not needed right now. We need to know how important it is to set up the right lighting in film productions, why many good projects were ruined because of a poor interpretation of this element and why many small and modest projects were a completely success because of the right use of compositing and lighting.

Even if we don't need to know all the technical laws, we must know that as with any other element in render processing, a bad use of its settings could end in never-ending renders because of the amount of ambient occlusion, ray tracing, or calculation on indirect lighting.

Therefore, it's a good idea to use the Blender Internal render because this simplifies all these processes to avoid calculating the real physics for lighting.

If we have to talk about how to set up lights in Blender, we could come up with something simple in three or four steps. For example, select the type of lamp we want to use, position the light and direction, select the color of the light, and modify values like energy.

In fact, it's more complex than this of course, but we will use those steps as the starting point to know how the lights are managed in Blender.

11.1 LAMPS

In this panel, we can select between different lamp types. We have to know that depending on the selected type, we will have different options and controls.

The available lamp types in Blender are *Point*, *Sun*, *Spot*, *Hemi*, and *Area*.

From this panel, we could modify the light color and apply the energy value. The energy value is equivalent to the amount of light the lamp emits.

The light type also depends on the Falloff selected. Available values for the falloff are *Lin/Quad Weighted*, *Custom Curve*, *Inverse Square*, *Inverse Linear*, and *Constant*. This value is also dependent on the Distance value. The falloff property is only available for Point and Spot lamp types.

We also have some options to enable us to refine our light setup, like *Negative* to cast the negative light, allow Blender to use lamp on those objects in the same layer with *This Layer Only*, create *Specular* highlights, or enable *Diffuse* shading (Figure 11.1).

11.2 SHADOW

If we talk about lights, we have to talk about shadows. To produce a convincing project, we have to set up a balanced system between lights and shadows.

In this Blender panel, we can choose if we do not want to use shadow at all with No Shadow or use ray tracing to cast shadows with Ray Shadow button.

If we have Ray Shadow selected, then we can select the color of the shadow being cast by the lamp. In the same way, we can play with Sampling properties like the number of samples,

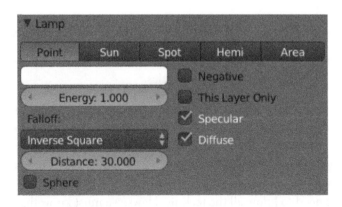

FIGURE 11.1 Different types of lamps we can use in Blender. Each one contains its own properties and results vary one from the other.

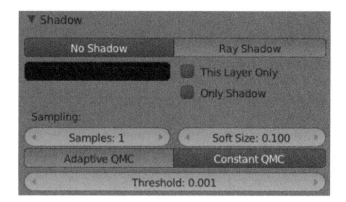

FIGURE 11.2   The shadow panel where we can modify and adapt the shadows of the scene. If we play with lights, we need to take shadows into account.

size, or method being used—Adaptive QMC that is faster for processing or Constant QMC that generates less noise.

This panel will not be available if we select a Hemi lamp (Figure 11.2).

11.3 ENVIRONMENT LIGHT

We could think about the environment light as a property that provides light in all directions, wrapping the whole scene. This light is calculated in the same way as the Ambient Occlusion (AO) with the small but important difference that Environment lighting checks the ambient value of the material shading properties, indicating the amount of color the material receives.

We can also select the color of the environment light projected and the energy value. The available options for environment light color are *Sky Texture*, *Sky Color*, and *White* (Figure 11.3).

11.4 AMBIENT OCCLUSION

The AO is a very interesting ray-tracing calculation that makes renders look great. This is not a very technical explanation but the fact is the AO does not exist in real life, so it just simulates a nonphysical effect to make renders look better.

The thing we must understand is that AO doesn't have anything to do with lights, because it even works if we don't have any lamp on our scene but it's commonly used together with lamps to improve renders' appearance.

The AO is located in the World context and requires the ray-tracing option enabled in the Shading panel of the Render context.

FIGURE 11.3   With the environment light, we manage the whole light on the scene. As we know, it manages the light provided in all directions over the scene.

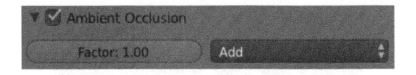

FIGURE 11.4 Even though the ambient occlusion does not exist in real life, it is a very common feature to improve the final renders' look.

Then, we can play with the AO color that is located in the World panel of the world context. This makes Blender use that color for the AO calculation.

In this panel, we have some properties to play with. We can adjust the Factor value and the method to mix the material shading between Add or Multiply (Figure 11.4).

11.5 RESOLVING ISSUES WITH LIGHTS

When we work with lights, it's usual to set up a trial-and-error environment, so we can modify and adapt our lighting environment properties later. But it's also common to have some issues with the lighting environment in film production.

While producing the RAT bProficiency project, we had several issues with lighting, probably because we were relative beginners in film production but we finally managed to solve them. We don't mean they were the best solutions, because we could probably have made them look better, but we did solve some issues with very practical fixes.

We have to admit that we were using a very messy environment light, because it was our first experience as shown in Figure 11.5.

FIGURE 11.5 A completely messy environment light for the RAT bProficiency project. Even though it was a beginner project, it ended up with Platform Michelangelo Studio.

FIGURE 11.6 Issue fixed with a point lamp. Notice the bottom picture makes the lamp to raytrace lamp object making the material simulate a warm scene.

We had to solve, for example, an issue with the lighting over the table where everything looked a bit gray. We couldn't manage to have a nice and warm ambience over the table. We finally came up with the solution of adding an object, basically a lamp, and use a Point lamp as shown in Figure 11.6.

Notice the picture at the bottom makes the object's shadows a bit smooth, integrating each to the other while the picture at the top looks harder. Notice the shadow of the cup over the cheese.

This is a very rare issue but be sure that the most famous film production deals with these kind of issues during production. Setting up a really nice environment light is a very hard task but as important as any other such animation. In fact, we could say, even more important because, as mentioned earlier in this book, the visual aspects will be the first contact with the final user.

Those visual aspects the final user has access to at first glance are very valuable to determine a complete success or a failure (Figures 11.7 through 11.9).

FIGURE 11.7 Environment light for the *Big Buck Bunny* open movie developed by the Blender Institute. Notice the point lamps used in the middle of the scene grouped in a circle shape.

FIGURE 11.8 Environment light for the shaman scene in the *Sintel* open movie developed by the Blender Institute. Notice, we have here some interesting point and spot lamps dispersed over the scene to create the warm ambience.

FIGURE 11.9 Rendered scene with Sintel and Shaman from the *Sintel* open movie developed by the Blender Institute.

## CHAPTER 12

Compositing Nodes

To UNDERSTAND WHAT NODES are is not easy, but we can think about them as small filters with the ability, and used single or grouped to modify our render's final result, generating the final composition expected.

Nodes are necessary elements in almost every project for some reasons. First, they apply those visual changes that improve the initial state. On the other hand, it's a bit hard to get into the detail level in a straightforward way, so the use of nodes is more than important in such cases in order to obtain this plus in quality.

There are nodes of very different types and their functionality varies depending on the group they are stored in. Some projects only require the use of a small number of nodes to adjust the final composition, but others require a very complex group of nodes resulting in a complete network. In this case, the team working with compositing and nodes need to know the final result they need to achieve. The process of making a complex node network is called *Noodle*.

Nodes are very important in animation films and projects because applying the right nodes in the right place will improve the overall ambience improving the feeling between product and viewer. The project already has passed through a very hard process of pre-production, modeling, rigging, and animation, but the final appearance, the one that will be in direct relationship with the viewers, is created by the compositing and lighting team.

Depending on how big the animation studio is, these teams may be structured in differed departments or grouped just in a single one. Anyway, they must work to apply that level of detail giving the product the final appearance to make it attractive to viewers.

This topic has been the subject of forums and talks, because we find two different ways of approaching the topic. One argues about the necessity of that visual aspect, based on the importance of the story not the visual aspect. But sometimes, the story is misunderstood because the film is overwhelmed by the visual aspect.

Anyway, it seems like there is no doubt that the visual appearance should be taken into consideration in some measure. We won't enter into that discussion because it's not our objective right now. We'll simply see how we can alter and improve the final result using Blender's nodes.

When we say that we can improve the visual aspect using nodes, we don't mean using nodes will solve previous mistakes. It's not magic. We must know how to combine them for a successful result because a bad use of nodes might result in a very poor final product.

We can find three node types:

- *Input Nodes*: They are nodes providing information but they do not receive any information from others. That means these types of nodes are connected to others but they don't receive connection.

- *Output Nodes*: They process information to offer a final result. These nodes receive external connection but they don't require to be connected to any other node. They manipulate information and the final result is shown by themselves.

- *Processing Nodes*: These nodes process and filter information to produce a different result. These nodes receive an external connection and they are connected to others at the same time.

12.1 SETTING UP NODES

To use nodes in Blender, we must select some parameters making Blender receive and manipulate information about our nodes. In the first place, we need to go to Properties editor to the Render context. There we will see the Post-Processing panel where we need to have the option Compositing enabled. With this option, we make sure Blender will use our nodes in the render process as shown in Figure 12.1.

After enabling the Compositing option, we will go to the Node editor to enable the Composite Nodes by clicking i the Image icon and enabling the Use Nodes option. There we will find other useful options for our work with nodes like Free Unused, which will free the memory space to avoid processing unused nodes, or the Backdrop option that will generate the node result as background in the Node editor, so we can get a first approach on how our work with Nodes is going as shown in Figure 12.2.

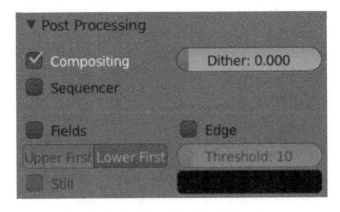

FIGURE 12.1   Enable Compositing from Properties editor, Render context, and Postprocessing panel.

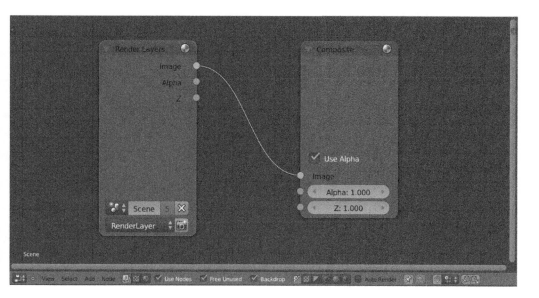

FIGURE 12.2 Basic options for Node editor. Enabling Composite Node, and Use Nodes is enough to tell Blender to use nodes in the render processing.

12.2 USING NODES

Now, we will see the structure of a single node and its elements as shown in Figure 12.3. We will learn how to work with them so we can create a node structure or the desired noodle.

A node is composed of the following:

- *Titlebar*: Here, we can see the name of the node and some buttons and options to hide content like the *Collapse Node* and *Hide Preview*.

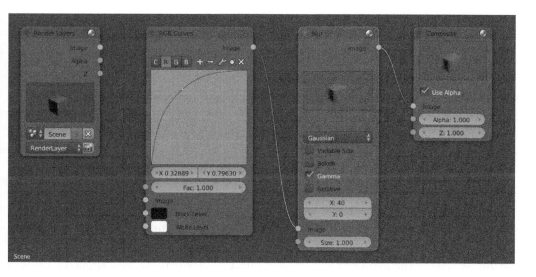

FIGURE 12.3 Structure of a node. Different elements compound the node and determine node behavior.

- *Toggle Preview*: This shows or hides a preview of the node.

- *Node Toggle*: This completely collapses the node leaving only the name visible.

- *Input Sockets*: The small circles in the left bottom side are the so-called input sockets and they have the responsibility to accept the input connection from other nodes.

  - *Blue sockets*: These accept vectors.

  - *Yellow sockets*: These accept colors.

  - *Grey sockets*: These accept single values like alpha.

- *Output Sockets*: Like the Input Sockets, the small circles on the right upper side are the so-called output sockets, and they determine the type of output used by the node.

  - *Blue sockets*: These produce vectors.

  - *Yellow sockets*: These produce colors.

  - *Grey sockets*: These produce singe values like alpha.

- *Image Preview*: As mentioned earlier, nodes include a small preview of the image showing the result after the node has processed the information depending on the node parameters and options.

- *Buttons and menus*: Depending on the type of node selected, we will see different parameters and options here. We will adjust specific values to optimize the expected result we want our node to apply to the final compositing.

- *Threads*: A curved line illustrates the connection between an output socket from node A to the input socket of node B.

As shown in Figure 12.3, we can see the structure of the different nodes. In our example, we have a scene with a cube. We have applied an orange material and rendered the image. Once in the Node editor, we see four types of nodes used. In the first place, we have a Render Layers node, where we only have output sockets, in our case the render or the image of our rendered scene.

We connect the Image output socket to the input socket of another node, this time the RGB Curves node. Notice that sockets must be the same type, in our case Image. Then we modify the color curve for the Red layer. The RGB node is connected by the output Image socket to the input socket of the Blur node, where we apply a blur effect to the compositing.

As we can see in the preview of the Blur node, the initial image has been altered for both the diffuse level of the Red layer and the blur effect itself, where we have applied a value of 40 in the X axis.

Finally, we connect from the Image output socket of the Blur node to the input socket of the Composite node. Using the latest one, we say to Blender to use our noodle tree information in the final render processing. In fact, if we render again using F12 key, our final result will be different from the very beginning because Blender has used the noodle information in the render processing resulting in the new composite.

It's important to understand what the sockets are and how they work in the noodles development. We can resume sockets as connection points where we link information between nodes. As mentioned earlier, sockets from the left side are input sockets and the ones on the right side are called output sockets.

To make the process of creating new sockets easier, Blender shows us the different types of sockets by applying different colors, depending on the type of information we expect to manipulate in such connectors.

There are some basic colors:

1. *Yellow*: This is related to the color information. Here we can manipulate information for input and output as they always have a color relation.

2. *Grey*: This is usually used for numeric values, but could also contain information for a value map or a ramp color. This type of connectors is usually used to manipulate alpha.

3. *Blue*: This is related to information about vectors and coordinates.

Both input and output sockets might be connected only to others sharing the same type unless we use a special case denominated as *Converter*. Sometimes, Blender knows how to manipulate such exceptions by applying the converter automatically, but not always.

A very interesting point while manipulating nodes is that such sockets usually have a name describing their action. They are like a clue to the information that is to be manipulated in both input and output as shown in Figure 12.4.

To add nodes to our noodle, we can use two methods. In the first place, we can make that from the menu in the header of the Node editor with option Add and then select the type of node we want to add. On the other hand, we might add a new node if we keep the cursor in the Node editor and press the Space key where we can select the type of node from a small pop-up menu.

To connect nodes, we know that we should join output sockets from one node to input sockets from another node. We also know that in most cases they should be of the same type. For that, we just click using LMB over a specific output socket and keeping it pressed we connect to the input socket of another node. We should see an association line called *thread* indicating that we are sharing information between the selected nodes.

If we would like to disconnect both sockets, we could make it in two ways. One by one select any of the sockets by clicking with LMB and moving it a bit to raise the button and

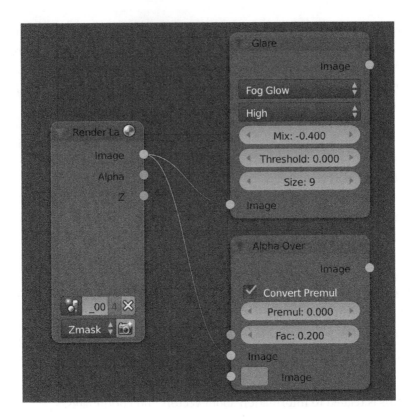

FIGURE 12.4 Each socket contains a small name describing the action or property we could manipulate. Notice in this picture that the sockets we are manipulating are related to image.

disconnect. Another way is by using Ctrl+LMB where we see something like a cutter. If we move that cutter to our thread, the connection line, we will see it's disconnected meaning that both nodes are not sharing information anymore.

Nodes are elements we can organize in our Node editor, so we can move, duplicate, group, or delete so we keep our noodle clear and easily readable.

12.3 NODE TYPES

12.3.1 Input Nodes

Input nodes are those producing information. This information is exported to other nodes so that it can be manipulated in order to produce a completely new information. These nodes are easily recognizable because they have only output sockets (Figure 12.5):

- Render Layers Node
- Image Node
- Texture Node
- Value Node

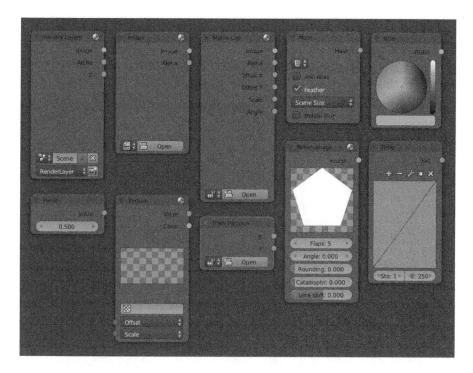

FIGURE 12.5 The available input nodes. As mentioned earlier, input nodes are those producing information.

- RGB Node
- Time Node

12.3.2 Output Nodes

The output nodes are the ones showing the information processed by the rest of nodes (Figure 12.6). These nodes are really useful to check the approximated result of specific operation or to check how our noodle is working at a determined point.

- Viewer Node
- Composite Node
- Split Viewer Node
- File Output Node

12.3.3 Color Nodes

These nodes are the ones manipulating the color information like contrast, layers, colors, alpha, or intensity (Figure 12.7).

- RGB Curve Node
- Mix Node

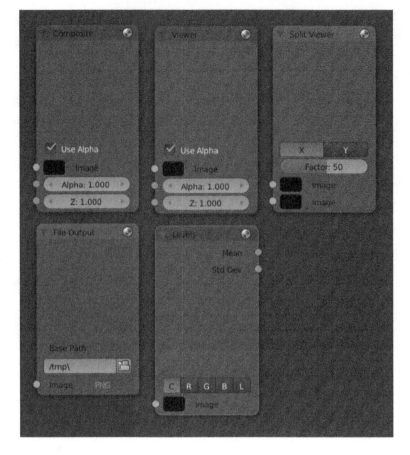

FIGURE 12.6 The available output nodes. As mentioned earlier, output nodes are the ones showing information processed by the rest of nodes.

- Hue Saturation Node

- Bright/Contrast Node

- Gamma Node

- Invert Node

- Alpha Over Node

- Z-Combine Node

12.3.4 Vector Nodes (Figure 12.8)

- Normal Node

- Vector Curves Node

- Map Value Node

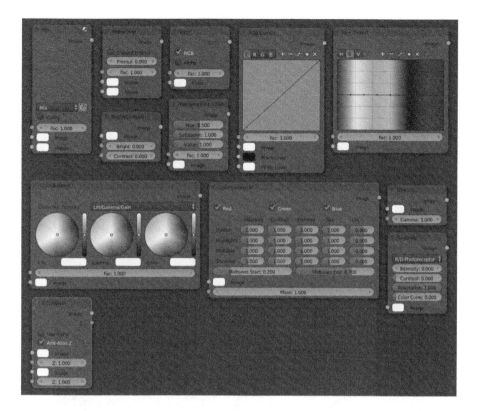

FIGURE 12.7 The available color nodes. As mentioned earlier, color nodes are the ones manipulating color information.

12.3.5 Filter Nodes (Figure 12.9)

- Filter Node
- Blur Node
- Bilateral Blur Node
- Vector Blur Node
- Dilate/Erode Node
- Defocus Node

12.3.6 Convertor Nodes (Figure 12.10)

- ColorRamp Node
- RGB to BW Node
- Set Alpha Node
- ID Mask Node

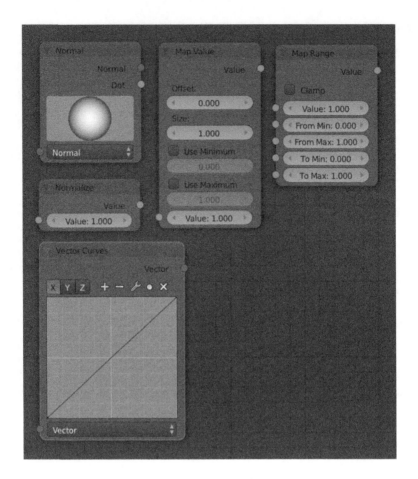

FIGURE 12.8 The available vector nodes.

- Math Node
- Combine/Separate Node

12.3.7 Matte Nodes (Figure 12.11)

- Difference Key Node
- Chroma Key Node
- Luminance Key Node
- Color Spill Node
- Channel Key Node

12.3.8 Distortion Nodes (Figure 12.12)

- Translate Node
- Rotate Node

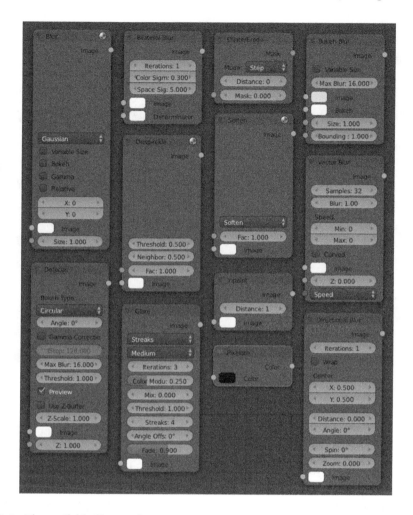

FIGURE 12.9 The available filter nodes.

- Scale Node

- Flip Node

- Displace Node

- Map UV Node

It's also interesting to see some of the Blender Foundation's open movies node trees. For example, as shown in Figure 12.13, the *Creatures Factory* open movie is very distinctive with the glow and neon effects. In the picture, we can see those nodes working within the noodle to finally obtain the desired glowed effect.

In the same way, the *Big Buck Bunny* open movie developed by the Blender Institute and Blender Foundation uses a very distinctive compositing noodle that makes it looking warm and sunny as shown in Figure 12.14. Notice the use of nodes like Blur, RGB Curves, Mask, and Glow, for example.

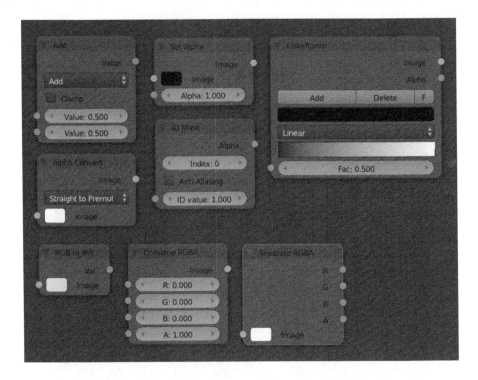

FIGURE 12.10 The available convertor nodes.

Another example is shown in Figure 12.15, where we have to take an special view to the lightwrap node and the blur one. This picture represents a very warm environment light within the shaman tent. Atmosphere created with the noodle tree is awesome and perfectly suits the scene requirements.

For a Lighthouse CGI Animation, formerly Platform Michelangelo Studio, project code-named Haiku, we came with a very complex noodle tree specially for some characteristic effects for convulsions and such as shown in Figure 12.16.

Some of the nodes used in the compositing were animated, as shown in the mentioned picture. So we can check how node properties could also be animated by placing the mouse over and inserting the right keyframe with the I Key.

For that project, we used and animated node properties for Lens Distortion, Defocus, Translate, or Displace. Also, ColorRamp and Map Values were used to adjust colors environment together with blur nodes to create a depth effect.

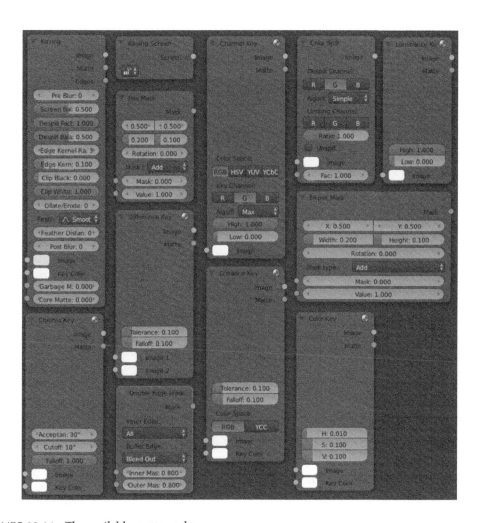

FIGURE 12.11 The available matte nodes.

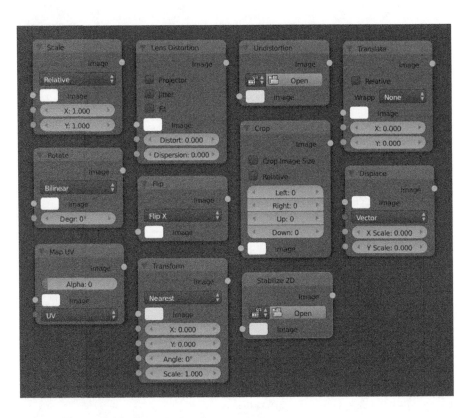

FIGURE 12.12   The available distortion nodes.

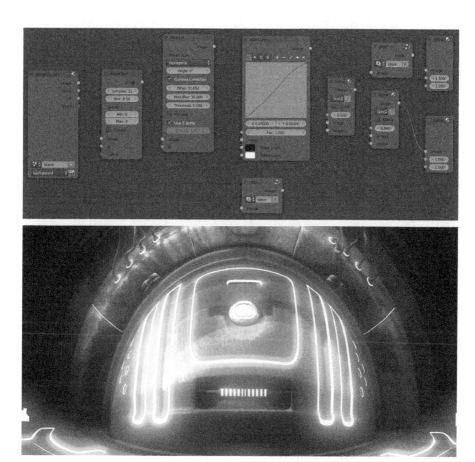

FIGURE 12.13 The compositing nodes for a *Creatures Factory* open movie developed by Andy Goralczyk. Notice the neon and glare nodes that are very representative of the film compositing.

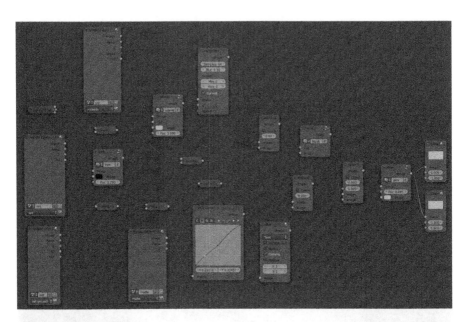

FIGURE 12.14 The compositing nodes for *Big Buck Bunny* open movie developed by the Blender Institute.

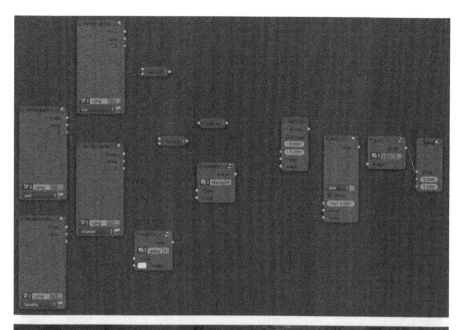

FIGURE 12.15 The compositing nodes for *Sintel* open movie developed by the Blender Institute.

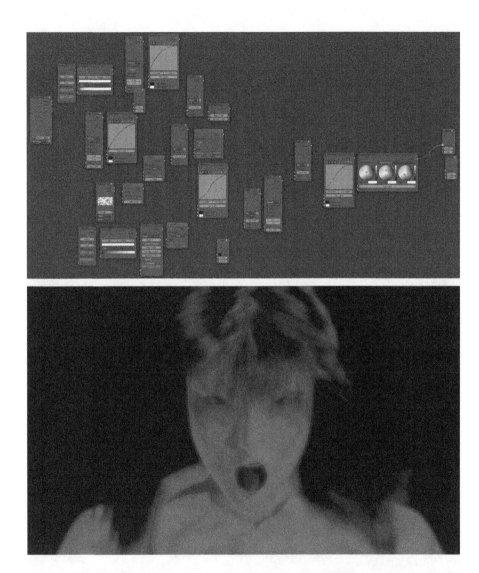

FIGURE 12.16 The compositing nodes for *Haiku Poem* movie developed by Lighthouse CGI Animation.

## CHAPTER 13

Using Particles and Dynamics

W E CAN HARDLY IMAGINE a 3D film without physical simulation. In Blender, when we say physics, it does not only refer to actual physical phenomena but also to the grass, fur, or hair.

The question is, can we imagine any of the 3D films we already know or have watched without physics? We could simplify this broad question by answering the following specific ones:

1. Did the characters have hair or were they furry?

2. Was there cloth simulation?

3. Was it raining at some point in the film?

4. Did you see smoke or wind phenomena at some point in the film?

5. Did you see particle effects in the environment?

These are just some questions, but if you answer *Yes* to any of them, then that film is using physics. Even if your answer is *No* for all of them, the film might have still used physics at some point.

We'll now discover how Blender manages the different options regarding physics, and we'll set the basis of the knowledge so the next time we watch a 3D film, we'll know at a glance where physics is being used.

Understanding physics in Blender is difficult if we look at it from a technical point of view, so we will just see what options are available. Our purpose here is not to develop any physical laws in Blender, but to understand Blender's physical and dynamic effects, which are used in almost every film production.

Technically speaking, Blender offers different kinds of physical simulation, as shown in Figure 13.1. Some of these may deserve elaborating as they are used on a day-to-day basis, like particles and soft bodies, but for now we will look at each of them in brief:

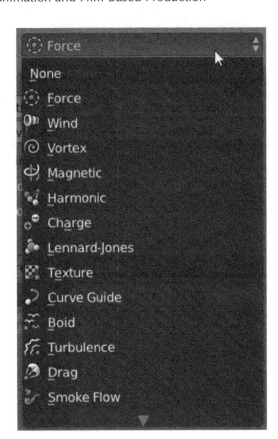

FIGURE 13.1 Force field types. We can select the force type from the drop-down menu within the Force Fields panel.

- *Dynamics*: Also called as force field are phenomena used to modify physical behavior.

- *Particles*: With particles we can simulate hair, furry characters, grass, or other particles in the environment.

- *Soft body*: A really interesting feature dealing with almost everything that bends or deforms depending on other physics, like collision. For example, we can simulate balls falling and bouncing on the floor.

- *Cloth*: This is a specific type of phenomena to make dynamic clothes in addition to forces like wind, for example.

- *Fluids*: To simulate everything related to dynamic fluids. It doesn't need to be strictly water simulation, but different kind of fluids and viscosity can be simulated.

- *Smoke*: This is a perfect feature to simulate smoke and fire, but also dust.

- *Dynamic paint*: This is a recently added physics system for the simulation of objects that would have otherwise been quite difficult. It converts the object to canvas and brushes enabling us to simulate things like rain drops on the floor, feet in the snow, etc.

- *Green screen and track motion*: This is probably the best known effect. Maybe it's not strictly a physics phenomena, but we will include it in this chapter because it shares some principles of dynamics.

These are the most important but surely not the only physical simulations we will see in Blender.

It is important to understand that physics simulation is a feature with a high level of resource consumption. In other words, we need to make sure that the level of simulation we want is possible within the hardware capabilities.

13.1 DYNAMICS AND FORCE FIELDS

Force fields are a way to modify the current dynamics. So, for example, we can modify the behavior or appearance of any of our particle system or our cloth simulation by adding a Force Field modifier system to that simulation.

But we have to know that this is not mandatory. We can tell Blender to not apply force field to a specific particle system by disabling the correct force field type from the Force Weights panel within the particle context.

How do we enable Force Fields? First we need to go to the Physics context and then use the Enable physics for Force Field. The Force Fields panel will appear with specific options to determine the physics behavior.

As we see, we can first select the type of force field being used. The specific properties of each type depend on the selected element. Available force field types are Smoke Flow, Drag, Turbulence, Boid, Curve Guide, Texture, Lennard-Jones, Charge, Harmonic, Magnetic, Vortex, Wind, and Force. These are discussed briefly next.

13.1.1 Drag

This is a force creating some resistance to particles motion.

Here the most characteristic options are Linear and Quadratic. Other options are similar to the ones used in other force fields.

13.1.2 Turbulence

This is a very easy effect to understand. This basically makes a turbulence effect using 3D noise, so our particles are randomized over 3D space.

Some parameters to take into account are Size, which determines the amount of noise, and Flow, which converts the force to velocity flow.

The Turbulence field has more or less the same options as other force fields do, like Strength, Noise, and Seed.

13.1.3 Boid

This force field is a bit complex to understand. We won't be learning about it in depth here, but we have to know that it could be used to simulate swarm or bands, like insects or birds.

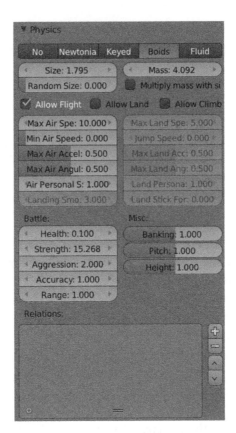

FIGURE 13.2 The Boid requires some properties to be enabled in the Boids option of the Physics panel within the Particles context.

Boids might work with positive and negative values, but the point is that we have to manage the Boids properties in the Physics panel within the Particles context, as shown in Figure 13.2.

Here we have several properties and options to determine the final Boids calculation.

The Boid properties for the Force Fields panel within the Physics context are the same as for Force.

13.1.4 Curve Guide

This is an effect used to guide particles to move along specified paths. This is something that we see in film productions; it is not that important but is commonly used—we want to have some control over our particles and we don't want our simulation going out of control.

For instance, imagine an environment where you want dynamic particles or liquid to follow a path. We can use Curve Guide to define a path that the particles should flow along. This effect is commonly used in commercial introductions and the like.

We have some specific, interesting options for this effect like Minimum Distance, Free or Falloff Power. A combination of these parameters will determine the final result.

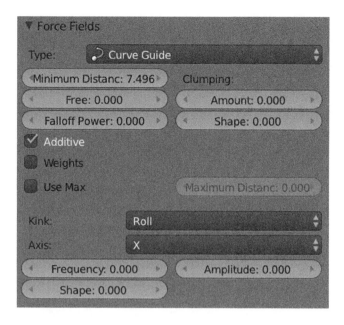

FIGURE 13.3 Force Fields panel using the Curve Guide. Notice that the Kink option has further options to configure.

It's important to understand that particles have a lifetime. In this case, our particles will be following the defined path during their lifetime. So parameters like velocity and length of the path should be taken into consideration.

We also have options to refine our Curve Guide simulation like Additive, Weights, and Use Max.

But what is different in all these methods are the Kink dropdown options. These will determine the form of the force field:

- *Curl* is used to determine the radius of influence.

- *Radial* simulates a 3D standing wave.

- *Wave* simulates a 2D standing wave.

- *Roll* simulates a single dimensional wave.

- *Nothing* is used to disable the Kink feature.

When using a kink option from the dropdown, apart from the Nothing option, we will have further options to manage that kink feature. Available options are Frequency, Shape, and Amplitude (Figure 13.3).

13.1.5 Texture

This is a very interesting force field. We can use a texture to create a complex force field depending on our needs.

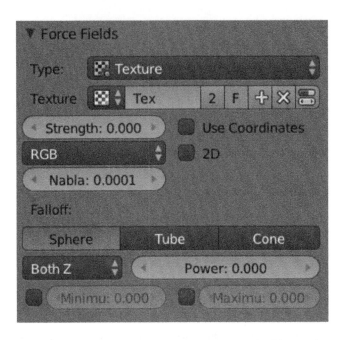

FIGURE 13.4 The Texture field panel allows us to use textures to build complex and exclusive force fields.

This field works with three axes represented by RGB—red for the *x*-axis, green for the *y*-axis, and blue for the *z*-axis.

We can define how the texture field should be calculated in the Texture Mode drop-down menu. The available values are Curl, Gradient, and RGB.

RGB uses three colors in predefined directions. To make this work, we need an RGB texture.

Gradient calculates the force intensity depending on the grayscale.

Curl is used to calculate the force using the rotation of RGB vectors.

If we select the Gradient or Curl option, we have to consider the Nabla option as well, which defines the size of the offset used in the force calculation.

We can see two options in this panel—Use Coordinates and 2D. The first makes Blender use the emitter object coordinates, rotation, and scale to calculate the texture force field. The second limits Blender to use just the *x*- and *y*-axes to calculate the texture field (Figure 13.4).

13.1.6 Lennard-Jones

The Lennard-Jones force field has a short-range behavior, and this range is determined by the size of particles, for example.

This force basically works like an attractive or repulsive force depending on the combination of the particles size and distance. It tries to maintain a reasonable distance between particles and only works if they are relatively close.

13.1.7 Charge

This option basically attracts or repels particles based on positive and negative charges of the particles. This force field can be used only on particles with charge and becomes useless for particles without charge.

13.1.8 Harmonic

This is a very special force assigned to particles. It basically represents the pendulum phenomenon. When using this field, we have to note that the particles in the target do not influence each other.

Here, we must keep in mind that the Damping value will result in the particles being stopped upon contact with the object. An interesting option specific to this force is Rest Length.

Rest Length controls the rest of the harmonic force, that is, when the value is set to 0, the particles form a shape, and when the value is positive, the particles repel and scatter away. Think about magnetics (Figure 13.5).

13.1.9 Magnetic

This field will be easy to understand if we think about magnets. We can attribute positive or negative charges to objects to make them attract or repel particles.

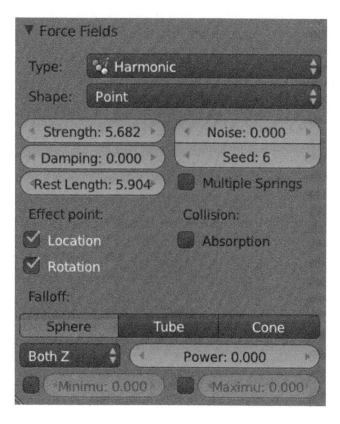

FIGURE 13.5 The Harmonic field has almost the same buttons as other force fields except the specific Rest Length option.

13.1.10 Vortex

This is used especially to create vortex points on an object to twist around the object's local z-axis. This force is commonly used to simulate twisters or other spiral phenomena.

13.1.11 Wind

To understand wind is really simple. The wind force uses a constant in a determined direction, along the object's local z-axis. We can visually determine the strength of this force because the circles shown in the 3D view may vary in space.

Wind applies a constant force in a single direction, along the object's local z-axis. The strength of the force is visualized by the spacing of the circles.

13.1.12 Force

This is a pretty simple type of force field. It is used to create a constant positive or negative force toward the center of an object.

Here, we can select the shape or direction being used to calculate the force. Available options are Every Point, Surface, Plane, and Point as shown in Figure 13.6.

All of these force fields have four common properties—Strength, Flow, Noise, and Seed. The combination of these values will determine the added parameters affecting the force. For example, we can apply a random noise to the force or modify the calculation seed.

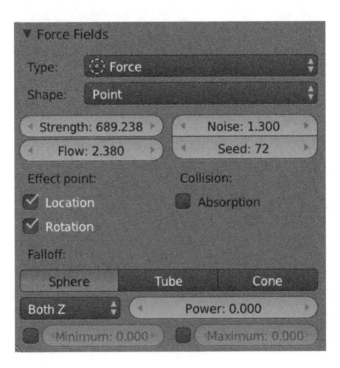

FIGURE 13.6 Force Fields panel where we can determine the type of force being used and set up all other specific parameters for the physics behavior.

As mentioned earlier, Dynamics and Force Fileds share some common properties and settings. But they don't work exactly the same in all Force Felds but have relatively common values, so it's easy to understand what they do:

- *Strength:* As the name suggests, it's just the strength of an effect. This option accepts both positive and negative values that will determine the direction of the particles.

- *Flow:* This setting converts the force of an effect to flow velocity.

- *Noise:* This adds a 3D noise, rendering particles with some kind of randomized noise.

- *Seed:* Blender changes and auto generates a new pattern for this effect.

- *Collision Absorption:* When this option is enabled, particles will be absorbed by an object upon collision.

- *Falloff:* If the fall of power is greater than 0, three different options are made available through this feature—Sphere, Tube, and Cone. This option will render one of these shapes to the particles. We can also define the direction and the minimum and maximum distance for the particles.

13.2 COLLISIONS

This is not a force field, but we have to know that when using particles, soft bodies, or cloth simulation, we have to deal with collision objects. Some important things to take into account when working with dynamic elements and collisions are as follows:

1. Objects should be in the same layer so that the simulation might be calculated, that is, we need those objects placed in the same layer so Blender is able to proceed with the simulation. In Blender, it's not possible, at the moment of authoring this book, to calculate simulations with objects being placed in different layers.

2. We have to limit the particles' effect to a group of objects.

3. To get a perfect deflection in soft bodies is practically impossible because they usually penetrate or keep away from colliding objects.

4. To use deflection with hair particles simulation, we can animate them like soft bodies, so they are taken into account.

Blender usually saves simulations in cache. Therefore, it's important to remember that when we modify any property in the particle system or fields, we need to recalculate the simulation by freeing the cache.

This is done with the Free Cache button within the Cache panel (Figure 13.7).

When we define an object as a collision object, Blender offers different options to control its behavior. To set a perfect balance between particles, soft bodies, cloth simulations, and collisions is not always easy; it is a trial-and-error process. Let's briefly look at the options available for collision object:

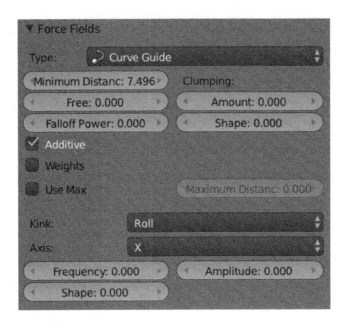

FIGURE 13.7   Cache panel within the Particles properties context. This panel is useful to regulate the machine performance by freeing cache or baking.

- *Permeability*: This option determines the fraction of particles passing through the collision mesh.

- *Stickiness*: This option is used to define how many particles stick to the collision object.

- *Kill Particles*: This option will kill particles upon contact with the collision object.

- *Damping Factor*: This option determines the damping value during a collision. It does not deal with the velocity of the particles.

- *Random Damping*: This option applies randomized damping, like a kind of noise.

- *Friction Factor*: This will adjust the friction between particles during collision. So the movement along the surface vary from viscose to smooth.

- *Random Friction*: This option applies randomized friction, like a kind of noise.

There are some interesting options in the Collision panel for soft body collisions.

- *Outer*: Determines the size of the outer collision.

- *Inner*: Determines the size of the inner collision.

- *Absorption*: This option determines the percentage of force that gets lost, or absorbed, when colliding with the collision object.

13.3 PARTICLES

In this section, we will be learning about what particles are. We already know that Blender supports two kinds of particles: emitter and hair. However, we could also define particles as elements emitted from the mesh of an object. As dynamic elements, they should be working together with force fields and should accept physics, so that a combination of these three results in the desired visual effect.

In fact, some very common elements in film making like fire, smoke, mist, and other similar effects are done with dynamic particles using the emitter type. On the other hand, simulating hair, strands, fur, or grass is usually done with particles using the hair type (Figure 13.8).

The way particles are generally visualized in the 3D view depends on many factors like the velocity of the particles, the movement of the emitter, gravity or air resistance, and the influence of force fields or collisions or modifiers like lattices.

There are three ways to render particles: Halos, Meshes, and Strand.

When we apply a particle system to any object, we should know that this is not the only particle system that the object could have. We can add several particle systems to the same object for different purposes. So we can use a particle system for the furry skin of a

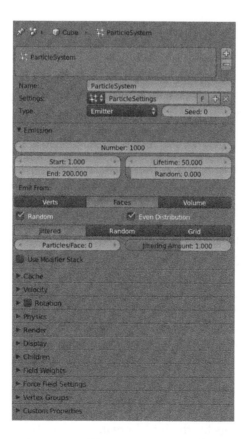

FIGURE 13.8　Particles properties context. We can manage everything from our particle system from this context.

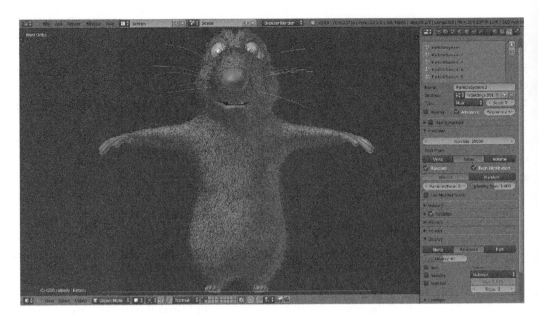

FIGURE 13.9 Different particle systems used in RAT bProficiency project over the same character.

character, another one to make the whiskers, and a third one refining the hair for some different vertex groups.

In fact, we used such a system for our RAT character as shown in Figure 13.9.

To create a new particle system, we first need to select the object we want to apply the particle system to. Then we go to the Particle properties context and create a new one by clicking the New button, or the "+" icon, as shown in Figure 13.9.

First, we have to determine when we have to add a particle system, the purpose of such a system, and evaluate if it's really needed. What do we need? Because this will determine the kind of particles type to be used. By default, Blender works with two different particle types:

- *Emitter*: Here particles are small elements emitted by the emitter object to the 3D space depending on very different settings. This system makes particles go from the start to the end frame in the scene along their lifetime.

- *Hair*: This system is usually used and rendered as strands.

Like any other dynamic and physics feature in Blender, every type has different panels and options.

13.3.1 Emission

This panel stores the settings for the initial organization of the particles system. With this panel, we basically define how we want particles to enter a scene. But we can also define the end, the lifetime, or apply random values.

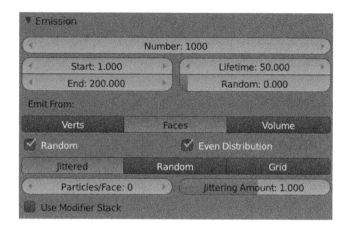

FIGURE 13.10 Emission panel, where we can control the initial state of the particles system.

This system produces small particles emitted from the emitter object to the 3D scene for a specific amount of time. As mentioned earlier, we can control the number of particles to emit. This number represents the maximum of the parent particles. We will see that each parent particle could be split into child particles.

The Start and the End options determine the time frame for which particles will be simulated. A very important property is the Lifetime value, which determines how long the particles will live.

When we work with emitter type of particles, we have the option to define from where they should be emitted. This gives us control over the organization and distribution of the particles. The available options are Verts, where particles are emitted from vertices of the mesh; Faces, where particles are emitted from the faces of the mesh; and Volume, where particles are emitted from the volume of the mesh.

Once we have selected from where we want the particles to be emitted, we have some more options to choose for the distribution of the particles. A very interesting property is the Random option that determines if the particles should be emitted by applying some kind of noise or using a linear method. We can also choose between random parts of the emitter object and the amount of jitter applied in the simulation (Figure 13.10).

13.3.2 Velocity

This panel contains options to set up the initial state of the particle system. This will determine the first look of the particles depending on the particle system type. It's commonly misunderstood with the initial particles' size.

We have some groups or properties here like Emitter Geometry and Emitter Object.

Probably the most important option here is the Normal value. This will determine the initial starting speed. This value complements with the X, Y, and Z values from the Geometry Object.

The Random option applies a random value to the initial speed (Figure 13.11).

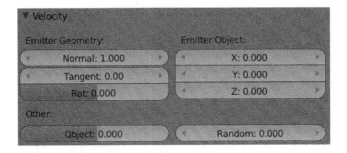

FIGURE 13.11 Velocity panel, where we can control the initial speed of the particle system.

13.3.3 Rotation

Here we will find some special properties to deal with the rotation of the particles according to their lifetime. These can be used to define how particles should rotate from the start to the end of their lifetime.

We can select initial values from the Initial Orientation dropdown list. Available values are None; Normal; Normal-Tangent; Velocity/Hair; Global X, Y, and Z; or Object X, Y, and Z.

The Angular Velocity determines the magnitude of the velocity. Available values are None, Velocity, Horizontal, Vertical or Global X, Y, and Z.

As we discussed in the Curve Guide Force Field, we have to set the Angular Velocity if we want particles to follow the defined curve path (Figure 13.12).

13.3.4 Physics

When we want to move particles or to simulate any physical action, we have to use this panel. There are several ways to make particles move, but what determines their actual behavior is the Physics panel.

We have some kind of different systems to simulate, namely, Newtonian, Keyed, Boids, and Fluid.

The Newtonian system makes particles move according to physical laws and principles. The Keyed system is applied to those E dynamic or static particles whose animated targets are other particle systems. The Boids system is used for particles with a limited artificial

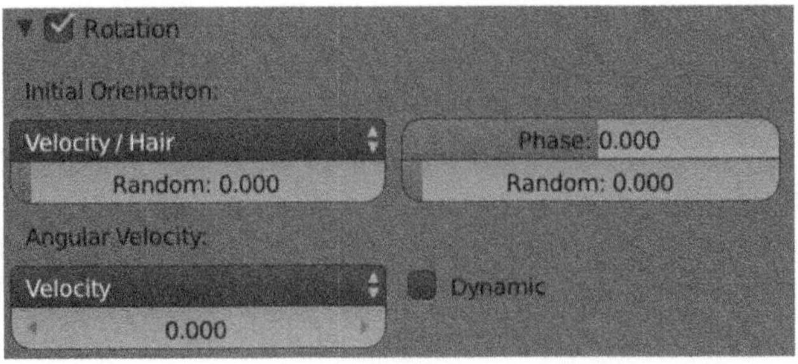

FIGURE 13.12 Rotation panel, where we control the rotation of the particles along their lifetime.

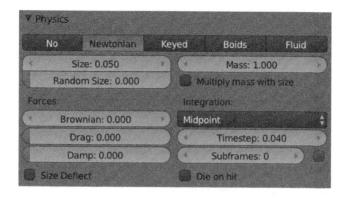

FIGURE 13.13   Physics panel, where we have control over the physical laws in the simulation.

intelligence expecting some behavior. Finally, the Fluid system is used to simulate fluid dynamics.

Based on our requirements, we will need an appropriate combination of these parameters together with the Force Field dynamics in order to achieve the desired result.

Some of the most important properties in this panel are Size, which determines the size of the particles and Mass, which determines the mass of the particles. Each system contains properties specific to the selected principle (Figure 13.13).

13.3.5 Render

In this panel, we can manage how the particles system will be passed to the rendering process.

We can assign a material to the particle system from the *Material* index. This will make the particle system use this specific material while rendering. We also have the option to enable rendering for the *Emitter, Parents, Unborn* or *Died* particles as well.

We also have some options to define how the particles will be rendered. Each type will contain its own properties defining the final look of the particles in the rendering process. The available values are None, Halo, Line, Path, Object, Group, and Billboard (Figure 13.14).

13.3.6 Display

This panel tells Blender how the particle system should be visualized in 3D. It is important to know that even will not see particles in the 3D view, but they are there, and if enabled, will be rendered in 3D.

We can choose from different types of 3D view depending on our selection. The available modes are None, Rendered, Point, Circle, Cross, and Axis.

Here probably the most important option is the Display slider, which determines the percentage of particles to be displayed in the viewport.

We also have options such as Size, Velocity, and Number that will display different elements in the viewport. For example, the size of the particles is displayed with the particle being wrapped with a circle (Figure 13.15).

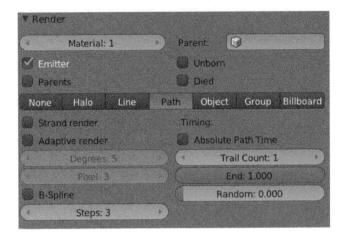

FIGURE 13.14 We can control how particles are rendered from the Render panel. Different systems are also available for rendering purposes.

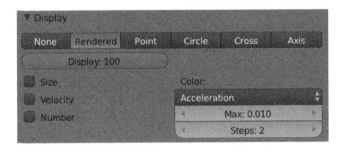

FIGURE 13.15 The way the particles are displayed in the 3D viewport is determined by the settings we apply in this panel.

13.3.7 Children

As mentioned earlier, the particle system is a compound system composed of both parent and children particles. In this panel, we can control how many child particles each parent particle can have.

Some very important properties to take care of are the Display and Render values. The Display value will determine how many children particles should be visualized for each parent in the 3D view and the Render value will determine how many of them will be rendered in the final rendering process.

There are options to modify how the children behave with respect to their parents, such as Clump, Shape, Length, or Threshold.

In order to obtain the desired effect, it's good to play around a bit with values within this panel because there are so many combinations where getting the desired effect is just a matter of time.

Sometimes it's good to have a mixed system, that is, a compound particle system. For example, we could have a particle system with 100 parents and 100 children per parent instead of a particle system with 100,000 parents (Figure 13.16).

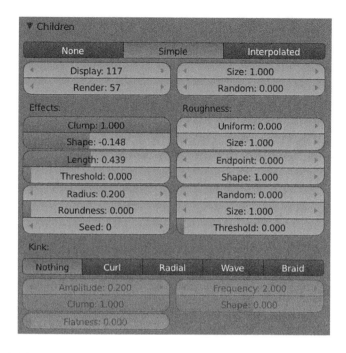

FIGURE 13.16   Children panel stores enough parameters to deal with parent/children relationship.

13.3.8 Field Weights

This panel allows us to control how much of the force field effects affect to our particle system. As mentioned earlier, the particle system could be affected by any of the force fields available within Blender, but in this panel we can define specific values by increasing or decreasing the effector weight.

Here the most important values usually are Gravity and All. This latest one scales all effector weights (Figure 13.17).

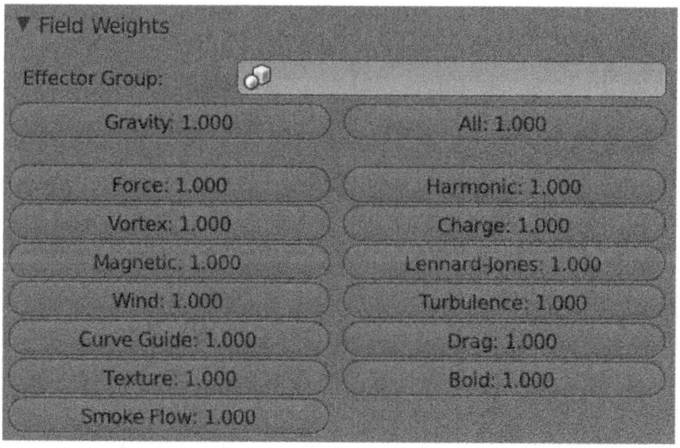

FIGURE 13.17   We can control how much of the force field effects affect our particle system with this panel.

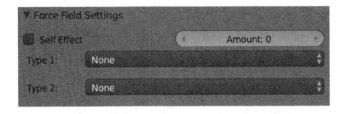

FIGURE 13.18 We can apply special Force Fields to our particle system and make the effect affect its self-elements.

13.3.9 Force Field Settings

We can allow our particle system elements to behave like any Force Fields effector. We can also enable the option of each particle affecting other particles in the same system. Blender allows us to apply two force field systems to our particle system.

For example, we can apply a self-effect field, like a Vortex or Wind, to our particle system (Figure 13.18).

13.3.10 Cache

We can't imagine particles or dynamics without cache. What Blender does is it saves the generated simulation in cache to make calculations easier. This is a really useful and vital activity when working with particles and dynamics, so we can safely execute the simulation once again from cache.

The cache panel has some very useful operators like Bake, Bake All Dynamics, and Free All Bakes.

When we bake a simulation, we're telling Blender to save that simulation on disk in something like log files in order to visualize that same simulation as many times as we want. What we have to remember is to free the cache when we modify any parameter in the particles or dynamic properties. This will make Blender to recalculate the simulation according to the new changes (Figure 13.19).

13.4 SOFT BODY

First thing that comes to mind when we hear soft bodies is a ball bouncing on the floor. When we talk about soft bodies, we talk about simulation of soft and rigid objects with a deformable property.

The way Blender manages it is by applying different forces, outer and inner, so the vertices of the object simulate the shape corresponding to a specific state, depending on other soft body objects or collision objects.

An interesting thing about soft bodies is that the generated shape could be converted to a new solid object. So when we have the bouncing ball deformed over the floor in a specific frame, we can select that object and create a new one with just the same shape.

When do we need to use soft bodies? Or, in other words, where are soft bodies used in filmmaking? Possible answers to these questions are as follows:

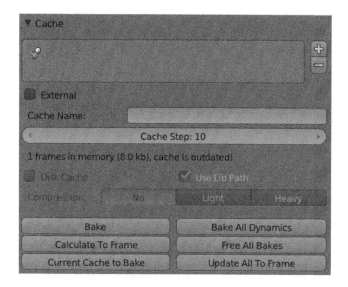

FIGURE 13.19   Cache panel allows us to manage simulation bakes to maintain machine performance. The cache helps avoid extra calculations in simulations.

- To deform and make elastic objects
- To create cloth simulation reacting to force fields like wind, for example, a flag
- To create dynamic hair

In Blender, we have some objects or data type supporting soft body. Basically those contain vertices or control points like Meshes, Curves, Surfaces, and Lattices.

Applying soft body simulation to an object is easy by using the Soft Body button within the Physics properties context (Figure 13.20).

13.4.1 Soft Body Solver

This is a very important panel because its settings determine how effective the simulation is.

Using the Min Step and the Max Step, we set the number of steps per frame in the simulation, so we can customize them to make soft bodies avoid fast-moving collision objects, for example.

Another important setting is the Error Limit. This value will tell us how precise the simulation will be based on collisions. We must define this value because it's really important to achieve professional results (Figure 13.21).

13.4.2 Soft Body

This panel also contains important simulation properties.

We can modify here the Friction, Mass, and Speed values that are directly applied to the simulation. With the Friction value, we can calculate the surface friction for collision objects

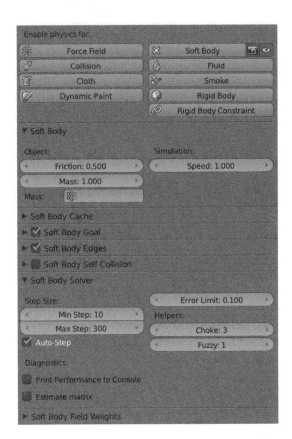

FIGURE 13.20   Enabling soft body is easy from the Physics properties context.

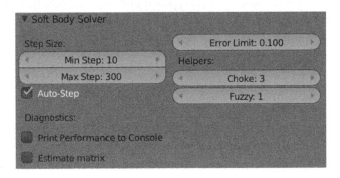

FIGURE 13.21   Soft Body Solver panel, which determines the level of accuracy of the simulation.

or between soft body objects. In the same way, the Mass value determines the mass of the object. Modifying this value will result in a very different kind of simulation (Figure 13.22).

13.5 CLOTH

Blender has its own system for cloth simulation. Cloth simulation is a very difficult task to achieve. We can basically simulate everything related to clothes with this built-in feature.

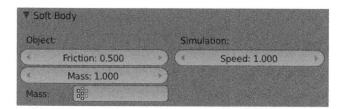

FIGURE 13.22 Soft Body panel contains common properties to deal with like Mass, Speed, and Friction.

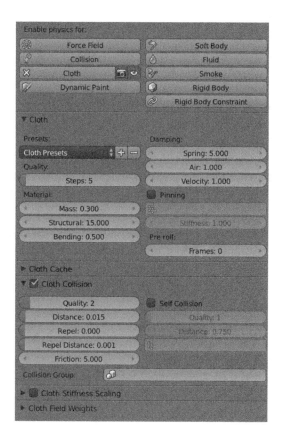

FIGURE 13.23 Cloth simulation is also supported by Blender.

To enable Cloth simulation, we just need to use the Cloth button within the Physics properties context (Figure 13.23).

First, we can select from Blender's presets for Cloth simulation. The available values are Cotton, Denim, Leather, Rubber, and Silk, as shown in Figure 13.24.

These presets automodify some values, so we can use them as a starting point to our custom simulation.

We can also add new or delete new with the New or Delete buttons. Once we have selected a preset, we have to define some values to render the desired effect. For Cloth simulation, almost every value has to be taken into consideration.

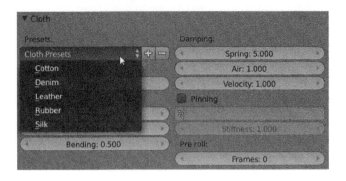

FIGURE 13.24   Some prebuilt in cloth presets we can use as basis.

The Damping group with Spring, Air, and Velocity or the Material group with Mass, Structural, or Bending needs to have the correct combination of values to achieve the desired result.

So for example, having a high Spring value will result in a smooth simulation but will obviously consume more resources. Here, the cache and baking come in handy. We should also modify the Air resistance that basically slows down things that are falling down. The amount of wrinkles can also be managed with the Bending value, a higher Bending values means bigger wrinkles.

Another interesting panel to work with in cloth simulation is Cloth Collision. Here we can define the amount of collision iterations to be calculated. It's important to enable this option even when we have other objects with collision settings; this won't work unless we have Cloth Collision enabled within the Physics properties context (Figure 13.25).

It's important to take care of the amount of iterations we apply because higher values mean best quality, but also more resource consumption.

It is also possible to add force fields to cloth simulation from the Cloth Field Weights panel, where we can manage how they affect our simulation. As simple example is to apply a very small value for Gravity, so falling down of the cloth becomes slow; this is similar to applying a very high value for Air resistance (Figure 13.26).

The simulated object can be converted to another one with the current shape as the default mesh. In other words, if we started with a subdivided plane, applied a cloth simulation, and now we want to use the simulated shape at a determined point, we could do so by using the Alt+C keys and then selecting Mesh from Curve/Meta/Surf/Text.

This is really useful if, for example, we want a scene in a restaurant where we need more than one table. We could simulate a single tablecloth and then convert it to an object, duplicating it as many times as needed. It's easier than trying to simulate a huge number of tablecloths individually.

13.6 FLUIDS

To achieve a convincing fluids simulation is not an easy task. There are a lot of factors to consider. Something we have not discussed so far is that some studios have an experience department to develop these kinds of physics effects (Figures 13.27 and 13.28).

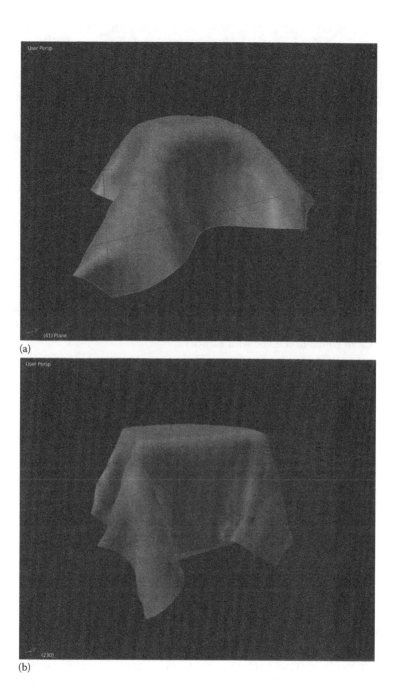

FIGURE 13.25 Cloth simulation made with Blender. (a) The Denim cloth preset. (b) Leather default preset.

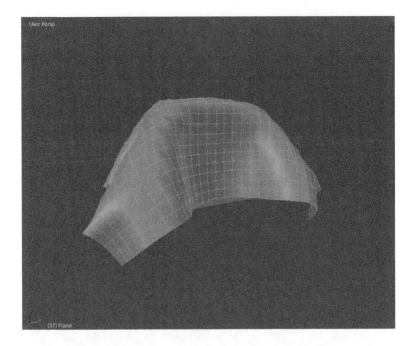

FIGURE 13.26 Cloth simulation made with Blender.

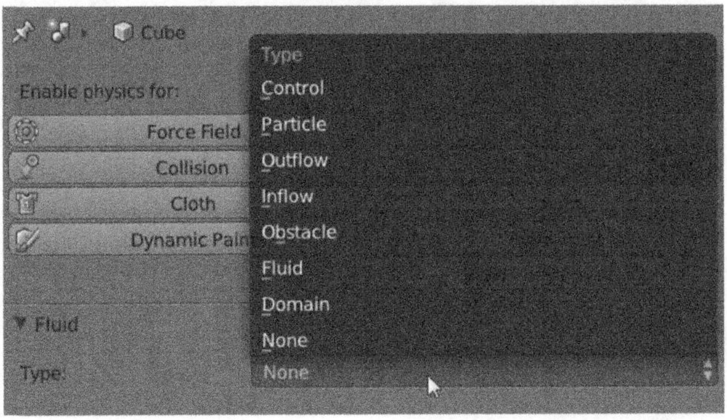

FIGURE 13.27 Different fluid types. We have to select the fluid type depending on our needs.

In Blender, we can simulate Fluids by enabling that option from the Physics properties context.

There are different fluid types to choose from. For example, if we need to simulate a simple water jets, we will need to enable a domain as well (Figures 13.29 and 13.30).

A basic example is to add a Cube, make it Domain, then add another within the previous one and use the Fluid type in the smaller one. Then we can go to the domain object and bake the simulation.

Like in other kinds of simulations, we can set up an obstacle in our fluid simulation. It's quite obvious how obstacles work, so to enable it, add a new object and select the Obstacle type from the drop-down menu (Figures 13.31 through 13.33).

FIGURE 13.28   Basic fluid example with Domain and Fluid types.

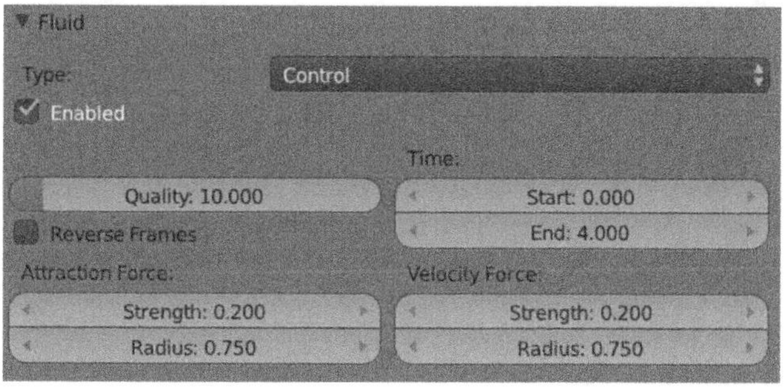

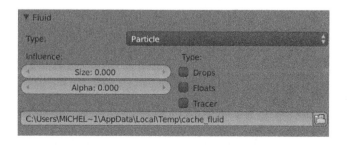

FIGURE 13.29   Fluid Control type.

FIGURE 13.30   Fluid Particle type.

FIGURE 13.31   Fluid Outflow type.

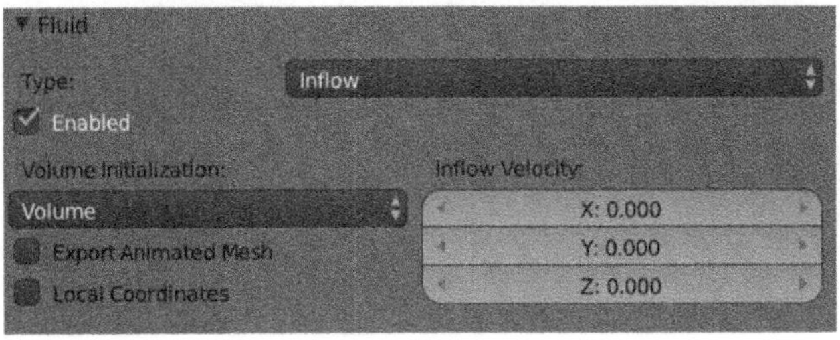

FIGURE 13.32   Fluid Inflow type.

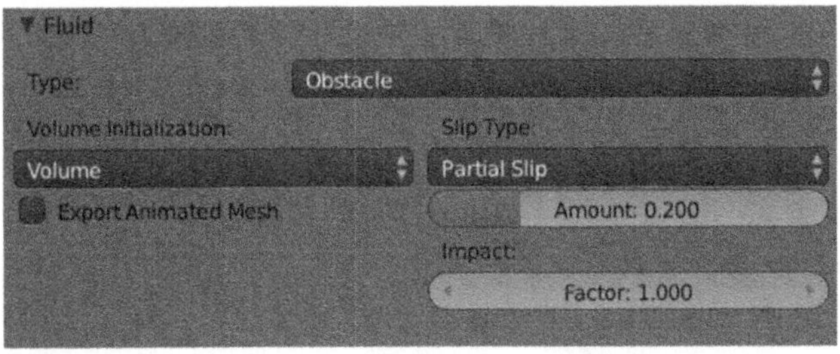

FIGURE 13.33   Fluid Obstacle type.

If we bake our simulation now, we will notice that the obstacle object affects the fluid element as it is a simple collision object, as shown in Figure 13.34.

In the Domain, we control the final resolution of the fluid simulation. A very important value to take into account is the Final Resolution (Figures 13.35 and 13.36). It's obvious that raising that value will result in the best quality, but also progressively consumes more memory, as shown in Figure 13.37. So it's important to know how to set a perfect combination of values.

We also have a Preview value, that is, the quality used in the 3D viewport. Sometimes we don't need to view the full quality when editing our fluid simulation, so we raise the Final resolution value only for rendering, keeping a lower value in the Preview.

Notice we can control when the simulation is supposed to start and end and its speed, for which we have the Start, End, and Speed sliders (Figure 13.38).

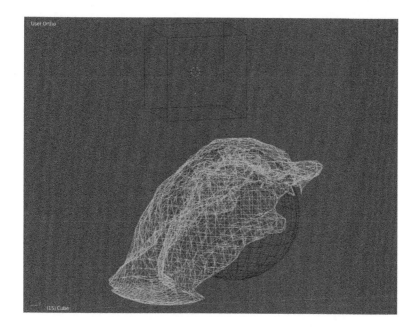

FIGURE 13.34   Fluid simulation using an intermediate object as Obstacle.

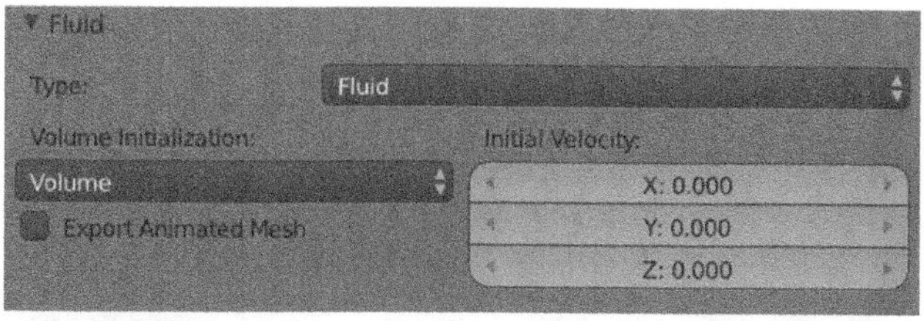

FIGURE 13.35   Fluid Fluid type.

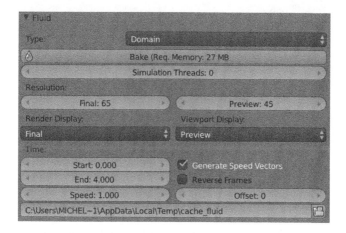

FIGURE 13.36   (See color insert.) Fluid Domain type.

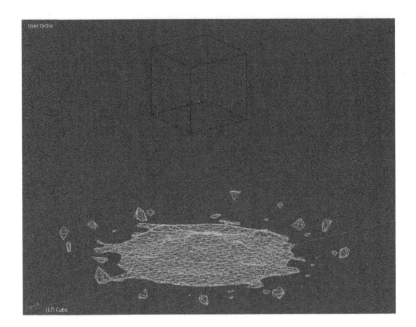

FIGURE 13.37   Fluid Domain type with a higher Final Resolution value.

FIGURE 13.38   Fluid simulation developed by Andrew Price at blenderguru.com.

13.7 SMOKE

In Blender, the smoke physics simulation is not only useful to simulate the smoke itself, but also dust, mist, fire, and similar phenomena.

To simulate fire, for example, we need to deal with volumetric textures as well (Figure 13.39).

The principle to create smoke is the same as that for fluids or cloth simulation. We have a domain, a flow, and collision options. Again, the quality of the smoke will depend on our hardware capabilities because a very detailed smoke, like any other simulation, consumes a lot of computer memory.

13.7.1 Flow

To create a flow effect of the smoke, we need to add a Cube to make it a Domain. Then we can add a plane at the bottom within the previous Cube and apply the Flow type of smoke (Figure 13.40). As mentioned before, if we want a higher-quality smoke, we need to enable the Smoke High Resolution option within the Physics properties context as shown in Figure 13.41.

We also can add obstacles or collision objects to our smoke simulation. Basically, add a new object and select the Collision type of smoke to make it work as expected. We have to be sure to include the collision object within the smoke Domain so that Blender can calculate the simulation, as shown in Figure 13.42.

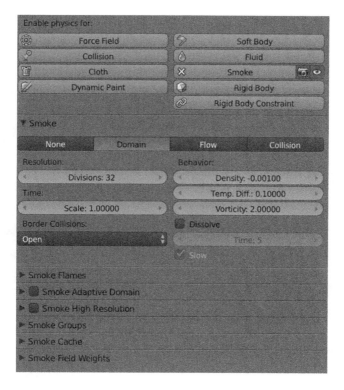

FIGURE 13.39   Smoke Domain type.

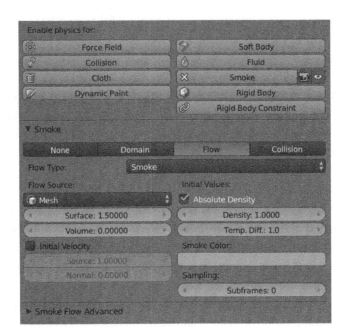

FIGURE 13.40 Smoke Flow type.

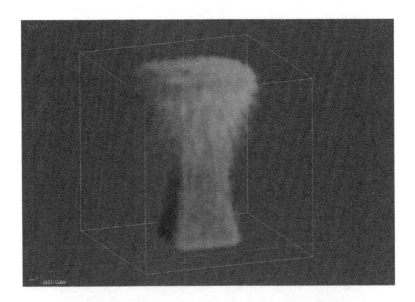

FIGURE 13.41 Smoke simulation made with Blender. The resolution depends on our settings and computer resources.

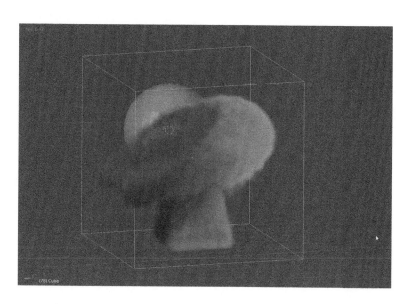

FIGURE 13.42 Smoke simulation made with Blender. Collision objects can also be used in smoke simulation.

## CHAPTER 14

Render

WE FINALLY HAVE A project moving to the end with the render process. That means, the project has successfully passed all previous stages. The rendering process might be a more stressful moment than developing the project itself. Depending on the purpose and size of the animation project, the rendering process could be done in different ways, from a single computer to different connected computers or ending in a professional render farm.

When we say the render process might be stressful, it is because studios have usually developed the project with months of hard work, and the render process is the end of that effort. The expected result is either a complete success or a failure at the end of the render process.

Usually, this process is done at the end of production, which means the team does not have the time to refactor possible issues. Big studios usually solve this with pre-render tests but small studios work in a very straightforward way. There is no time for errors, so the render process needs to be fine. The generated stills should not contain errors or the whole production will be ruined.

To avoid that, as mentioned earlier, it's important to test everything to do with lights, textures, or materials to avoid glitches at any point. So it's not enough doing a render test of just a couple of frames in a scene but also for very different frames in the timeline, especially where we know any camera changes, any light changes, or anything might end in strange results.

This prerender tests will save a lot of time and money for producers and it's definitively the difference between success and ruin of the project.

In Blender, we have very different ways of rendering an animation project:

1. Blender Internal

2. Cycles

3. External render engines

The Blender internal render is good enough for small projects and produces very nice results. There are other specific renders that produce very different results and they are emerging

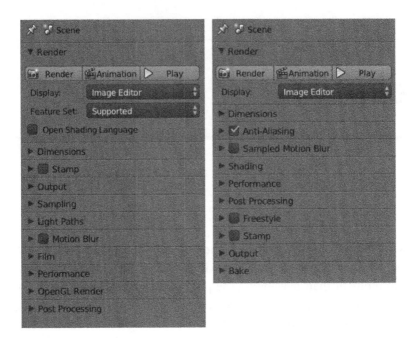

FIGURE 14.1 Different panels in the Render context for different render engines. The left picture represents the Render context for Cycles render. The image on the right represents the Render context for Blender Internal render.

to improve not only the quality but also the processing of the render allowing to generate complex renders with less computer resources.

The Render context within Blender changes depending on the render engine selected as shown in Figure 14.1.

14.1 BLENDER INTERNAL

The Blender internal render is the one built-in in Blender by default.

Until the external render engines emerged, a lot of animation projects were developed using this internal render engine. It offers all guarantees to suit any small project, in the small or medium animation studios. In fact, the projects developed by the Blender Foundation were developed and rendered using this render engine.

It's true that architecture or technical renders has been using external ones for several reasons.

The important thing now is to know what each render engine offers because they end in very different results. The same scene may differ when rendered using the Blender Internal render if we compare with Cycles and this also differs compared to external render engines.

Then, the most important thing is to have a clear idea on the render engine that suits our needs.

FIGURE 14.2   Blender Internal Render.

14.1.1 Render

We can determine the type of render we will be using by selecting between the three available options, namely, *Render*, *Animation*, and *Play*.

The first renders the current frame in the selected Display, where we find options like *Keep UI*, *New Window*, *Image Editor*, and *Full Screen*.

The Animation button renders from the start to the end of the frame range exporting to the format selected in the Output panel.

The Play button just plays back the rendered frames (Figure 14.2).

14.1.2 Dimensions

In this panel, we can set up some very important options determining the length and final aspect of the render.

First, we can set the Resolution, setting the width and height (X and Y) in pixels. A very interesting option is that in determined moments we can reduce it without the need for modifying those values but the Percentage scale value. This is really useful for render tests.

Another interesting option is the Frame Range that determines where the playback starts and ends. We can also adjust here the frames to skip while rendering.

In this panel, we can play with Aspect Ratio and Frame Rate setting the number of frames per second used in the final render (Figure 14.3).

14.1.3 Antialiasing

If we enable this option we tell Blender to combine multiple samples per pixel that improves the render quality avoiding strange issues or artifacts.

We can select the amount of antialiasing between 5, 8, 11, and 16 in the same way that we switch the filter used in the combination. The available filters are *Mitchell–Netravalli*, *Gaussian*, *Catmull–Rom*, *Cubic*, *Quadratic*, *Tent*, and *Box* (Figure 14.4).

14.1.4 Sampled Motion Blur

It's used to simulate motion (Figure 14.5). This is a particular effect to avoid static renders when they should appear like motion. This is a slow process but produces a very realistic result with blurred images.

Here, we should take into account the Motion Samples option, which sets the number of samples that we tell Blender to use for each frame.

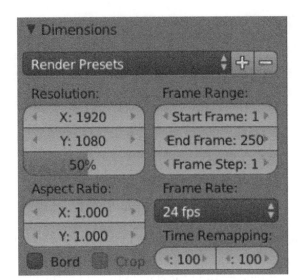

FIGURE 14.3 Dimensions panel within the Render context.

FIGURE 14.4 Antialiasing panel.

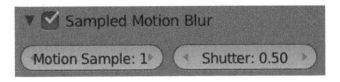

FIGURE 14.5 Sampled Motion Blur panel.

14.1.5 Shading

We can enable or disable different options to include or discard different properties being processed while rendering.

We can basically enable *Textures* to affect material properties, calculate *Shadows*, use *Subsurface Scattering*, calculate *Environment Map*, or enable *Ray Tracing* (Figure 14.6).

14.1.6 Performance

We can set up how the render will deal with our machine in this panel.

First, we can select the number of Threads or let Blender auto-detect. Second, we can play with memory and tell Blender to Save Buffers, Free Image Texture, or Free Unused Nodes, so the render processes free memory as needed (Figure 14.7).

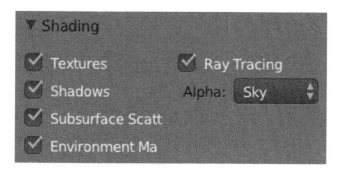

FIGURE 14.6 The Shading panel used with Blender Internal Render.

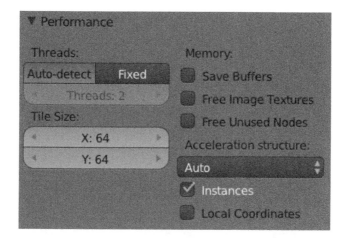

FIGURE 14.7 Performance panel.

14.1.7 Post Processing

This panel is very important if we want to enable options like Compositing or Sequencer.

The compositing option is very important as it allows Blender to use the compositing nodes while rendering; otherwise, they will be ignored and the whole compositing is done with this information (Figure 14.8).

The same happens with the Sequencer option.

14.1.8 Freestyle

This is a completely new render engine that generates a 2D render for the given 3D scene (Figure 14.9). This render is usually generated by different lines and patterns that result in a very interesting render style.

14.1.9 Stamp

If we enable this option, we can print the information text within the render image. The available info to print is *Time, Date, RenderTime, Frame, Scene, Camera, Lens, Filename,* and *Marker.*

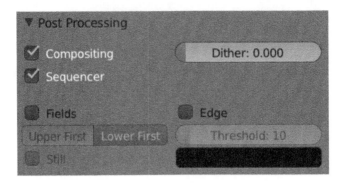

FIGURE 14.8 Post Processing panel where we can enable Compositing or Sequencer.

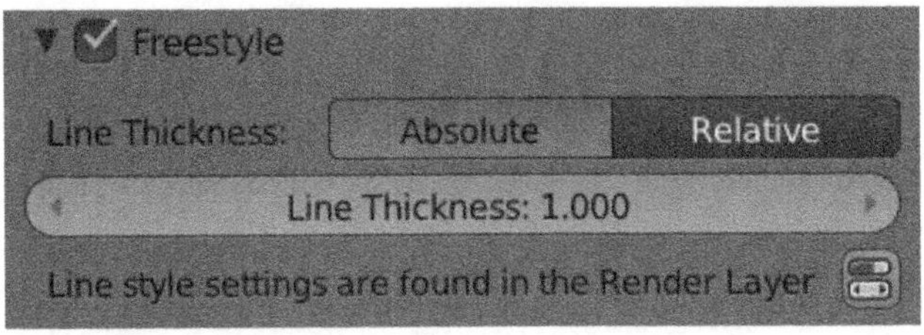

FIGURE 14.9 Freestyle panel.

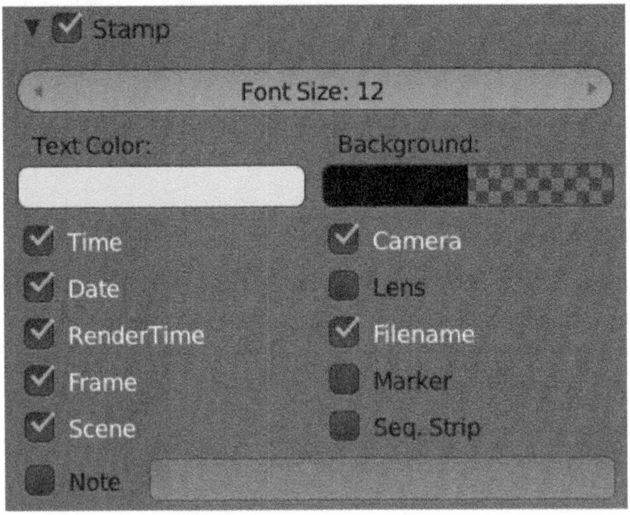

FIGURE 14.10 Stamp panel helps printing information in the rendered images.

We can adjust and edit the font size, color, and background (Figure 14.10).

14.1.10 Output

We can set up where we want to store the resulting images, like directory, filename, compression of the files, or the file format (Figure 14.11).

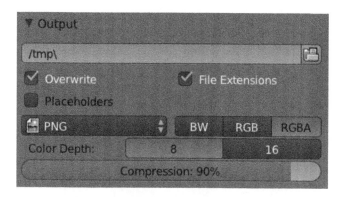

FIGURE 14.11   Output panel.

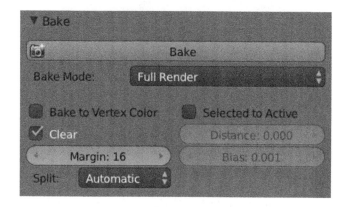

FIGURE 14.12   Bake panel.

14.1.11 Bake

Blender uses Bake to precompute the process so that the user gets the final result faster (Figure 14.12). In Blender, we can bake several things, that is, we can precompute and save it in the cache for later use.

14.2 CYCLES

Cycles is a relatively new render engine. Currently, Blender offers this engine as an add-on enabled by default because it's still being developed.

We must take care because selecting Cycles as the render engine could give very different options than the ones Blender uses in contexts like materials and textures as shown in Figure 14.13.

Notice the panels for Light Paths, Film, and OpenGL Render that are exclusively for Cycles render engine.

Cycles principle is based on the GPU rendering, that makes use of the graphic card for the rendering process. The result is a very fast rendering compared with the CPU ones.

We can divide the current GPU rendering process into two modes, CUDA and OpenCL, or in other words the mode of choice for Nvidia and AMD/ATI, respectively.

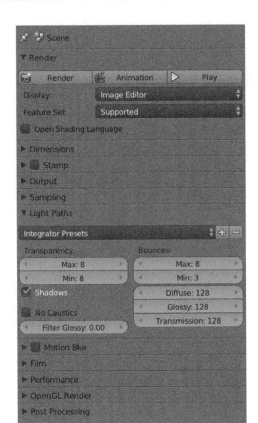

FIGURE 14.13   Render properties context while Cycles render engine is selected.

As mentioned earlier, we are not going to discuss in depth about Cycles. It is enough to know that Blender supports other render engines even when they are applied as add-on or they are simply external renders.

As mentioned earlier, some of the Properties context changes depend on whether Cycles or Blender Internal render engine is selected. As shown in Figure 14.14, the material contexts vary and consequently the results in the final render will do too. As shown in Figure 14.15, the same panel with nodes enabled allows us to control the shaded appearance.

14.3 EXTERNAL RENDER ENGINES

14.3.1 Freestyle

Freestyle is a new way of rendering by creating a nonphoto realistic render. It basically draws lines and edges and uses an interface to allow control of the different options and parameters determining the final appearance of the render.

The good point of this new style of rendering is the great chance of customization to draw the lines and edges resulting in this peculiar style.

We can use two different modes within the Freestyle engine—the Python scripting and the Parameter editor.

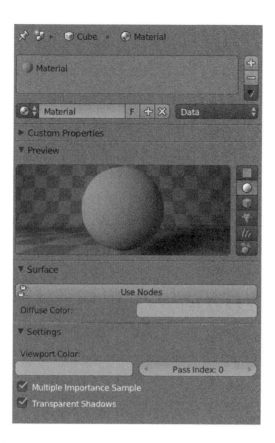

FIGURE 14.14   Material properties context while Cycles render engine is selected.

The Python scripting supports predefined scripts written in Python producing results close to styles like cartoons or the Japanese brush.

On the other hand, the Parameter editor mode allows flexible customization for lines and edges (Figure 14.16).

It's important to know that at the moment of authoring this book, this engine is only available for Blender Internal Render. So, in essence, we are talking more of a feature than a real render engine.

14.3.2 Yafray

The thin external engine has been used by Blender users for years in architecture and interior designs. The number of artists and professionals using the Blender Internal Render to produce such material is really low.

The render information provided by Blender could be used by this render engine but this doesn't mean that we don't have to manage and set up different properties in Yafray too in order to obtain the desired result.

Anyway, our purpose is not to list all the external render engines applicable to Blender but to understand that the option to use external render engines with our Blender's render information exists.

FIGURE 14.15 Material properties context while Cycles render engine is selected using the nodes option.

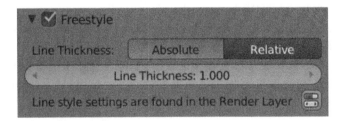

FIGURE 14.16 Freestyle panel within the Render properties context.

14.4 RENDER SETTINGS AND TIPS

14.4.1 Using Layers to Organize Our Render

For small projects, any 3D film contains a lot of assets and they should be organized in layers. This is equivalent to the render process that, depending on the desired result, might need to organize some render layers to apply the right compositing nodes or add the specific info for processing (Figure 14.17).

FIGURE 14.17 Freestyle panel within the Scene properties context. We can manage everything related to this feature here like Line appearance and the Freestyle mode.

It's quite common to render the whole environment behind our character in a separate layer to apply a compositing effect of blur and deep noise later. If we render everything in the same layer, this effect is too complex to accomplish.

This is just an example why we need to organize the render layers according to what we want to produce because each shot in each scene for the 3D film has its own requirements, sometimes so many that we can't enumerate them (Figure 14.18).

14.4.2 When Something Goes Wrong

When we develop a scene, setting up the lighting environment when animations are completely done and compositing with nodes doesn't guarantee that the scene will render according to what we are expecting.

There are several issues that could make our rendered scene looking weird, sometimes unexpected and sometimes undesired but the truth is that for a large film production appearance, more issues are to be expected (Figure 14.19).

In fact, the issues appearing while rendering are in direct relationship to the size of the project. It's obvious that the possible number of issues in film productions with hundreds of scenes will be much more than in others with a very small number of scenes.

FIGURE 14.18 **(See color insert.)** This picture represents an example of FreeStyle render result. Notice the toon style that Blender is capable of achieving using this feature.

FIGURE 14.19 Picture modeled with Blender and rendered using the Yafray extension. Image provided by http://blenderartists.org by the user enricoceric.

FIGURE 14.20   Some rendering issues for *Sintel* open movie developed by Blender Foundation.

Anyway, we all learn from such errors and sometimes it's very productive because some refinements and adjustments are developed to solve a specific rendering issue as shown in Figure 14.20. In the figure, notice the issue with the textures of the eyes and face.

Sometimes things go wrong not at the rendering process but earlier, for example, while animation and poses stored have any issues, it will result in a weird render as shown in Figure 14.21.

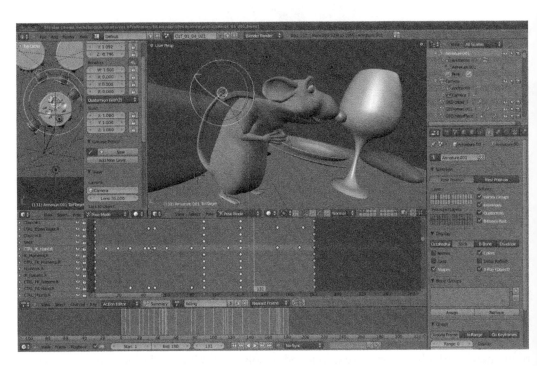

FIGURE 14.21 Animation and posing issues in the RAT bProficiency project. This weird pose will end in a very weird render.

## CHAPTER 15

Final Movie Compositing

I N THE SAME WAY we saw that Blender has a powerful node editor capable of modifying or adding effects to stills or video, Blender also has a very interesting editor for postprocessing. This stage of any movie production is usually developed with external and specific tools. Companies spend a lot of money on this kind of software because even though we know that each stage of film production is important, postproduction will make the final product ready and accessible to the public. Every detail needs to be double checked to adjust composition, audio, soundtrack, vfx, and everything must be in place and postproduction software needs to be powerful enough to operate with all these factors.

In Blender we have the Video Sequence Editor totally integrated with the application. As in any other Blender editor, we can access the VSE and manipulate it as we saw in Chapter 3 and Section 3.4.7. This editor works with blocks of strips, so we can assemble them to build our final movie. When studios produce a film, they end up with a large number of small pieces of animations, probably for some specific scenes in the movie, actions, battle, dialogue, and so on, so it's usual to assemble previously rendered animation streams within a single Video Sequence Editor session to finally add video effects such as fades, transitions, credits, or audio to complete the final film production.

As mentioned earlier, the Blender's VSE is a fully video editing system integrated in the application and very powerful, and this is a good reason to try it instead of using external, expensive, and privative licensed applications. Another good reason is that as in many other features in Blender, the VSE can also be improved using add-ons and plug-ins or totally adapted because of Python scripts.

15.1 USING BLENDER IN POSTPRODUCTION

To understand how to successfully complete our film production we need to know how the Blender's VSE works. We already talked about it in Chapter 3 and Section 3.4.7 but we will see it in depth now. The first thing we can check when we open the VSE is that the workspace is divided horizontally into channels numbered on the left. We will put our animation strips and streams within each channel. At the bottom, we see some numbers too that are meant to be the movie time or movie frames, which we can modify according to our needs.

An interesting point is that Blender's VSE not only accepts very different types of files like the traditional Audio-Video Interleaved (.avi), Apple QuickTime (.mov), single image

(.jpg, .png, .tiff, etc.), a sequence of images of any format (01.jpg, 02.jpg, 03.jpg, etc.) but also a Scene in the current .blend file or an audio file. We can also work with the format we want and mix them in the same VSE session, so we could be working over a .avi strip overlapping a single .jpg or a sequence of them and apply a Alpha Over effect.

When we add any of the supported formats, the strips are colored following a pattern, that is,

- *Blue* for any of the movie formats
- *Gray* for a single image
- *Purple* for a sequence of images
- *Green* for an audio file

15.1.1 Effects

The option of editing and applying effects to recently rendered strips is an awesome feature we can enjoy within Blender. It has a lot of built-in effects that we all know from other editors because they are really common in this kind of software.

When we add new affects to Blender, we have to know that some add new strips to the editor, some use just a single strip, and some use a couple of strips. Anyway, we can improve our project by applying the final postproduction visual effects:

1. Add

2. Subtract

3. Alpha Over

4. Alpha Under

5. Cross

6. Gamma Cross

7. Over Drop

8. Wipe

9. Glow

10. Transform

11. Color

12. Speed Control

13. Multicam Selector

14. Adjustment Layer

15.1.1.1 Add

This effect automatically merges the color of two strips and must be used with an image strip.

This effect is usually used to increase or decrease images' brightness or to add black and white masks. A peculiarity is that we can apply that to the whole image or just to some areas.

15.1.1.2 Subtract

This is an effect used to subtract color from a specific strip or to create the negative of any image.

15.1.1.3 Alpha Over and Alpha Under

The Alpha effect deals with all those transparent zones in our strips, that is, for a scene, in those areas without anything solid on them. In such cases, the alpha has a value of 0. On the other hand, for an image or movie strip, the whole strip is opaque resulting in an alpha value of 1.

This effect is very common to apply over layers to integrate the new strip together the second one as if they both were the same. That depends on the use of Alpha Over or Alpha Under.

The Alpha Over one means that new strips are layered up. We can play here with the Factor value that determines the amount of background and foreground to show.

The Alpha Under is just the inverse. The new strips are layered down but works similar to the previous one. We can play here also with the Factor value.

15.1.1.4 Cross

This is an effect to fade from one strip to another depending on the overlapping number of frames.

15.1.1.5 Gamma Cross

This is a very similar effect but uses color correction while fading. It's a very popular effect specially for fading from or to black. The transition is really smooth and reduces the eye impact.

15.1.1.6 Multiply

As in other software, this effect multiplies the value of two colors. There are a couple of ways in which to use the Multiply effect. The most common ones are using it with a mask and using it with solid colors.

We have to take care of this effect because we notice a bit of luminosity reduction on the whole strip.

15.1.1.7 Wipe

This is a kind of transition effect between strips. In Blender, we have some different pre-built-in transitions available like *Clock, Iris, Double Wipe,* and *Single Wipe.*

15.1.1.8 Glow

This effect is specially used to make some parts of the image look bright and glowing. We have some properties to determine the type of glow used, like *Threshold*, *Clamp*, and *Blur distance*.

15.1.1.9 Transform

This is a particular type of effect. In fact we can apply several different effects with it. With Transform, we can switch, scale, or rotate the images of the strip.

In that, we have several properties to play with. We just need to select the Transform strip and go to the Effect Strip panel within the transform properties panel. There we can play with some properties like Interpolation, Translation Unit, Position, Scale (we can apply an uniform scale), and Rotation.

15.1.1.10 Color

This effects crates a solid colored strip. By default it's completely solid but we can play with the Opacity property within the Edit Strip panel to apply some transparency. Notice that depending on the type of Blend used, we will have different results that may vary from what we expect.

15.1.1.11 Speed Control

This effect is really useful to control the time that the strip is reproduced. We can apply here the typical effect or make the strip play faster or slower than its normal value.

We have to remember that the Speed value of 1 makes the strip play slower. But making it greater than 1 plays the strip faster. If we apply this to play faster we have to take into account that some frames will be ignored. This is important to avoid or to fix possible issues when using this type of effect.

15.1.1.12 Multicam Selector

This is a relatively new effect added into Blender that deals with something people have been asking for years. We can use this effect to deal with the multicam editing within Blender.

15.1.1.13 Adjustment Layer

This kind of effect makes all the strips below the selected one work as its input. So if we think of a practical case where we could use it, for example, imagine we want to use a color effect over several strips, we could apply an adjustment layer on top and then apply a color effect.

15.1.2 Audio

We have been talking about everything to do with preproduction, development, and postproduction of filming, but everything we have talked about is related to visuals.

Postproduction filming has an important aspect that we might take into account—the audio, sounds, and music.

Now, Blender incorporates an audio sequencer editor, in which we can import .wav or .mp3 files. A very interesting option is that we can even incorporate that audio within the movie and use a F-Curve to modify the volume properties.

When we add a sound strip within the sequence editor, we have to take care of the Sound panel. Here we have some interesting options to play with.

We can make the sound part of the current blend file by using the Pack button. Another interesting option is to enable the Caching feature, that decodes and loads the file into RAM.

For a quick visual of the sound waves, we can enable the Draw Waveform that makes the sound waves visually represented within the strip in the sequence editor.

Some other common properties for sounds are also available such as Volume, Pitch, and Pan.

A very important thing we have to remember now is that in the recent versions of Blender, almost everything is animatable, so if we want to fade two sounds, we can play with keyframes and the volume property.

## CHAPTER 16

Python

SOMETHING THAT PEOPLE DON'T think about is the role of scripting in film productions. In fact, we can consider it as a forgotten task for people.

Blender has been developed using Python as one of the main programming languages and the software's entire interface and tools are accessible using Python modules. Like many other 3D software such as 3D Max, using MAXScript, Blender could be extended using Python.

Such extensions might be for very specific purposes or to improve Blender functionalities, like modules, and to add completely new features. Many of the current built-in features of Blender started as Python projects to extend a determined area of Blender and were finally incorporated into the trunk of the code.

This shows us how extensible Blender is and it's promising future potential. And one of the most interesting things about extending Blender is that we can do it just using Python scripting. We could write a plug-in in Python, load it into Blender, and run it to extend it, say, by adding new panels for specific purposes. This avoids the need to make changes to Blender's source code and recompile the whole code to have the new changes available.

One of the most important areas where Blender uses Python extensions are add-ons. In fact, Blender includes an add-ons editor where we can find different add-ons for the various functionalities of Blender.

We have add-ons related to objects and for rendering, animation, etc. But what is an add-on?

An add-on is a Python script that we can enable or disable to enhance a particular functionality in Blender when needed.

So, for example, if we need to have a panel with buttons to display or hide different bones of an armature, we could write a Python script, an add-on in fact, to add such a panel with the required buttons.

The Blender Foundation assesses and validates the huge amount of add-ons written by volunteers. Those considered stable are included and officially supported by Blender, and the others are made available through the website as part of the catalog because they are not considered stable enough to be part of a Blender release, but these are also good and can be pretty useful.

We can always check the catalog for any specific add-ons we want; they are generally released under the GPL license. Once downloaded, we can modify and adapt the add-on to suit our needs.

Another interesting thing about add-ons is that they can be a starting point to learning about coding your own add-ons.

There are specific add-ons for each purpose. We can use modules or libraries to import available presets for Blender's tools, scripts used as startup files when Blender is launched, or custom scripts we just require to run from a text editor.

Depending on the purpose of the scripts, we can have them stored in different folders. There are many ways to install add-ons—we can import a script to a text editor and run it there, but we can also install add-ons from the User Preferences editor.

16.1 PYTHON API

We will not be discussing what Python is, but rather what we can do with it in Blender, and, more interestingly, how it is used in film productions.

Extending Blender functionalities with Python has its benefits, which that range from improving features with missing functionalities to creating completely new tools and managing objects in the 3D view.

The intention here is not to go in depth into the Blender/Python API but to understand how Blender can deal with this awesome functionality, because film productions use a lot of scripting, and sometimes more than people could imagine.

We will now look at some basic concepts, how to manage them in Blender, and how they could be used in any film production.

16.1.1 Accessing Data

First, we need to have a clear idea about what this means. A basic feature is that everything a button can do in the Blender interface is also doable via Python scripting.

For example, pressing the Render button in Blender starts the rendering process, but this can also be done without having to press the button—with Python scripting.

Let's look at an example script. To access the current loaded data, we can use the module bpy.data that is completely available within Blender.

```
# For Blender's default cube scene
>>> bpy.data.objects
<bpy_collection[3], BlendDataObjects>

>>> bpy.data.cameras
<bpy_collection[1], BlendDataScenes>

>>> bpy.data.lamps
<bpy_collection[1], BlendDataMaterials>

# Trying to access on to non valid data
>>> bpy.data.lights
```

```
Traceback (most recent call last):
  File "<blender_console>", line 1, in <module>
AttributeError: 'BlendData' object has no attribute 'lights'
```

Any programmer will find this easy. If you are not a programmer, it takes just a little more time to understand, but it's not that complex to understand the following.

Collections are like arrays that we can access using the index or the string. We must be careful about this because as said in the API manual, the index may change while running Blender.

```
>>> list(bpy.data.cameras)
[bpy.data.cameras['Camera']]

>>> list(bpy.data.objects)
[bpy.data.objects['Camera'], bpy.data.objects['Cube'],
    bpy.data.objects['Lamp']]

# Accessing using string index
>>> bpy.data.objects['Camera']
bpy.data.objects['Camera']

# Accessing using integer index
>>> bpy.data.objects[0]
bpy.data.objects['Camera']
```

16.1.2 Accessing Attributes

Now, we have to imagine that we have something like an object. Our object is a collection of attributes like name, x-axis location, rotation, and scale.

Then we can also access our datablock attributes using Python like we could do using any other user interface button. Imagine scaling a cube. We can do this by pressing the S key but also by accessing the scale attribute using Python.

```
>>> bpy.data.objects[0].name
'Camera'

>>> bpy.data.scenes["Scene"]
bpy.data.scenes['Scene']

>>> bpy.data.materials.new("MyMaterial")
bpy.data.materials['MyMaterial']
```

16.1.3 Creating or Removing Data

This is a very interesting function, especially for beginners of Blender's Python API. All of us programmers know that we can create new objects by instantiating the class.

In Blender, we can't create new datablocks in this way but only using the methods on the collections in bpy.data.

```
>>> bpy.types.Object()
Traceback (most recent call last):
  File "<blender_console>", line 1, in <module>
TypeError: bpy_struct.__new__(type): expected a single argument
```

This results in a Traceback error. In this case, we should be using the following script instead:

```
>>> bpy.data.meshes.new(name="hello")
bpy.data.meshes['hello']
```

16.1.4 Context

This is a very interesting aspect because even though we sometimes access datablock attributes by name, it's more usual to access them based on the user's behavior. The context is always available and usually represents each active object, scene, or element and consequently its attributes.

```
# If we have selected the Cube
>>> bpy.context.object
bpy.data.objects['Cube']

# If we have selected both, the cube and the lamp
>>> bpy.context.selected_objects
[bpy.data.objects['Cube'], bpy.data.objects['Camera']]

>>> bpy.context.scene
bpy.data.scenes['Scene']
```

An important point to note is that context is read-only. So, assigning new values directly will throw an error but modifying it using the data API will work.

```
bpy.context.object = obj will end in error.
bpy.context.scene.objects.active = obj will work fine.
```

16.1.5 Operators

These are the tools the user usually manipulates through Blender's user interface buttons, menus, or keyboard shortcuts. So, they are also accessible by Python scripting using the module bpy.ops. A very interesting feature is to use the Ctrl+Space keys to autocomplete this task in the Python Console within Blender. This will show us available operators and the structure of data.

```
>>> bpy.ops.scene.delete()
{'FINISHED'}
>>> bpy.ops.object.lamp_add()
{'FINISHED'}
>>> bpy.ops.material.new()
{'FINISHED'}
```

16.1.6 Example

```python
import bpy

class OBJECT_PT_object(bpy.types.Panel):
    bl_label = "Render Isolated Objects"
    bl_space_type = "PROPERTIES"
    bl_region_type = "WINDOW"
    bl_context = "scene"

    def draw(self,context):
        layout = self.layout

        obj = bpy.context.active_object

        row = layout.row()
        row.operator("obj.isolate_object",text="Render")

        view = context.space_data

class selectObj(bpy.types.Operator):
    bl_idname = "obj.isolate_object"
    bl_label = "object selected"

    def execute(self,context):
        obj = bpy.context.active_object
        ob=obj.name
        self.report({'INFO'}, "Object and Lamps ready to render")
        bpy.ops.object.select_name(name=ob)
        bpy.ops.object.select_by_type(extend=True, type="LAMP")

        return {'FINISHED'}

def register():
    bpy.utils.register_class(selectObj)
    bpy.utils.register_class(OBJECT_PT_object)

def unregister():
    bpy.utils.unregister_class(selectObj)
    bpy.utils.unregister_class(OBJECT_PT_object)

if __name__ == "__main__":
    register()
```

This script registers the operator within Blender, meaning it's fully integrated; so we can call it from the operator pop-up menu or add it to the toolbar.

Another example could be registering a panel. To place this panel within a context, we have to tell Blender where we want it to be placed. In this case, note the variables with the prefix "bl".

```python
import bpy
from bpy.props import *

nf="0"
fps=int(24)


class OBJECT_PT_Framing(bpy.types.Panel):
    bl_label="Scene Framing"
    bl_space_type="PROPERTIES"
    bl_region_type="WINDOW"
    bl_context="scene"

    def draw(self,context):
        layout=self.layout

        obj=context.object
        scene=context.scene

        split=layout.split()
        col=split.column()

        col.prop(scene, "prop_seconds", slider=False)

        col.operator("op.calculate_frames",text="Calculate")


class SCENE_OT_calc(bpy.types.Operator):
    ''''''
    bl_idname = "op.calculate_frames"
    bl_label = "Calculate"

    def execute(self, context):

        scene=context.scene

        propSeconds=scene.prop_seconds
        nfint=int(propSeconds*fps)
        nf=str(nfint)
        scene.frame_end=nfint

        return {'FINISHED'}
```

```
###################################################
#### REGISTER #####################################
###################################################
def register():
    bpy.utils.register_class(SCENE_OT_calc)
    bpy.utils.register_class(OBJECT_PT_Framing)

    bt=bpy.types.Scene

    bt.prop_seconds = IntProperty(
        name="Seconds", description="Number of seconds the
            scene will be",
        min=0, max=59, default=0)

def unregister():
    bpy.utils.unregister_class(SCENE_OT_calc)
    bpy.utils.unregister_class(OBJECT_PT_Framing)

if __name__ == "__main__":
    register()
```

This will register a new panel in the Object context, according to the example `"Hello World"`.

16.1.7 Types

Python has its own data types but we can add more in Blender for easy access to datablocks, that is, in Python, we have data types like boolean or integer but we are able to add our own ones so we can use them within Blender data structure.

16.1.7.1 Native Types

```
    blender float/int/boolean -> float/int/boolean

    blender enumerator -> string

    >>> C.object.rotation_mode = 'AXIS_ANGLE'

    blender enumerator (multiple) -> set of strings

    # setting multiple camera overlay guides
    bpy.context.scene.camera.data.show_guide = {'GOLDEN', 'CENTER'}

    # passing as an operator argument for report types
    self.report({'WARNING', 'INFO'}, "Some message!")
```

16.1.7.2 Internal Types

These are used on internal datablocks and collections like bpy.types.

```
>>> bpy.context.object
bpy.data.objects['Cube']

>>> C.scene.objects
bpy.data.scenes['Scene'].objects
```

16.1.7.3 Mathutils Types

These are used for vectors, quaternion, Euler's, matrix, and color types, which are accessible from mathutils and used in attributes such as bpy.types.Object.rotation.

Here's an example of a matrix-vector multiplication:

```
bpy.context.object.matrix_world *
    bpy.context.object.data.verts[0].co
```

Example:

```
# modifies the Z axis in place.
bpy.context.object.location.z += 10.0

# location variable holds a reference to the object too.
location = bpy.context.object.location
location *= 5.0

# Copying the value drops the reference so the value can be
  passed to
# functions and modified without unwanted side effects.
location = bpy.context.object.location.copy()
```

16.1.8 Animation Using Python

In Python, key frames for animation processes can be added in two different ways.

Simple example:

```
obj = bpy.context.object
obj.location[2] = 0.0
obj.keyframe_insert(data_path="location", frame=10.0, index=2)
obj.location[2] = 1.0
obj.keyframe_insert(data_path="location", frame=20.0, index=2)
```

Using low-level functions:

```
obj = bpy.context.object
obj.animation_data_create()
obj.animation_data.action = bpy.data.actions.new(name="MyAction")
fcu_z = obj.animation_data.action.fcurves.new(data_path="location",
    index=2)
fcu_z.keyframe_points.add(2)
fcu_z.keyframe_points[0].co = 10.0, 0.0
fcu_z.keyframe_points[1].co = 20.0, 1.0
```

16.2 BLENDER/PYTHON API IN FILM PRODUCTION

As mentioned at the beginning of this chapter, we can hardly imagine a film production without scripting. In our case, we can hardly imagine a Blender movie released without scripting.

Python scripting is required at some point in any production process. Maybe the most common use of Python in film production is related to rigging and animation. Riggers not only provide an armature structured in layers using the right widgets, but sometimes it's very interesting to develop new features or panels with Python as well, to manage bone layers, behavior constraints, bone groups, etc.

Let's take the example of the Mushroom project for Lighthouse CGI animation, where Python scripting was used to manage the main character's armature. The script contains different panels within the Transform context in order to manage specific areas of the armature.

So, for example, we developed a Bone Layer to manage everything related to bone layers, allowing us to show/hide bone layers easily as shown in Figure 16.1.

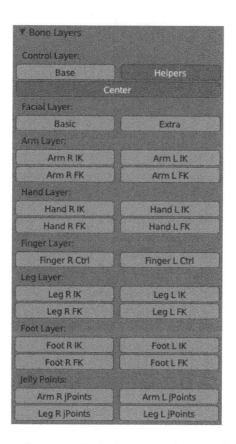

FIGURE 16.1 Bone Layers panel generated by Python script. This panel allowed the Lighthouse CGI animation crew to deal with armature layers easily.

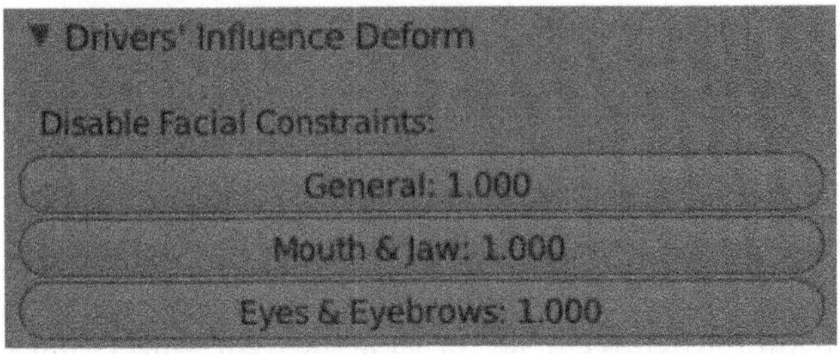

▼ Drivers' Influence Deform

Disable Facial Constraints:

General: 1.000

Mouth & Jaw: 1.000

Eyes & Eyebrows: 1.000

FIGURE 16.2   Drivers' Influence Deform to allow enabling/disabling of facial constraints.

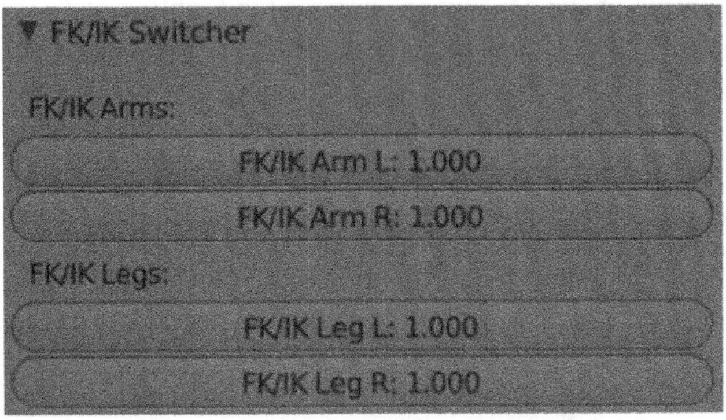

▼ FK/IK Switcher

FK/IK Arms:

FK/IK Arm L: 1.000

FK/IK Arm R: 1.000

FK/IK Legs:

FK/IK Leg L: 1.000

FK/IK Leg R: 1.000

FIGURE 16.3   FK/IK Switcher panel generated with Python, which allows switching from FK to IK solver for arms and legs.

Another panel generated using Python script was the one for Drivers' Influence Deform. This was an interesting panel containing some sliders to enable or disable facial constraints for General, Mouth & Jaw, and Eyes & Eyebrows, as shown in Figure 16.2.

Another interesting feature we thought about was something to easily switch between IK and FK. So we came with the FK/IK Switcher panel also generated with Python, where we had control of the FK and IK for arms and legs, as shown in Figure 16.3.

But we also had a necessity for joint deform. That is, to allow deform arms and legs in a very wavy way (i.e., undulating), so we developed easy access to those properties using Python script, as shown in Figure 16.4.

Depending on body poses, we wanted to manage elbows and knees easily. We developed another panel generated via Python containing three widgets for controlling those parts. Usually, we have a single widget, or point, to control elbow or knee, but in our case we were required to use three, so we generated the three-way Controlled Pole panel as shown in Figure 16.5.

The following code is the one used to generate all of the armature helpers we have seen.

```
import bpy

class MollyRigProperties_BoneLayers(bpy.types.Panel):
    bl_space_type = 'VIEW_3D'
```

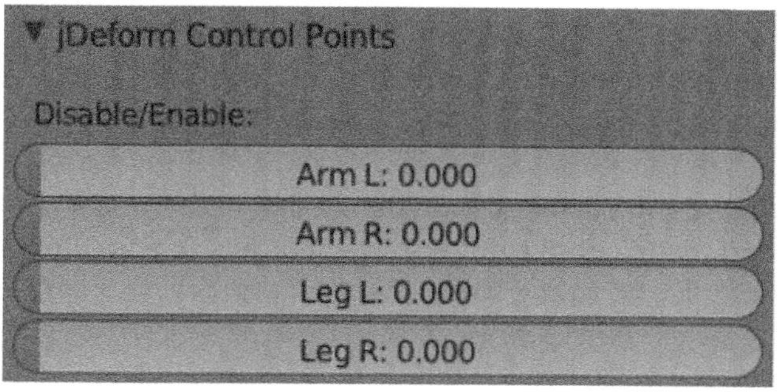

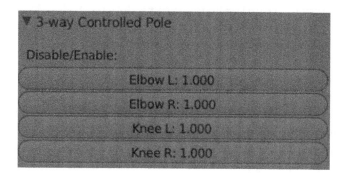

FIGURE 16.4 jDeform Control Points panel to allow waved deform in arms and legs. Custom properties were easy to access with this panel.

FIGURE 16.5 The 3-way Controlled Pole panel allows to control elbows and knees with three different widgets or points.

```python
bl_region_type = 'UI'
bl_label = "Bone Layers"

@classmethod
def poll(self, context):
    try:
        ob = context.active_object
        mode = context.mode
        return (ob.name == "Molly_Armature" and mode == "POSE")
    except AttributeError:
        return 0

def draw(self, context):
    pose_bones = context.active_object.pose.bones
    layout = self.layout
    col = layout.column()

    col.label(text="Control Layer:")
    viewprop = col.row()
    viewprop.prop(context.active_object.data, "layers",
```

```
            index=16, toggle=True, text="Base")
      viewprop.prop(context.active_object.data, "layers",
            index=15, toggle=True, text="Helpers")

      viewprop = col.row()
      viewprop.prop(context.active_object.data, "layers",
            index=0, toggle=True, text="Center")


      col.label(text="Facial Layer:")
      viewprop = col.row()
      viewprop.prop(context.active_object.data, "layers",
            index=7, toggle=True, text="Basic")
      viewprop.prop(context.active_object.data, "layers",
            index=23, toggle=True, text="Extra")

      col.label(text="Arm Layer:")
      viewprop = col.row()
      viewprop.prop(context.active_object.data, "layers",
            index=3, toggle=True, text="Arm R IK")
      viewprop.prop(context.active_object.data, "layers",
            index=4, toggle=True, text="Arm L IK")

      viewprop = col.row()
      viewprop.prop(context.active_object.data, "layers",
            index=19, toggle=True, text="Arm R FK")
      viewprop.prop(context.active_object.data, "layers",
            index=20, toggle=True, text="Arm L FK")

      col.label(text="Hand Layer:")
      viewprop = col.row()
      viewprop.prop(context.active_object.data, "layers",
            index=5, toggle=True, text="Hand R IK")
      viewprop.prop(context.active_object.data, "layers",
            index=6, toggle=True, text="Hand L IK")

      viewprop = col.row()
      viewprop.prop(context.active_object.data, "layers",
            index=21, toggle=True, text="Hand R FK")
      viewprop.prop(context.active_object.data, "layers",
            index=22, toggle=True, text="Hand L FK")

      col.label(text="Finger Layer:")
      viewprop = col.row()
      viewprop.prop(context.active_object.data, "layers",
            index=10, toggle=True, text="Finger R Ctrl")
```

```python
        viewprop.prop(context.active_object.data, "layers",
            index=11, toggle=True, text="Finger L Ctrl")

        col.label(text="Leg Layer:")
        viewprop = col.row()
        viewprop.prop(context.active_object.data, "layers",
            index=1, toggle=True, text="Leg R IK")
        viewprop.prop(context.active_object.data, "layers",
            index=2, toggle=True, text="Leg L IK")

        viewprop = col.row()
        viewprop.prop(context.active_object.data, "layers",
            index=17, toggle=True, text="Leg R FK")
        viewprop.prop(context.active_object.data, "layers",
            index=18, toggle=True, text="Leg L FK")

        col.label(text="Foot Layer:")
        viewprop = col.row()
        viewprop.prop(context.active_object.data, "layers",
            index=8, toggle=True, text="Foot R IK")
        viewprop.prop(context.active_object.data, "layers",
            index=9, toggle=True, text="Foot L IK")

        viewprop = col.row()
        viewprop.prop(context.active_object.data, "layers",
            index=24, toggle=True, text="Foot R FK")
        viewprop.prop(context.active_object.data, "layers",
            index=25, toggle=True, text="Foot L FK")

        col.label(text="Jelly Points:")
        viewprop = col.row()
        viewprop.prop(context.active_object.data, "layers",
            index=12, toggle=True, text="Arm R jPoints")
        viewprop.prop(context.active_object.data, "layers",
            index=13, toggle=True, text="Arm L jPoints")

        viewprop = col.row()
        viewprop.prop(context.active_object.data, "layers",
            index=28, toggle=True, text="Leg R jPoints")
        viewprop.prop(context.active_object.data, "layers",
            index=29, toggle=True, text="Leg L jPoints")

class MollyRigProperties_diDeform(bpy.types.Panel):
    bl_space_type = 'VIEW_3D'
    bl_region_type = 'UI'
    bl_label = "Drivers' Influence Deform"
```

```python
    @classmethod
    def poll(self, context):
        try:
            ob = context.active_object
            mode = context.mode
            return (ob.name == "Molly_Armature" and mode == "POSE")
        except AttributeError:
            return 0

    def draw(self, context):
        pose_bones = context.active_object.pose.bones
        layout = self.layout
        col = layout.column()


        col.label(text="Disable Facial Constraints:")
        col.prop(pose_bones["RootController"], '["EnableCons"]',
            text="General", slider=True)
        col.prop(pose_bones["RootController"], '["JawCons"]',
            text="Mouth & Jaw", slider=True)
        col.prop(pose_bones["RootController"], '["EyelidsCons"]',
            text="Eyes & Eyebrows", slider=True)

class MollyRigProperties_FKIK(bpy.types.Panel):
    bl_space_type = 'VIEW_3D'
    bl_region_type = 'UI'
    bl_label = "FK/IK Switcher"

    @classmethod
    def poll(self, context):
        try:
            ob = context.active_object
            mode = context.mode
            return (ob.name == "Molly_Armature" and mode == "POSE")
        except AttributeError:
            return 0

    def draw(self, context):
        pose_bones = context.active_object.pose.bones
        layout = self.layout
        col = layout.column()

        col.label(text="FK/IK Arms:")
        col.prop(pose_bones["RootController"], '["IK_Arm_L"]',
            text="FK/IK Arm L", slider=True)
```

```python
        col.prop(pose_bones["RootController"], '["IK_Arm_R"]',
            text="FK/IK Arm R", slider=True)

        col.label(text="FK/IK Legs:")
        col.prop(pose_bones["RootController"], '["IK_Leg_L"]',
            text="FK/IK Leg L", slider=True)
        col.prop(pose_bones["RootController"], '["IK_Leg_R"]',
            text="FK/IK Leg R", slider=True)
class MollyRigProperties_jDeform(bpy.types.Panel):
    bl_space_type = 'VIEW_3D'
    bl_region_type = 'UI'
    bl_label = "jDeform Control Points"

    @classmethod
    def poll(self, context):
        try:
            ob = context.active_object
            mode = context.mode
            return (ob.name == "Molly_Armature" and mode == "POSE")
        except AttributeError:
            return 0

    def draw(self, context):
        pose_bones = context.active_object.pose.bones
        layout = self.layout
        col = layout.column()

        col.label(text="Disable/Enable:")
        col.prop(pose_bones["RootController"], '["jDeform_Arm_L"]',
            text="Arm L", slider=True)
        col.prop(pose_bones["RootController"], '["jDeform_Arm_R"]',
            text="Arm R", slider=True)

        col.prop(pose_bones["RootController"], '["jDeform_Leg_L"]',
            text="Leg L", slider=True)
        col.prop(pose_bones["RootController"], '["jDeform_Leg_R"]',
            text="Leg R", slider=True)
class MollyRigProperties_3wayPole(bpy.types.Panel):
    bl_space_type = 'VIEW_3D'
    bl_region_type = 'UI'
    bl_label = "3-way Controlled Pole"

    @classmethod
    def poll(self, context):
```

```python
    try:
        ob = context.active_object
        mode = context.mode
        return (ob.name == "Molly_Armature" and mode == "POSE")
    except AttributeError:
        return 0

def draw(self, context):
    pose_bones = context.active_object.pose.bones
    layout = self.layout
    col = layout.column()

    col.label(text="Disable/Enable:")
    col.prop(pose_bones["RootController"],
        '["3wayPole_elbow_L"]', text="Elbow L", slider=True)
    col.prop(pose_bones["RootController"],
        '["3wayPole_elbow_R"]', text="Elbow R", slider=True)

    col.prop(pose_bones["RootController"],
        '["3wayPole_L"]', text="Knee L", slider=True)
    col.prop(pose_bones["RootController"],
        '["3wayPole_R"]', text="Knee R", slider=True)

def register():
    bpy.utils.register_class(MollyRigProperties_BoneLayers)
    bpy.utils.register_class(MollyRigProperties_diDeform)
    bpy.utils.register_class(MollyRigProperties_FKIK)
    bpy.utils.register_class(MollyRigProperties_jDeform)
    bpy.utils.register_class(MollyRigProperties_3wayPole)

def unregister():
    bpy.utils.unregister_class(MollyRigProperties_BoneLayers)
    bpy.utils.unregister_class(MollyRigProperties_diDeform)
    bpy.utils.unregister_class(MollyRigProperties_FKIK)
    bpy.utils.unregister_class(MollyRigProperties_jDeform)
    bpy.utils.unregister_class(MollyRigProperties_3wayPole)

if __name__ == "__main__":
    register()
```

For a general overview, you could have a look at the Blender Institute open movies to know how scripts are used in 3D film productions. About 46 scripts for different purposes like input and output, modules, operators, user interface, and utilities were developed for a project codenamed Durian. And about 41 Python scripts were developed for a project codenamed Peach.

This is very representative of the importance of scripting in film production.

While working on the second episode of *The Doctor Show*, we noticed the need for a render for estimating the time for animatics. That is, we usually need to know how much time a determined animatics is going to need. A lot of times we had to do animatics with lengths of 200 and 400 frames and to know the time this might take is really useful for the production pipeline.

For this reason, we wrote a short Python script to be used as an add-on within Blender.

```python
import bpy
from bpy.props import *

class OBJECT_PT_Render(bpy.types.Panel):
    bl_label="Estimated Time"
    bl_space_type="PROPERTIES"
    bl_region_type="WINDOW"
    bl_context="render"

    def draw(self,context):
        layout=self.layout

        obj=context.object
        scene=context.scene

        split = layout.split()
        col = split.column()

        # col.prop(scene, "prop_frames", slider=True)
        col.prop(scene, "prop_days", slider=False)
        col.prop(scene, "prop_hours", slider=False)
        col.prop(scene, "prop_minutes", slider=False)
        col.prop(scene, "prop_seconds", slider=False)

        col.operator("renderop.calc_render_time",text="Calculate",
            icon="RENDER_RESULT");

        row=layout.row()
        row.label(text="Estimated Render Time:")
        row=layout.row()
        row.label(et)

class RENDER_OT_calc(bpy.types.Operator):
    '''Calculates the estimated render time'''
    bl_idname = "renderop.calc_render_time"
    bl_label = "Calculate"
    bl_register = True
```

```python
def execute(self, context):

    scene=context.scene

    propDays=scene.prop_days
    propHours=scene.prop_hours
    propMinutes=scene.prop_minutes
    propSeconds=scene.prop_seconds

    startFrame=scene.frame_start
    endFrame=scene.frame_end
    nF=int(endFrame-startFrame+1)

    rt=[propDays,propHours,propMinutes,propSeconds]

    rtd=rt[0]
    rth=rt[1]
    rtm=rt[2]
    rts=rt[3]

    rtd=rtd*86400
    rth=rth*3600
    rtm=rtm*60

    rtime=rtd+rth+rtm+rts
    rtime=rtime*nF

    if rtime<60 :
        rtSec=rtime

    if rtime>=60 & rtime<3600 :
        rtMin=int(rtime/60)
        rtMinrest=rtime-(rtMin*60)
        rtSec=rtMinrest
        rtDay="0"

    if rtime>=3600 & rtime<=86400 :
        rtHrs=int(rtime/3600)
        rtHrsrest=rtime-(rtHrs*3600)
        rtMin=int(rtHrsrest/60)
        rtMinrest=rtHrsrest-(rtMin*60)
        rtSec=rtMinrest
        rtDay="0"

    if rtime>=86400 :
        rtDay=int(rtime/86400)
```

```
            rtDayrest=rtime-(rtDay*86400)
            rtHrs=int(rtDayrest/3600)
            rtHrsrest=rtDayrest-(rtHrs*3600)
            rtMin=int(rtHrsrest/60)
            rtMinrest=rtHrsrest-(rtMin*60)
            rtSec=rtMinrest

        et=str(rtDay) + "days " + str(rtHrs) + "hrs " + str(rtMin)
            + "min " + str(rtSec) + "sec "
        global et

        return {'FINISHED'}

##################################################
#### REGISTER ####################################
##################################################
def register():
    bpy.utils.register_class(RENDER_OT_calc)
    bpy.utils.register_class(OBJECT_PT_Render)

    bt=bpy.types.Scene

    bt.prop_frames = IntProperty(
        name="Frames", description="Number of frames the animation
            is suposed",
        min=0, max=10000, default=250)

    bt.prop_days = IntProperty(
        name="Days", description="Number of days of the
            single render",
        min=0, max=30, default=0)

    bt.prop_hours = IntProperty(
        name="Hours", description="Number of hours of the
            single render",
        min=0, max=24, default=0)

    bt.prop_minutes = IntProperty(
        name="Minutes", description="Number of minutes of the
            single render",
        min=0, max=59, default=0)

    bt.prop_seconds = IntProperty(
        name="Seconds", description="Number of seconds of the
            single render",
        min=0, max=59, default=0)
```

```
def unregister():
    bpy.utils.unregister_class(OBJECT_PT_Render)
    bpy.utils.unregister_class(RENDER_OT_calc)

if __name__ == "__main__":
    register()
```

## CHAPTER 17

Film Promotion and Conclusion

ONCE WE HAVE EVERYTHING done, we are ready to promote our product. We have been talking about the whole production process, and now we have a final rendered and postprocessed product we want to show the world.

This is a very specific topic because it depends on the size of the project and the funding. For big projects, the promotion starts even before the production does, but for small projects it takes quite a bit of effort to find ways to go to the public.

We have discussed the costs to make even open movies that are almost self-funding projects but this doesn't ensure they will be a success because they are usually seen by a limited audience following the project or those with any kind of knowledge about the existence of the project.

The big studios, the big productions use very different ways for film promotion. They usually invest the same or even more in promotion than in production. The profits will come once the large audience knows about the product and, at some point, consume it.

Anyway, we will make some distinction between the usual ways to promote big or small film productions:

1. *Theater*: This is the final target for every film production though not always accessible. It's the golden egg for producers. Theaters require some specific business operations and deals and not all small productions have a financial budget to afford this option.

   Anyway, sometimes, the theaters themselves are the ones promoting some film as they did with Blender Foundation films.

   It's also possible to incorporate partners funding the film production and include some terms and conditions to premiere at any theater, but again, that depends on the marketing and how the film production has been defined.

2. *Television*: This is a very exclusive promotional way that is usually only accessible to very big productions. It's said that Hollywood spends billions of dollars every year per 30 s of TV advertising. But the truth is that has been the more effective way of promotion.

   It's also usual that film sequels use this channel for promoting special campaigns that announce the recently created film and televisions incorporate part of the previous film into their daily program.

The open movies can rarely be promoted on television unless they are very strong and are backed by a huge funding program. In such cases, other ways of promotion are also available and will probably be more effective because they are less time and effort consuming.

3. *Internet*: Nowadays, the best and most common way to promote film productions is through the Internet. The wide variety of methods available for advertising on the net makes it accessible to a large audience. Small studios have found in the Internet a way to not only promote their small products but also to make premiers or screenings.

Today, it's possible to ask for preorders of any movie that the open source makes. But it's also possible to find specialized websites to promote artistic works. This trying to find the required fundings for film production is an awesome option.

Internet offers a simple way of reaching out to millions of people with a couple of clicks. It also offers specialized websites, as mentioned earlier, for funding or to upload the final movie so people are able to access the film and watch it.

It's widely known that there are campaigns deployed against piracy of artistic works over the net. Of course, we encourage everyone to use the open source and free software because it's a perfect option to extend creativity, to increase knowledge about any topic, and to share products and life.

17.1 CONCLUSION

Blender offers enough warranties to be part of any studio pipeline for film production. In this book, we have seen how Blender is so versatile from initial processes to the final touch and compositing.

We have seen how Blender provides good solutions for modeling, rigging, animation, or texturing. We even saw how Blender could deal with all preproduction tasks, from scripting to developing concept art. Basically, every step that film production requires is possible and realizable using Blender.

We are not attempting to get rid of the current studios nor do we mean to suggest getting rid of everything else and using only Blender. Established studios have their own internal routines but we are sure they should be thinking about integrating Blender in their pipeline because we are sure they will find it more and more useful every day.

With the latest Blender releases, we are all experiencing some incredible changes because we see how it's improving not only in its user interface but also in its internal features. Motion tracking, particles, dynamics, physics, sculpting, and a lot of new features are being integrated into Blender every day by passionate people working as volunteers or, in a reduced number, as official Blender Foundation's developers.

Happy Blending!

Appendix

KEYBOARD COMMANDS

G	Translate or move
G + x, y, or z	Move along specific axis supplied
S	Scale
S + x, y, or z	Scale along specific axis supplied
R	Rotate
R + x, y, or z	Scale along specific axis supplied
X	Delete
M	Move to specific layer
NumPad 1	Front view
NumPad 3	Side view
NumPad 7	Top view
NumPad 5	Perspective or orthogonal view
Shift + F1	File browser editor
Shift + F2	Logic editor
Shift + F3	Node editor
Shift + F4	Console
Shift + F5	3D view
Shift + F6	Graph editor
Shift + F7	Properties editor
Shift + F8	Video sequence editor
Shift + F9	Outliner
Shift + F10	UV/image editor
Shift + F11	Text editor
Shift + F12	Dope sheet
MMB Click	Middle mouse button; manage the 3D view over the control point
MMB Scroll	Middle mouse button; zoom the 3D view
MMB + Shift	Pan the 3D viewport
LMB Click	Left mouse button; sets an action or activates operators and buttons
RMB Click	Right mouse button; select an object
RMB + Shift	Allow to select multiple objects
TAB	Switch modes
A	Select or deselect all
E	Extrude

U	Unwrap
Ctrl + R	Loopcut
B	Border select
Alt + B	Cut and show
Shift + B	Zoom selected area
F	Create new face or edge
Ctrl + Shift + F	Edge flip

References

Blain, J.M. 2012. *The Complete Guide to Blender Graphics*, A K Peters/CRC Press.

Blender Foundation, *Big Buck Bunny*, http://peach.blender.org.

Blender Foundation, *Elephants Dream*, http://orange.blender.org.

Blender Foundation, *Sintel*, http://durian.blender.org.

Blender Foundation, *Tears of Steel*, http://mango.blender.org.

Hess, R. 2011. *Blender Foundations: The Essential Guide to Learning Blender 2.6*, Focal Press.

Mullen, T. and Andaur, C. 2011. *Blender Digital Movie Making*, Wiley.

Powell, A.W. 2011. *Blender 2.5 Lighting and Rendering*, Packt Publishing.

Simonds, B. 2013. *Blender Master Class*, No Starch Press.

Wickes, R. 2011. *Foundation Blender Compositing*, Friendsoft.

Williamson, J. 2012. *Character Development in Blender 2.5*, Course Technology Cengage Learning.

Index